Andréi Nakov

MALEWICZ:
BEYOND CENSORSHIP

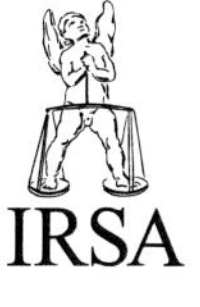

IRSA

•2021•

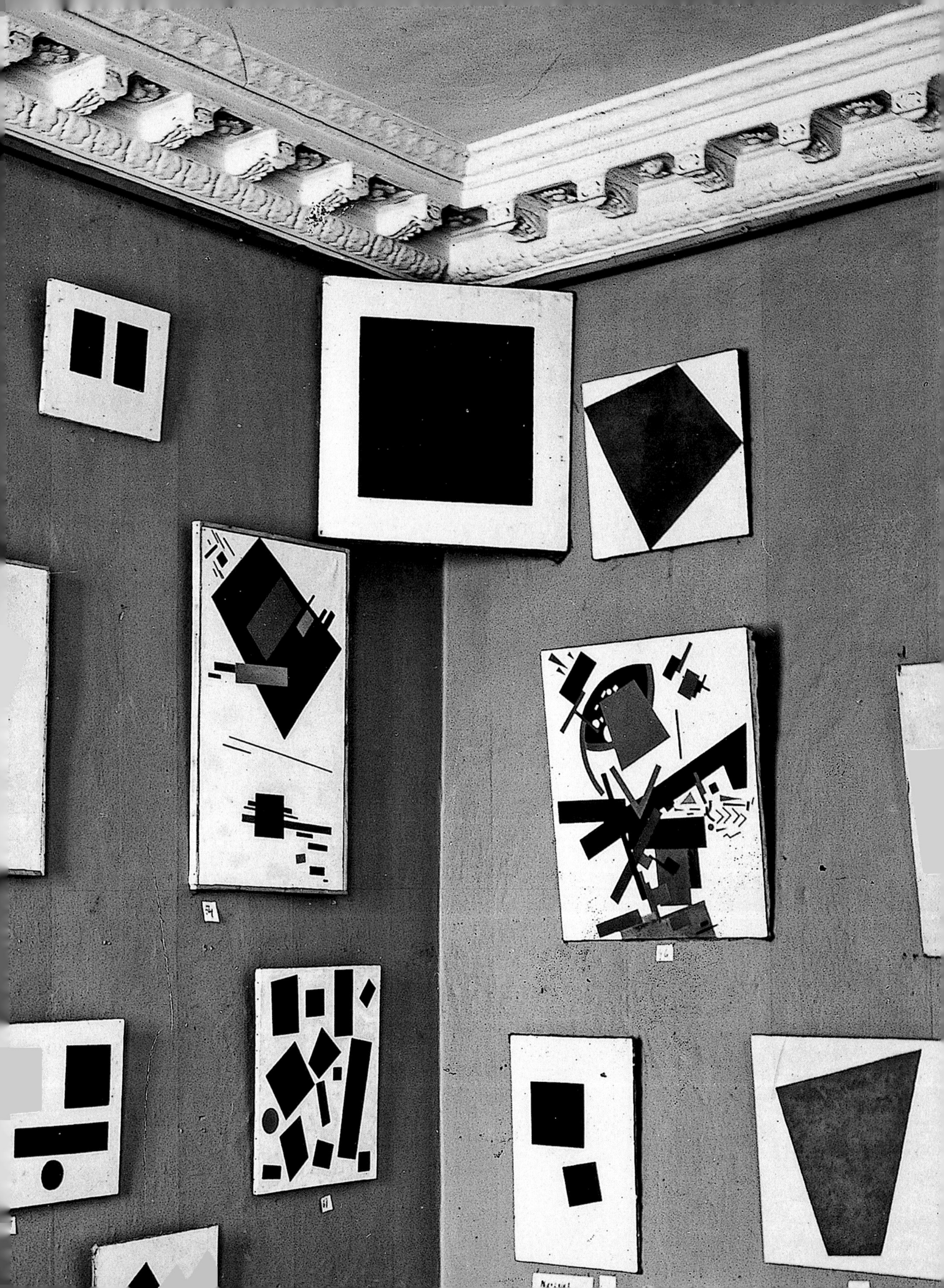

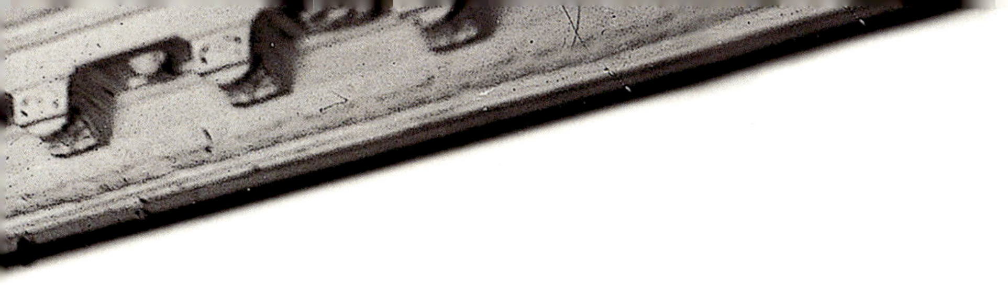

Andréi Nakov

MALEWICZ:
BEYOND CENSORSHIP

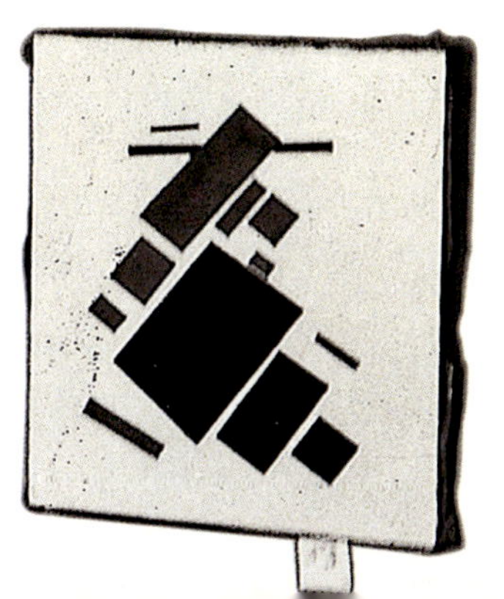

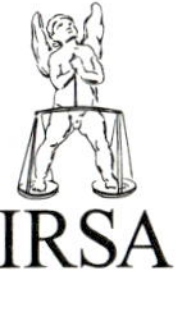

IRSA

•2021•

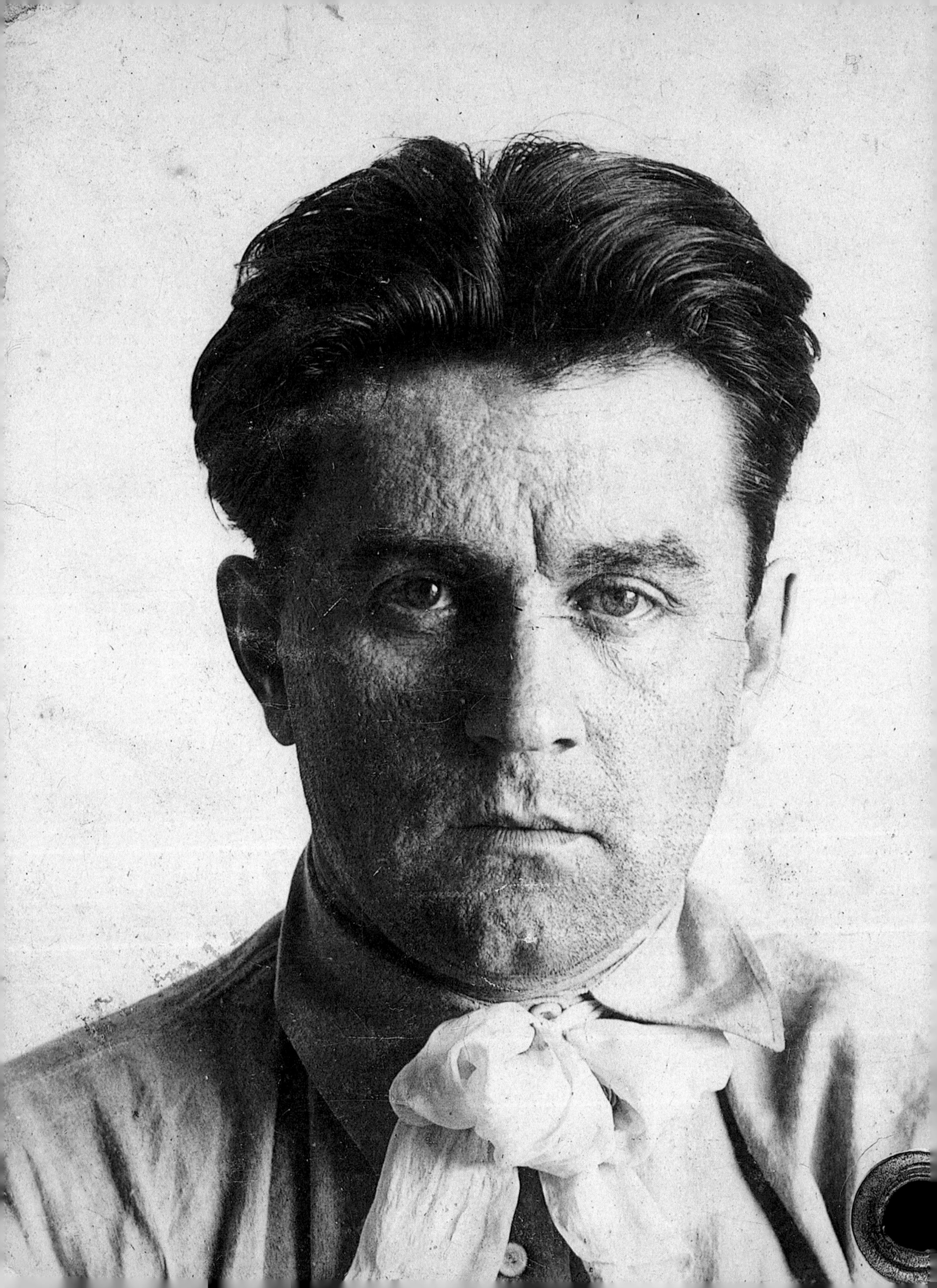

CONTENTS

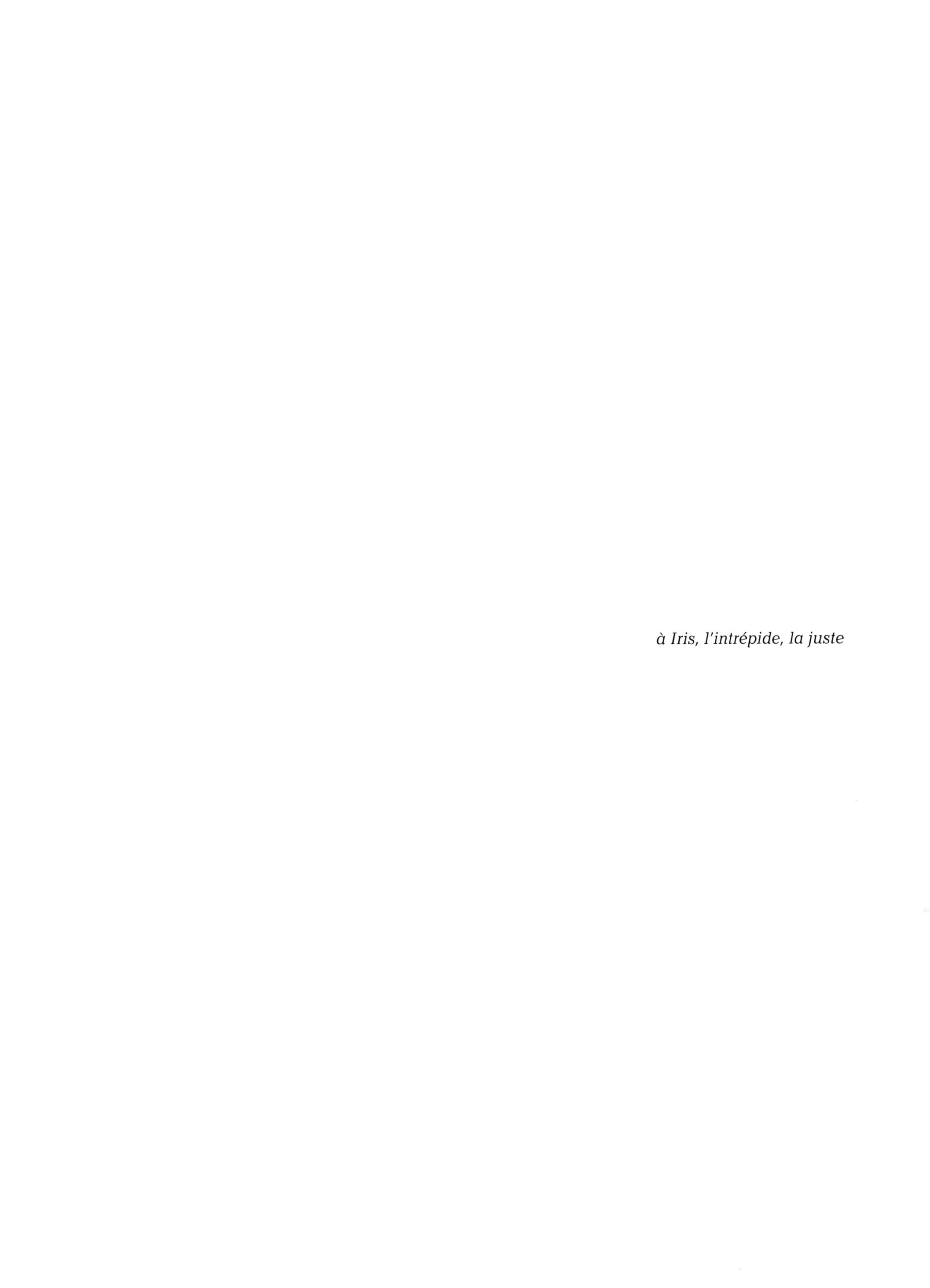

à Iris, l'intrépide, la juste

E ver since it was presented in public, in December 1915, the Suprematist œuvre has aroused a great deal of interest. Initially, this was a reaction of curiosity and surprise; immediately afterwards came the scrutiny of analysis and intellect, followed by incomprehension inevitably leading to rejection. Although Suprematism and the aesthetic ideas of Kazimir Malewicz[1] were highly respected in the avant-garde circles of his country during the artist's lifetime (and in Western Europe in the 1920s and 1930s), they were rejected and more often than not violently contested. This would remain the case for many, many years. Soon censored in Russia and even sooner forgotten, his œuvre nevertheless survived the socio-political disasters of the last century. In the past fifty years or so it has returned to the forefront of the artistic and literary scene. Like a lengthy archaeological process this rediscovery owes its existence to passions and fashions that unfailingly followed the wrong track on numerous occasions and in the dubious fantasies of partisan agendas. Often the latter ended by generating more misunderstandings, whether religious, visual (bluntly geometric), national-folkloristic and many other.

[1] For reasons that will immediately become clear to the reader, the author prefers to use the original Polish spelling of the artist's name here than the standard "Malevich", a phonetic re-translation from Cyrillic, by which he is known in the English-speaking world (translator's note).

The universal ambitions of an artist who straddled two cultures, a creator whose body of work offered in the 20th century's second decade an eminently logical conclusion to the vertiginous evolution of distinctly European modern art, had in some cases odd ramifications. Yet Malewicz's painting, and to an even greater extent his aesthetic system, resisted the fallacious interpretations of a century rife with social and cultural conflict – beginning with the famous *Black Square*, a canvas that was initially not a square and which the artist had pointedly and very lyrically named *Quadrilateral*.

This original and, to an even greater extent, inventive forerunner of Parisian Cubism continues to be subjected to the misunderstandings that surround the new logic of images, the Cubism that Braque and Picasso invented in Paris during the years preceding World War I. More remotely, the "Alogist" phase and the strange Idealistic concepts regarding the "metaphysical" colours upon which Malewicz built his system of Fauvist, Cubist and, later, Non-Objective painting, remain likewise insufficiently understood. Poorly explained, the painterly foundations of his aesthetic construction are for the most part simply ignored. At best their assimilation stems from expectations that are subject to an infinite number of misconceptions.

The metaphysical language that Malewicz used to formulate his aesthetic system comprises another barrier to Suprematism. A further level of difficulty hinges on the problem of translations. Not to mention the fact that the extensive theoretical work that the artist engaged in during the 1920s, a remarkable theorisation of modern art, is still largely unknown[2] to art historians hampered by a profusion of obstacles that constitute as many linguistic, cultural and above all conceptual prejudices. Built as an imaginary opposition, the connection between modern and ancient art appears to this day as a difficult bridge to cross. As heirs to what is unquestionably a continuity, scholars have for decades ignored some very simple facts.

In a nutshell, the field of investigating Suprematism remains open. What is more, when one approaches it one often has the impression of confronting a virgin forest. In order to facilitate this exploration, I have endeavoured to clear the access to Suprematism as much as possible by removing certain

[2] As yet a large number of writings derived from Malewicz's teachings await publication. The ones that are known, articles and didactic panels exhibited in Berlin in 1927, still need to be examined seriously by a history of modern art that as yet pays little heed to "artist's statements".

unwanted growths that, like false trails, have often created diversions or led to dead ends that prevent one from circulating freely in the Suprematist universe. At present the famous *Black Square* no longer seems like an open door but like a blind façade behind which the 20th century's visual imagination still lies concealed.

Ever since the publication of certain of my studies, especially the 2007 monograph[3] which I completed in the late 1990s, I have seen an accumulation of literary and strictly "cultural" interpretations that strike me as having strayed into secondary considerations reflecting nationalistic, folkloric, religious and recently "geometrical" and even "numeric" obsessions. It therefore seemed useful to indicate a number of self-generated themes the result of which has been to block the access to Malewicz's work, if not perversely at least unconsciously. Most of these misinterpretations stem from an ignorance of the essential principles of modern painting – the principles that guided Malewicz's art – as the artist makes amply clear in his writings. Returning to those writings seemed to me urgent as a way of opening the doors to Suprematism. One needs always to bear in mind that Malwicz's creative approach was based on the fact that before being a writer, teacher or polemist, he was a painter and reacted as such, i.e. in keeping with the logic of the visual arts of his time and the ones of his invention in particular. The materials of his imagination were visual, and it was from the revolutionary logic of modern art that his pioneering concepts arose. Images populated his imagination. As he himself states, he "untied the knots of wisdom and coloured the consciousness of colours". In the era of Cubism, he "destroyed things" and their "meaning", their essence and purpose. It was on this soil that the new painting arose. This in brief is the programme of the first part of this book.

In the second part I will bring corrections and additions to the *Catalogue raisonné* published in 2002. I will confirm or invalidate certain attributions, as there is no end to the evolution of knowledge. Inevitably the inventory of an œuvre as protean as that of Kazimir Malewicz is an open, if not infinite task. Keeping up with changes is not only a duty but more often than not it is also a pleasure. I am happy to share them with my readers.

[3] The original, French version of my monograph *Malevich, Painting the Absolute* was completed in 2001. The *Catalogue raisonné* (which was published in 2002) was initially meant to be part of this project. The original publisher having declined to pursue it further I was obliged to wait several years for the monograph to be issued in French by Thalia Editions in 2007 and in English by Lund Humphries in the UK (2010). To lessen my disappointment, I published an abridged version with Editions Gallimard in Paris, 2003.

1

BEYOND CENSORSHIP

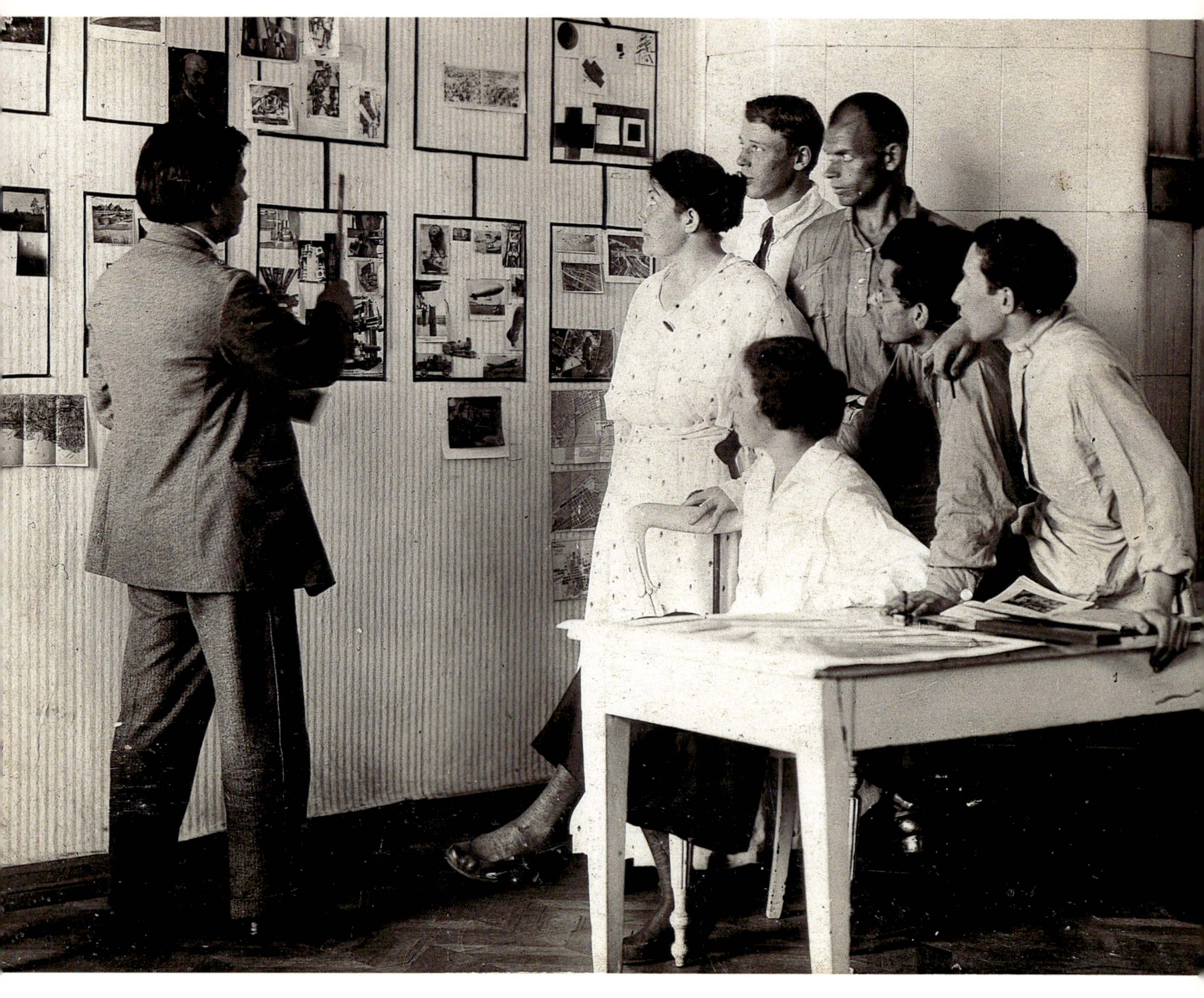

THE INCOMPREHENSION AND CONFUSIONS
THAT STEM FROM CENSORSHIP

Art is elitist by nature.
The artist does not cater
to the elite or to the multitude;
he follows his intuition.

Piet Mondrian
in *Cahiers d'art*, no. 1, 1935

Both understood and misunderstood, Kazimir Malewicz's œuvre has perhaps experienced to a greater degree than any other the fate that awaits any innovative art. Hidden behind the now famous *Black Square* it remains enigmatic. Attacked as soon as it came into existence, his creation, which was as radically new as it was complex, became the object, even before the artist's death, of fallacious interpretations. Like unexpected acts of sabotage these soon impeded its true understanding. The more indirect was this censorship the more easily it became part of the unconscious response of viewers, and the greater was its dissuasive impact. The residue of this artistic and philosophical hecatomb was felt for a long time. The present book aims to dissipate as much as possible the fog that still pollutes the approach to Suprematism. (I will discuss that movement in detail on page 51 and following.) Other, more superficial (i.e. hidebound) or more "biological" rejections (for instance that of Alexandre Benois) survived durably for they were rooted atavistically, so to speak, in "human nature" – the nature of a culture that Malewicz contested from the very beginning of his modernist ascent (1911).

1. Malewicz teaching his Leningrad students in spring 1925. The artist is seen from the back. Seated in the front row: Anna Leporskaya and Lev Yudin. Standing in the background: Konstantin Rozhdestvensky. Nakov Archives, Paris

Even before the artist's early death, his painting and the very traces of his aesthetic beliefs were expunged from the horizon of Western European culture, a situation that lasted decades. Due to its idealistic range the rhapsodic sweep of his aesthetic shared the fate of a good many other optimistic visions of art and humankind. As a result, this outburst of rare lyricism was severely repressed by the totalitarian reaction during the 1930s both in the East and the West. Only in the late 1950s did this *terra incognita* of creative energy begin to be rediscovered, and then it gave rise to archaeological reconstructions. For at that point, recreating the philosophical bases of the Suprematist aesthetic revealed itself to be a particularly arduous task insofar as, like prehistoric deposits, several cultural strata lay between Suprematism and the so-called materialist bias of the time – among them "geometrism",[4] "numerical" transformations and other "productivist" lucubrations of our "modern" world. The list of these false trails is too extensive to be examined here.

As surprising as it may seem, one of the innermost components of Malewicz's poetic, and therefore of his deep emotional makeup, has remained untouched up till now by the cultural or psychological – or merely biographical – investigations of modern scholars: the fact that the artist belonged to a Polish family. For, although he was indisputably one of the leaders of Russia's avant-garde, whose aesthetic action was a key element in the pantheon of modern art (owing precisely to the specificity of that current), he was unable to escape the particular character of his Polish origins and never tried to do so. Ignored by Russian and Soviet art historians, and by Western writers who quite uncritically took inspiration from them, the artist's cultural background, if only through his mother tongue, has so far not even been a minor object of study.[5] Yet it is obvious that for every artist, especially one as intuitive as Malewicz, the flowers of the imagination spring from the soil of childhood.

From the outset, then, the question of the artist's origin needs to be examined. Is there a direct connection between his background and his art? If so, of what nature is it? As a preamble to a fundamentally etymological approach to his family name, I would point out that it was charged with a primal meaning in his mother tongue, for in Polish Malewicz

[4] In my monograph *Malevich, Painting the Absolute* (trans. Michael Taylor with Helen Knox), 4 vols., London: Lund Humphries 2010 (hereinafter Nakov, *Malewicz*, 2007/2010), I mention certain "geometrist" aberrations in the approach to Suprematism. See in particular J. Milner, *Kazimir Malevich and the Art of Geometry*, London: Yale University Press, 1996.

[5] I broached this topic several times in my comments for a selection of Malewicz's writings in French translation, A. Nakov (ed.), *Malévitch. Écrits*, Paris: Champ Libre, 1975 (revised and expanded in 1986), and in more detail in my monograph (Nakov, *Malewicz*, 2007/2010). A brief summary of my findings also appears in my book *Malévitch, aux avant-gardes de l'art moderne*, Paris: Gallimard, 2003.

My study of archives kept in Kiev (in the church of St Alexander, which I compared with the city archives) enabled me to correct as early as the late 1990s the date of the artist's birth from 1878 to 1879. The archives concerning the artist's father, preserved in what is now western Ukraine, have yet to be published in their entirety. My conversations with the artist's sister, Victoria Zaitseva, were extremely helpful.

As for the selection of the artist's writing in French translation, I refer to the revised and expanded 1986 edition of the above-mentioned *Malévitch. Écrits* (reprinted in 1996). The reader is warned that the title of this edition, which the Parisian publisher Allia abusively and quite simply discourteously gave to a volume they published, has given rise to a confusion with an older publication (edited by J.-Cl. Marcadé) issued by the Lausanne publisher L'Age d'Homme, and with the two editions of my selection, which was the first to use the title *Malévitch. Écrits*.

signifies *to paint* and/or more exactly *painter*, a meaning that entailed a cultural commitment and, to an even greater extent, a destiny. As I have already indicated in my 2007 monograph[6] this connotation cannot have escaped the unconsciousness of a creative person (with all that this implied!) as keenly introspective as Malewicz (see the self-portraits of 1908–1910). Furthermore, at the end of his life, in lieu of a conclusion to his creative career, he inscribed his last self-portrait in 1933 *Khudozhnik* (The Painter)[7] in Cyrillic characters at the back of the canvas, accompanied by the symbol of a black square (for UNOVIS). The title is placed between quotation marks to stress the symbolic nature of the genre, and the whole thing is crowned with the artist's signature – *K. Malewicz* – in Polish. The various elements of this inscription, which indisputably form a totality, constitute a linguistic and cultural synthesis coexisting with an image that evokes the great tradition of the Italian Quattrocento (Piero della Francesca). The inescapable conclusion is that the artist made a humanistic gesture to cap a transnational œuvre, on œuvre that aspired to the infinity of a universal particularly dear to the artist.

Then there is the question of the artist's connection with the word "Suprematism". The term that did not exist in Russian before Malewicz introduced it in 1915 to designate his modernist invention, that is to say the planet of his dreams.

* * *

If Malewicz's work was able to thrive within the general trend of Russian modern art – and it is definitely one of the major moments of that trend – it was owing to the considerable international openness of its avant-garde currents, in particular the universalist aspirations of Russian Symbolism. Symbolism marks the point of departure if not the foundation of Malewicz's aesthetic action, just as it also leaves a deep imprint on the idealism and lyricism of those of his most creative contemporaries. More than a "movement" or "school" for his contemporaries, Symbolism was a supra-stylistic and supranational attitude, a vision of existence (a *Weltanschauung*) that opened

[6] I commented more in detail on this subject in Nakov, *Malewicz*, 2007/2010, vol. IV, chap. 30.

[7] *Cf.* Cat. PS-251, work in the collection of the Russian State Museum, St Petersburg, *cf. Kazimir Malevich in the Russian Museum*, ed. by Y. Petrova, St Petersburg: Palace Editions, 2000, p. 364. The catalogue numbers used here refer to my *Kazimir Malewicz – Catalogue raisonné*, Paris: Adam Biro, 2002 (hereinafter: Nakov, *Catalogue raisonné*, 2002).

the gates to the universal. The Symbolist mirror, an important metaphor for understanding that phenomenon, allowed artists to absorb and at the same time to reflect (i.e. to regenerate) a multitude of creative attitudes; it boosted the imagination by projecting it into new territories, new symbolic and therefore eminently visual dimensions. Similar in this respect universalist aspirations of (in Malewicz's eyes) Theosophy and the syncretistic tendencies that went with it, Symbolism was an intellectual centrifuge that made every combination and hope possible. Thus one must not be taken aback by the fact that the image of the mirror recurs triumphantly in 1923, through the symbolic force of transformative magnetism, in the last of the artist's Suprematist manifestoes, to which he gave the title "Suprematist Mirror". This ambitiously metaphysical heading, which seems somewhat startling at first, is comprehensible once one recalls the Symbolist roots of Malewicz's aesthetic. Having sprung from the metaphysical impulse of Symbolism the idealistic looking-glass references come full circle in the brilliance of a poetic illumination that projects itself extravagantly into a universality as generous as it is inexhaustible.

* * *

Kazimir Malewicz was born in 1879 to a Polish family (both his mother and father were Polish) and, although within the boundary of the Russian Empire, grew up in a distinctly Polish home. According to his youngest sister, Victoria, their father was an intensely "church-going Catholic" and a "Polish patriot", two characteristics that left a deep mark on the future artist. Kazimir was the eldest of eight brothers and sisters; his father, Seweryn Malewicz (1845–1902) was the youngest of several siblings, two of whom had distinguished themselves in 1863 in the last anti-tsarist uprising. Known as the "January Insurrection", this second great Polish revolt ended in bloodshed.[8] It led to a large number of deportations and expropriations of landowners, the "low nobility" to which the Malewicz family belonged. In the family saga

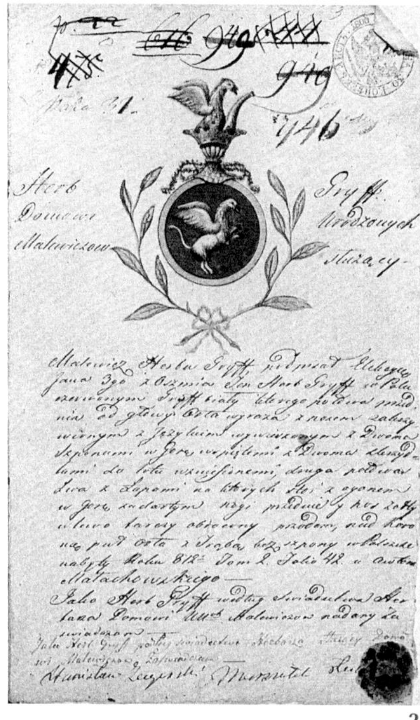

2.

2. The Malewicz family coat of arms crowned with a winged griffon, from deed dated 1746. State Archives of Zhitomir region, Ukraine

[8] The first uprising took place in 1830 and is known as the "November Insurrection". The later January 1863 Insurrection (*Powstanie styczniowe*) sealed the fate of the Polish nation for the next six decades. Large-scale immigration resulted from these two revolts.

as handed down (or embroidered upon) by the artist's father these two uncles appeared as heroes and martyrs of the national epic.

Their place in the artist's life was no doubt considerable. Tytus, the eldest, was an officer in the Russian army. He had been distinguished for his courage in the Crimean War. As an adjutant to the famous General Ushakov, he had been seriously wounded but had survived and been highly decorated. Owing to his military proficiency, he had commanded an insurrectionary battalion in the 1863 Polish uprising, which had fought the Russian army in the district of Zhitomir (today Western Ukraine but for several centuries a distinctly Polish territory). Another brother, Lucjan, a priest (Catholic of course), had been arrested "weapons in hand", a fact that had shocked public opinion at the time. After the uprising was quashed the two had been apprehended, put on trial before a war tribunal at Kiev, and severely sentenced. Tytus had managed to escape and seems to have fled to Western Europe. Search bulletins issued by the Russian police to their counterparts in France and Belgium would seem to indicate that like many Polish revolutionaries he found refuge in one of those countries. As for the unfrocked priest, Lucjan, he remained in the hands of the Russian authorities. Initially sentenced to twenty years imprisonment, he appears nonetheless to have been hung at Kiev.[9] His fate made a particularly deep impression of Kazimir inasmuch as the eldest son he had been destined by his father to a religious career like his martyred uncle. That this did not turn out to be the case was due to his mother, who encouraged the artistic penchant of her eldest child, whose life she later shared and whom she even outlived.

The patriotic and religious sentiments of Kazimir's father, as well as the teachings of the parish school he attended as a child, left their stamp on the future artist. Witness the recurring use of religious, indeed ecclesiastic, metaphors that crop up throughout his writings and artistic creations at every period. So frequent are they that they often recall the discourse of an inspired preacher. Indeed, it took an intuitive and intelligent poet as the *Oberiut*[10] Daniil Kharms to understand that behind the language of what could be described as "village sermons" there lurked a philosophy of such a sumptuousness and poetic incandescence that it still takes one's breath away.

---

[9] The documents relative to the trial mention a twenty-years' jail sentence, but according to the family version of the facts, as related to me by Victoria, the artist's younger sister and reconfirmed by Anna-Maria (Una) Uriman, his daughter, Lucjan Malewicz was hung, which is by no means unlikely. At all events Kazimir's father, Seweryn, organised an annual family pilgrimage to the cemetery of Baikove at Kiev where the hanging would have taken place.

[10] *Oberiu* (association for a Real – i.e. true – Art) was one of the last, if not *the* last, avant-garde poetic movements in pre-war Russia. Daniil Kharms and Malewicz were close in the late 1920s. In his notebooks the poet gives important information relative to his visits to the artist (see Nakov, *Malewicz*, 2007/2010, vol. 4).

Kazimir was not a practising Catholic but, symptomatically for his period and class, he was deeply marked by the religious spirit of his childhood parish school.[11] For him, the Christian religion in its Polish version proved a cultural framework. It was the national and above all cultural *habitus* that the Catholic Church offered every Pole throughout the 19th century, a long period when after the dismembering of the Polish state (the partitions in the late 18th century) it embodied a patriotic entity capable of epitomising the national myth, from whence it drew its social and cultural significance, thus playing a decisive role in the survival of the national consciousness. Indeed this ideal, properly spiritual dimension made it possible for Polish culture to survive other oppressions until the end of the 20th century.

So, since the late 18th century the region of Volhynia where Kazimir Malewicz was born and grew up was part of the Russian Empire, one of the "eastern confines" that had originally belonged to Poland and which after World War I and the October Revolution became the province of the new (western) Ukraine.[12] The educated milieu to which the artist's parents – especially his mother – belonged was largely open to Western (or "European", as it was called at the time) culture. Its social and economic life as well as its cultural references bore the stamp of this "Europeanization". The latter quickly became the unifying factor of a multinational community (Russian, Polish, Baltic, Jewish and other ethnic groups).

In the area of the visual arts, to which the young Kazimir was drawn very early, this mostly Russian-speaking society was to a large extent Francophile. Just as Vienna was the economic hub of this part of Europe (to a great extent east of the Rhine), Paris was without a doubt the centre of the then emerging literary and artistic fashions. The French capital was the nucleus of a large number of creative energies. It was there that the new culture was being forged. The latter spanned all frontiers, ethnic, social and national. The vista of a supranational modernity, a modernity based on an inescapable yearning for the universal, which at once characterised Viennese society (Freud and Mahler) as that of Kiev and St Petersburg, smoothed the way for artists of every stripe and every minority, as each individual was able to see himself or herself as an organic part of a groundswell towards an

11 After the death of the artist's father, his mother, Ludwika Malewicz (1858–1942), made several official requests to place her children on the list of the Polish "nobility". These did not reflect patriotic motivations so much as the hope of obtaining pensions for herself and her children.

12 The Malewicz family was established in the "Eastern Confines" (*Kresy wschodnie*), particularly the Zhitomir region, since the 17th century (see Nakov, *Malewicz*, 2007/2010, vol. 4, where this topic is discussed in conjunction with a selection of historical documents).

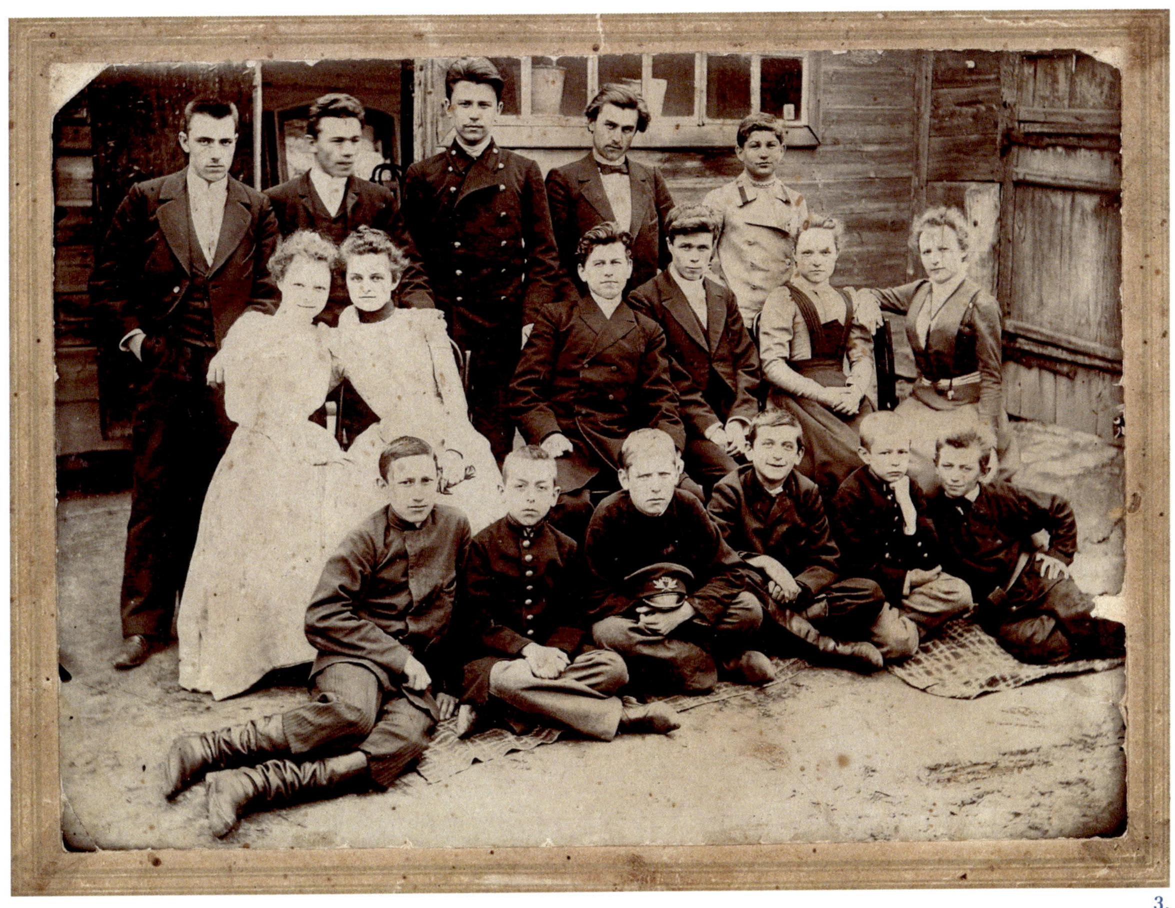

3. The Malewicz children photographed coming out of mass in a Kiev church, c. 1890–1895. Photo 12.2 × 17 cm. Kazimir Malewicz is the second on the right to the left of the last row. His brother Mieczysław is next to him. Nakov Archives, Paris

ideal universality. It was possible to feel as modern, to be at ease with the propositions and proponents of this modernism, in Dresden, Munich (Kandinsky, Jawlensky), Moscow, Kiev (Szymanowski, Horowitz, Exter) or elsewhere. So it is understandable that Malewicz, a new Rastignac in the cultural brotherhood simmering from East to West, should have had the constant dream, the obsession, of travelling to Paris to present his art there, that is to say to make a mark in the heart of the universal modernity which was, quite simply, his own modernity. The idea of a trip to Paris, in his eyes the apogee of an artistic commitment, was to become particularly urgent towards the end of his life when, sick and socially oppressed, he knew that surgery in the French capital could save his life. The example of his uncle Tytus who saved his life by fleeing to

the West, must have been present in the artist's imagination,
if not his subconscious.

A MODERNITY THAT LEAPS OVER BORDERS

*In poor Russian [...] he [Malewicz] read
from little notes he had prepared beforehand.*

Review of the *Knave of Diamonds soirée*,
20 February 1914[13]

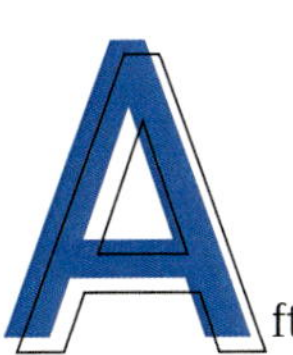

After settling as early as the age of 17 in the city of Kursk, where he earned his living working at a modest administrative job for the Moscow–Voronezh railway line,[14] Malewicz decided at 25 to move to Moscow in order to perfect his artistic training and, for the young Symbolist he was, to answer the "summons of destiny". In 1908 he joined the ranks of Moscow's avant-garde, very ambitiously.[15] Aged 29 at this point, he gave up transcribing his name in the Latin alphabet of Polish and began using Russian Cyrillic characters.[16] In 1912 Piet Mondrian, aged 40 by then, adjusted his name to the "French style". After experiencing the impact of Parisian Cubism, the latter decided to move to Paris and "modernised" the spelling of his family name by doing away with the Dutch double vowel "a" (Mondriaan). Manifestly, in both cases the affirmation of belonging to the ranks of modernity went hand in hand with an altogether personal declaration of allegiance to a new culture.

All his life Malewicz spoke with a Polish accent. This inevitably earned him sarcastic remarks from anti-modernist critics in Moscow and, less sardonically, from some of his avant-garde rivals (Larionov and other Futurists). In the 1920s his Russian friends addressed him affectionately as *Pan* ("mister"

[13] See the newspaper *Rannoe Utro*, no. 42, Moscow, 20 February 1914, p. 5.

[14] In the years 1980–2000 a number of fanciful art historians affirmed that Malewicz was a "draughtsman" whereas in actual fact according to archival documents he was simply a lowly "office clerk" (*kantorshchik*).

[15] He became a member of the MTKh (Association of Moscow Painters) and took part in its annual exhibition. See the detailed list of exhibitions at the end of my *Catalogue raisonné*, 2002.

[16] However, the back of many of his canvases from different periods – in particular works from the year 1914 such as *An Englishman in Moscow* (F-440) and *Vanity Case* (F-420) – are signed in Polish. *Vanity Case* was initially signed "K. Malewicz" in Polish on the back of the wooden panel but the signature was covered over when the painting was cradled.

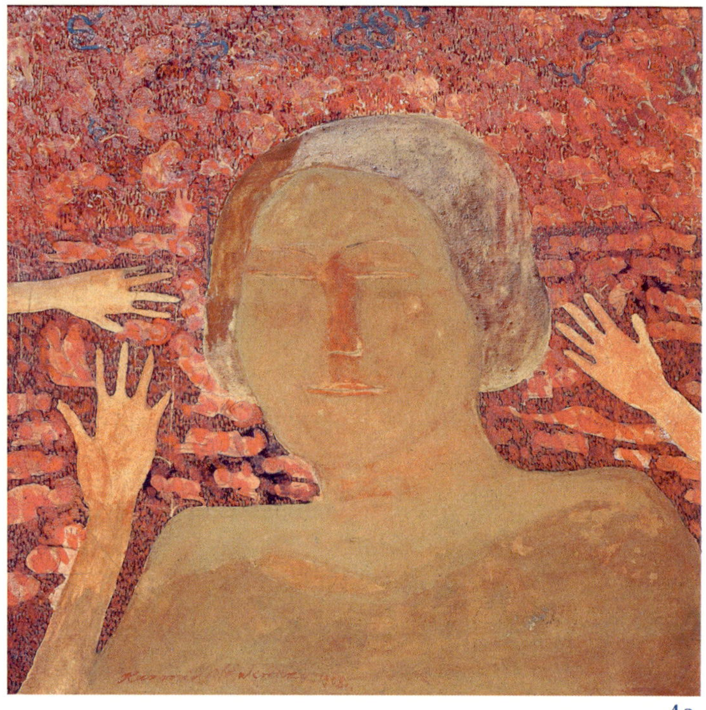

4a.

in Polish) to recall in a friendly manner his Polishness. Not incorrectly so, for Malewicz still tended to write not only private but also some professional letters in Polish, witness his correspondence with the Muscovite critic Paweł Ettinger, Polish-born though possessing an extensive European culture.[17] Until his dying day the artist, not feeling bound by any particular national allegiance, used to play slyly with linguistic approximations in Polish and Russian. This playful aspect of his cultural identity was widely noticed at the time and propelled his verbal inventions to the "transrational" level of Futurist poetry. But at no point was Malewicz's Polishness a provocative

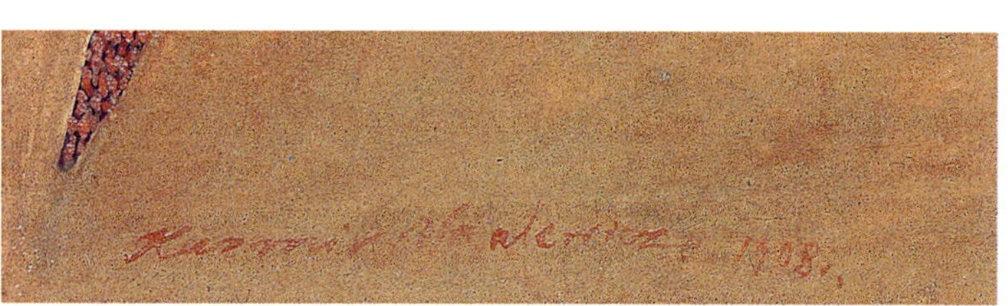

4b.

[17] See in particular two letters of March 1920 written in Polish (Ettinger Archives at the Pushkin Fine Arts Museum in Moscow). Szymon Bojko published the original Polish of both letters in German in "Zwei unveröffentlichte Briefe in polnischer Sprache an Paul Ettinger, Witebsk 1920", in *Von der Fläche zum Raum*, exh. cat., Gmurzynska Gallery, Cologne, 1974, pp. 53–56. The letters were reprinted, though only in a Russian translation, in the anthology *Malevich Klassicheskij avangard*, no. 3, Vitebsk, 1999, pp. 41–46. Only in 1983 were they published in Polish (*Kazimierz Malewicz*, Galeria GN, Gdańsk: Związek Polskich Artystów Fotografików; see note 23). In the 1920s Paweł Ettinger (1866–1948) was the Moscow correspondent of several German art reviews (notably *Der Cicerone*) to which he contributed articles on both Russian and Polish art. He exchanged letters with many Western correspondents, Rilke among them. He seems to have been regularly in touch with Malewicz and owned a work by the latter (F-119, *Children's Games*, now at the Pushkin Museum in Moscow).

[18] Y.-A. Bois broaches this subject in "Lissitzky – censeur de Malévitch?", *Macula,* nos. 3–4, Paris, 1978, pp. 191–201. However, the author does not venture beyond the preliminary stages of his investigation, for at the time the Symbolist origins of Malewicz's aesthetic system, not to mention the matter of the artist's language, were as yet closed books to Western scholars.

5 a and b.
a. *Children's Games*, 1908 (Cat. F-119), gouache and distemper on cardboard, 19 × 17.8 cm, former Paweł Ettinger Collection, Pushkin Museum of Fine Arts, Moscow
b. *Children's Games*, detail, signed in Cyrillic characters on the left *Kazimir* and on the right *Malewicz* (in Latin characters, i.e. in Polish)

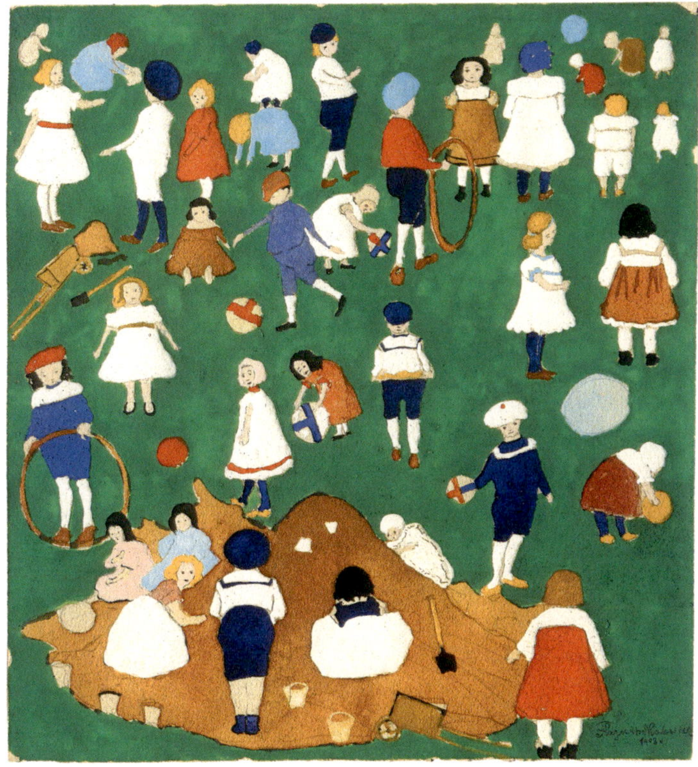

5 a.

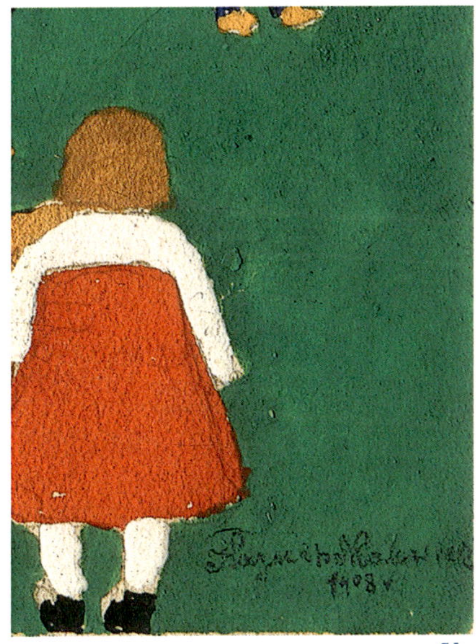

5 b.

attitude or mere façade; it was quite simply his inevitable way of being. It was neither emphatic nor a disguise.

The Polishisms of his manner of expressing himself was later to complicate the task of his translators, beginning with El-Lissitzky. In the early 1920s this favourite assistant of the artist's during the Vitebsk period would undertake the perilous enterprise of translating the master's principal manifestoes into German. Faced with linguistic as well as conceptual difficulties, Lissitzky soon gave up the project. Surely it was not just Malewicz's aesthetic vocabulary that proved too much for him, but also his style. The complexity of the post-Symbolist concepts underlying Malewicz's discourse was probably a major obstacle on Lissitzky's path.[18] Before long this specificity of Malewicz's written style was to contribute to the disparagements of the artist's "Socrealist" critics. Unable to subject his writings to a socially proscribed cultural reading, they subjected them instead to "class" abuse and in short order the artist's philosophical output was qualified as "unreadable", i.e. as the work of an "illiterate" person, a culturally eliminatory category to which his aesthetic system was surreptitiously confined, and this for decades. It was only a step to including his parents in the same bracket.[19] From being the director of a sugar refinery his father became a mere "worker". His mother, who had been raised in the family of a cellist and spoke French fairly well, was described as a "peasant". Inevitably the artist himself came to be viewed as "uncultivated" (*beskulturnyi*). A similar stratagem was employed on the other side of the German border: Nazi propaganda branded modern artists as "degenerates". In Malewicz's case, the downgrading of his writing to the level of "illiteracy" had grave consequences for the future reception of his aesthetic system. For roughly the next half century his texts were considered "unreadable" – and in fact were so to those who did not trouble themselves to understand them.

Another example of the cultural blindness, if not contempt, with which Malewicz's literary œuvre was received, is the strange attempt to re-translate one of his main written works into German. I refer to the recent academic (and rather cumbersome) retranslation of the expression "non-objective" (*bespredmetnyi*). The original translation figured in a small volume of Malewicz's writings in 1927 under the title *Die gegenstandslose Welt* published by the Bauhaus press. The artist himself, present in Berlin during the early stages of the translation, had an opportunity to discuss the choice of terms in the German version of his book[20] and to approve them. He settled on *Gegenstandslos* because it corresponded exactly to the Post-Symbolist idea conveyed at the time by the Russian *bespredmetnyi* expressing detachment, forsaking the world of objects (which Malewicz was later to call the "flesh-and-blood" world) and departing for *another* world. But for unknown reasons the recent translators, who were probably unaware both of the original Symbolist significance of *bespredmetnyi* for Malewicz or of its pre-Romantic roots in Germany (for example in the writings of Jean Paul Richter in the early 19th century), abandoned it in favour of *ungegenständlich*.[21] Recycled in 2014 on the cover of a thick exhibition catalogue, the latter seems to have gained ground since. More seriously to my mind, the authors of the new translation were probably

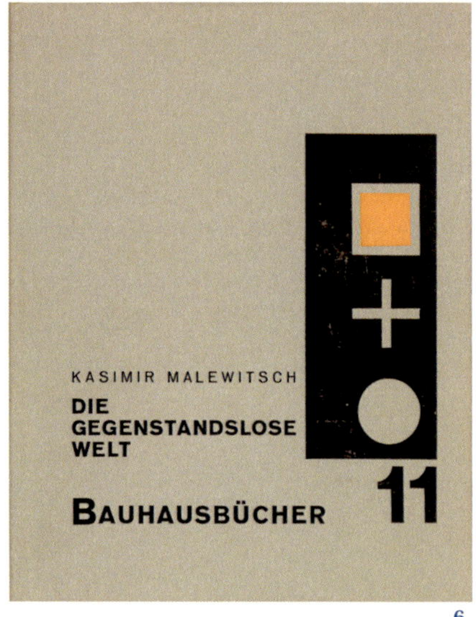

6.

6. K. Malewicz, original edition of
The Non-Objective World
(*Die gegenstandslose Welt*), Bauhausbuch
vol. 11, Munich, December 1927.
Cover design by László Moholy-Nagy

[19] In the late 1920s the Malewicz family adopted this transformation in social status as a protective cover. Both Kazimir and his youngest sister Victoria (who told me a great deal concerning this matter in the mid-1970s), played an active part in the invention of this social façade. This was in fact a common practice at the time (see how Tatlin resorted to a similar subterfuge in my *Tatlin's Reliefs: From Cubism to Abstraction* [trans. Michael Taylor], Kraków: IRSA, 2020, hereinafter Nakov, *Tatlin*, 2020). It is enough for the reader to be reminded that Kazimir's mother, being familiar with French, sometimes translated French articles to her son.

[20] Malewicz's collaboration with the translator, Alexander von Riesen, is documented. His choice of German terms and his manner of choosing them should be taken in consideration. I refer to them in volume 2 of my 2007/2010 monograph.

[21] Kazimir Malevič, *Got ist nicht gestürzt! Schriften zu Kunst, Kirche, Fabrik*, ed. by A. A. Hansen-Löve, Munich: Carl Hanser Verlag, 2004.

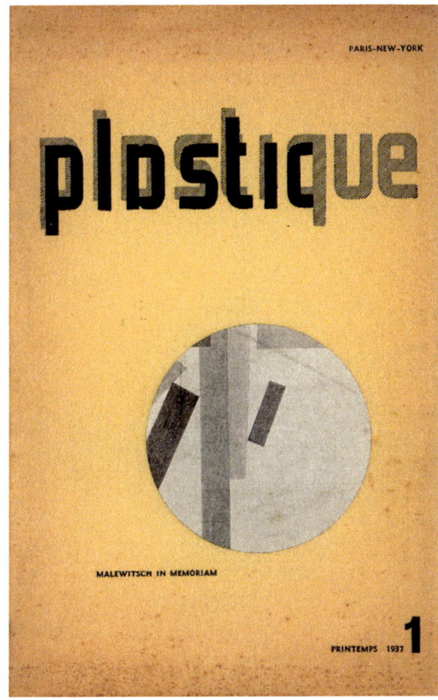

7.

7. Cover of the art review *Plastique*, no. 1 (subtitled "Malewitsch in memoriam"), Paris, 1937. Issue devoted to Malewicz

ignorant of the fact that *ungegenständlich*, with a negative, hence anti-modern connotation, appeared in the 1920s under the pen of Martin Heidegger, whose dismissive view of modern art escapes (or should at this point escape) no one.

Possibly the German translators drew their inspiration – whether directly or indirectly – from this source. At all events, where Malewicz is concerned, the fanciful ruminations of certain authors have produced bizarre results. In 1977 a publisher in Lausanne, Switzerland, brought out a rather voluminous book entitled *Malévitch et la philosophie* (Malewicz and Philosophy). In the very first pages the author, Emmanuel Martineau, declares he does not speak Russian and assures the reader that this has not been necessary for understanding the artist's philosophical writings. In his case a familiarity with the language was indeed unnecessary given that he hardly spoke about this topic. Heidegger was his true subject or rather obsession. As for Schopenhauer, one of the few European philosophers (if not the only one) that Malewicz actually cites by name, he was relegated in a tiny, perfectly irrelevant footnote.[22]

The conclusion that all this suggests is that such is the power of Malewicz's work, both in the purely visual and aesthetic fields, that it generates a level of interest such that it often escapes the expertise (in the modern visual arts and the aesthetics of Symbolism) of the scholars who attempt to deal with it. This means that Malewicz's aesthetic system has a dimension of its own; the fact that it has given rise to such a plethora of commentaries is, for that matter, proof of the essential poetic richness of his expression, a vital lyricism that resists all reductive approaches.

I am writing to you in Polish,
but for more than twenty years
of struggle in Russia,
in that "dark impasse",
I forgot the Polish language.

K. Malewicz, letter to Paweł Ettinger, Witales (Vitebsk), 3 April 1920[23]

Beyond the artist's vocabulary, which occasionally contains Polish expressions, it is first of all the peculiarities of his syntax that reveal the underlying Polishness of his writing, that

[22] Invited in 2004 by the Schopenhauer Gesellschaft in Frankfurt I devoted a paper to the topic of the German philosopher's influence on Malewicz in 2005. As a result of my subsequent research, this text would now be twice as long (see A. Nakov, "Malewitsch mit Blick auf Schopenhauer. Das Überschreiten der expressionischen und symbolistischen 'Verkleidung' der 'Welt der Dinge'", in *Schopenhauer und die Künste*, ed. by G. Baum and D. Birnbacher, Göttingen: Wallstein Verlag, 2005, pp. 163–200).

[23] Document in the archives of the Pushkin Museum, Moscow. Published in its original version in *Zeszyt teoretyczny Galerii GN*, Gdańsk, 1983, pp. 57–58.

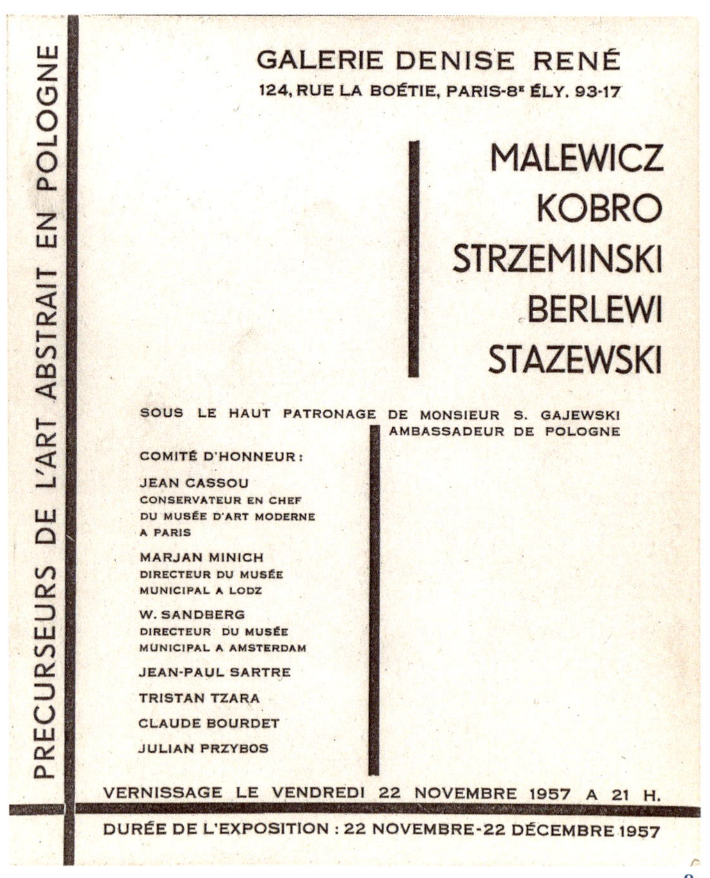

8.

8. Invitation to an exhibition of Polish painters, "Précurseurs de l'art abstrait en Pologne", the first showing of Malewicz's works in France. Galerie Denise René, Paris, 1957

underground river beneath his sentence constructions. These become more understandable once Polish words and especially Polish constructions – the manner of expressing oneself in Polish – are substituted for the Russian vocabulary. Now and then one even comes across Polish words written in Cyrillic. These words are of course not immediately comprehensible in a Russian text.[24] But for Malewicz the subterranean nature of the symbolic system and above all the logical structure of Polish belonged to the language spoken in his family. A letter from his youngest brother Mieczysław, who lived in Moscow, confirms this quite explicitly. Writing to Kazimir in July 1922 the latter excuses himself for writing in Russian, as the letter might be "used for administrative purposes".[25]

More interesting still is the structure of the symbolic layers in the artist's texts. With a successive gradation typical of

[24] In the late 1970s one of Malewicz's French translators assured me heatedly in the course of an informal discussion that some of the artist's writings were not always very "legible" and thus revealed a lack of culture (at least literary culture) on his part. As proof of this he instanced the artist's use of "words that simply do not exist" in the Russian dictionary. Responding to the example he showed me (the inscription in the margin of a Suprematist drawing), I answered that the word in question did in fact exist, though in Polish, Malewicz having simply written it in Cyrillic characters, whereupon the inscription became easily legible.

[25] See the letter dated 18 July 1922 in the Khardzhiev archives in Moscow (RGALI f.3145), published in *Arkhiv N. I. Khardzhieva* (N. I. Khardzhiev Archive), vol. 1, Moscow, 2017, pp. 208–211. This letter concerns the retrieval of Malewicz paintings which the art critic Aleksei Gan was reluctant to return to Nina Kogan and the artist's brother, who had been mandated by Kazimir Malewicz to get the paintings back from Gan after the 1920 Moscow exhibition.

the syncretic constructions of the second wave of Symbolism, these layers are piled on one another in a dizzying spiral of meanings. In a final burst of Suprematist enthusiasm, Malewicz's 1923 manifesto "Suprematist Mirror" is one of the best examples of this mode of thinking.

By way of comparison, one could cite certain writings of the Polish painter, theoretician and dramatist Stanisław Ignacy Witkiewicz, a somewhat unruly creative artist and exact contemporary of Malewicz's whose style of expressing himself is similar to the latter's "staggered" thought, especially after his "white" phase of 1918. The fact that the conceptual systems of the two artists resemble each other, though each in its own way, and that both spring from a Symbolist background, is surely no accident. The main difference between them lies in the visual results they arrived at: with his elaborate figurative creations Witkiewicz (who as a convinced Symbolist always refused pure abstraction) remains in a purely speculative category whereas Malewicz made a far more significant qualitative leap.[26]

[26] I broach this subject in my book *Abstrait/ Concret. Art non-objectif russe et polonais*, Paris: Transédition, 1981 and again in 2009 on the occasion of the Witkiewicz colloquium at Słupsk (Poland). A resumé of the latter ("Witkacy: close or distant?") appeared in Polish in 2013 (see *Witkacy: bliski czy daleki?, Materiały Konferencji*, Słupsk, 2013).

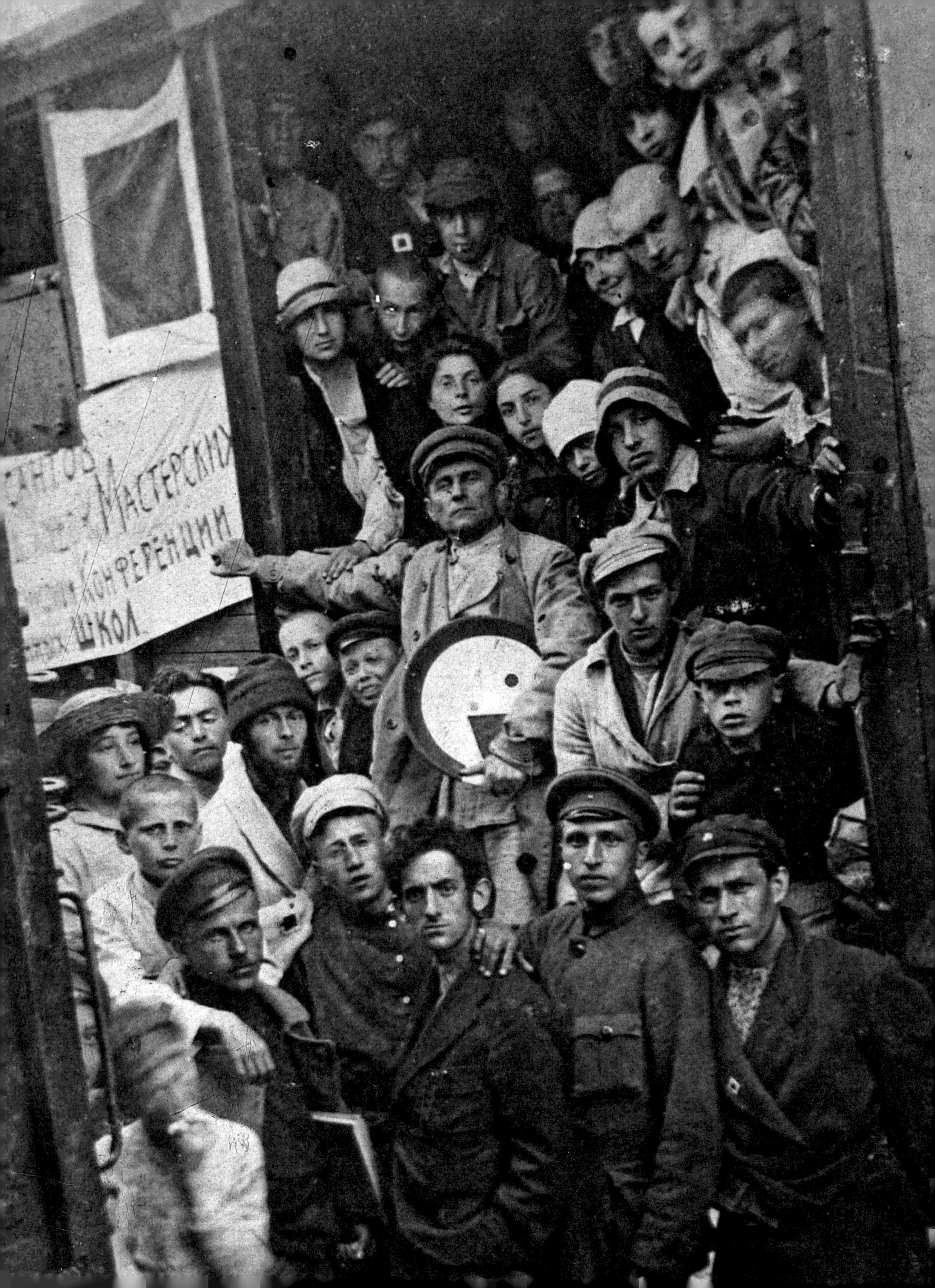
...НТОВ МАСТЕРСКИХ
...КОНФЕРЕНЦИИ
...ШКОЛ

LIBERATING ONESELF FROM ALL NATIONAL ALLEGIANCES

With the present [declaration] I hereby proclaim that I consider myself to have with drawn from every nation and religion. I belong to no people and do not consider any language to be my mother tongue.

K. Malewicz,
"UNOM 1 Declaration", 1920[27]

Given Malewicz's family background and his adherence to the modernist current that arose in the wake of Russian Cubo-Futurism, one of the major outcomes of which was Suprematism, we may well ask the question: what was his position concerning the question of a "national culture"? And first of all was this a *question* that artists of his aesthetic obedience posed at the time, and if so in what manner? Before anything else we need to eliminate a quantity of ideological interpretations. The poisonous fruit of cover-ups intended to foster an immediate feeling of incomprehension and create the impression that the writer is incompetent, amounted to what we must not hesitate to describe as socio-cultural sabotage. From the early 1930s on this task was abundantly carried out by a certain pseudo-Marxist approach. Yet the subject of "nationality" widely debated until the fall of the Berlin Wall simply did not exist for Malewicz and was indeed of no interest to the vast majority of European avant-garde artists (Brancusi, Kandinsky, Mondrian, Joyce, Arp, Tzara), all engaged in elaborating a culture that aspired to be universal and was *ipso facto* beyond all national limitations. This is not to say that the

9. The UNOVIS group leaving for Moscow, Vitebsk rail station, May 1920, gelatin silver print. Malewicz stands at the centre, holding a project for a Suprematist dish. To one side of the artist is Nikolai Suetin wearing a cap. Next to him is El Lissitzky (with a bonnet) and Nina Kogan (in a hat). Nakov Archives, Paris

[27] Included in the *Unovis No. 1* miscellany, 5 copies produced by hand at Vitebsk in May 1920.

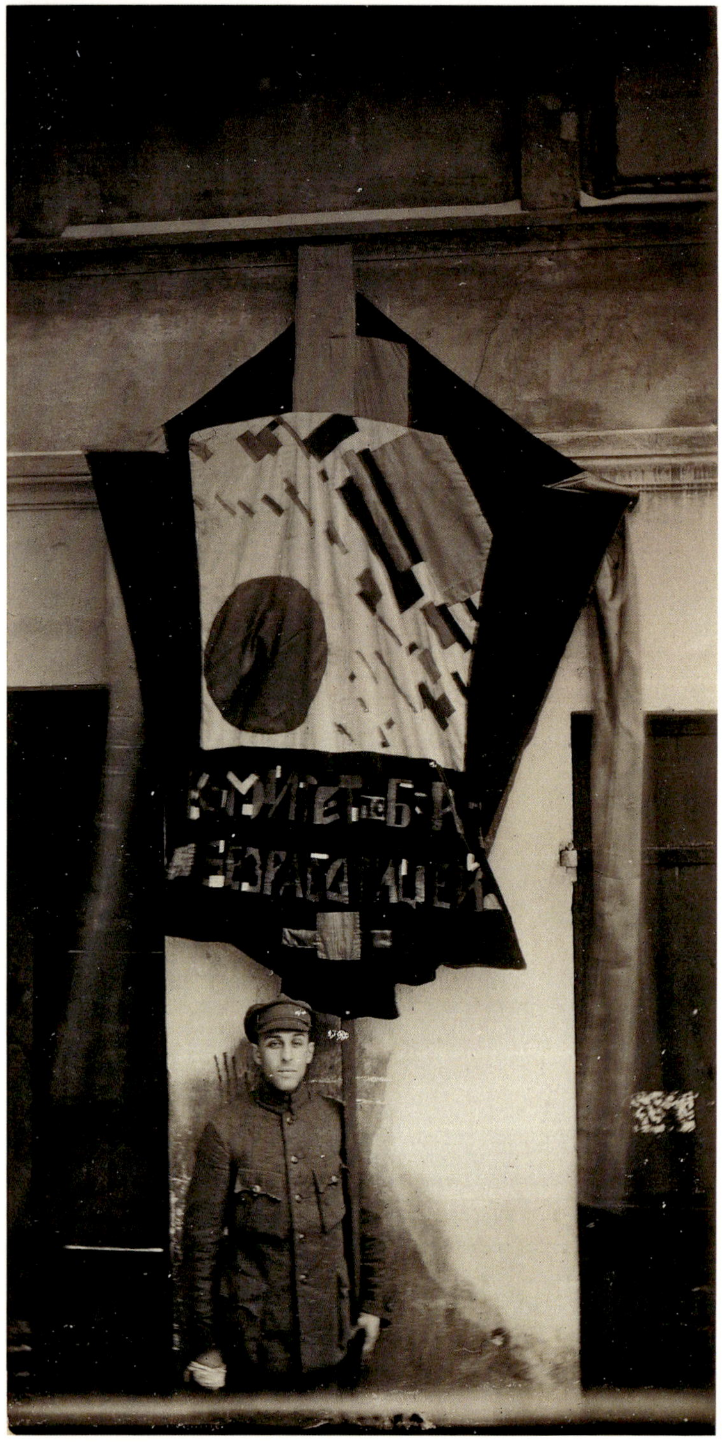

10.

10. Soldier under a Suprematist banner, week of the "Struggle against Unemployment", Vitebsk, January 1920, gelatin silver print, *Unovis No. 1* miscellany, Vitebsk, May 1920, private collection

11. El Lissitzky, cover of the *Unovis No. 1* miscellany, Vitebsk, May 1920, gouache on paper, 35.7 × 22.5 cm, private collection

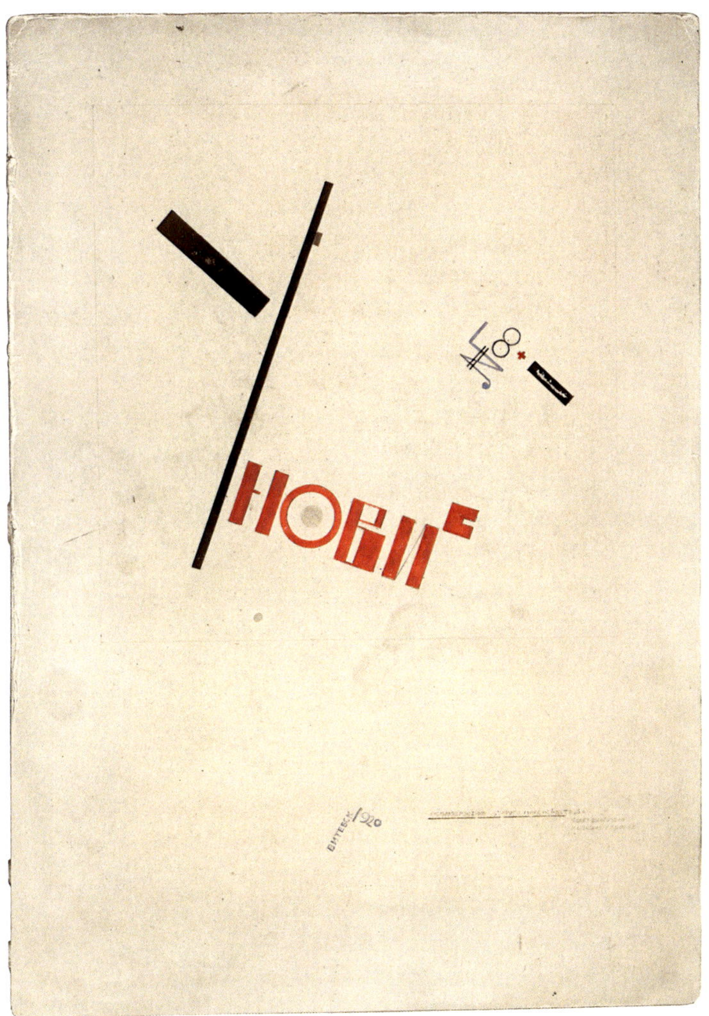

11.

different aspects of their work did not possess specific characteristics, since in every case they were the culmination of an original impulse and each of them sprang from creative roots of its own. At all events, the abstract art produced between 1915 and 1940 is evidence of the unquestionable universality of a transnational idiom: it is enough to compare the language of forms in the work of Kupka, Calder, Arp, Moholy-Nagy, and of course Malewicz, to be convinced of this. From both the visual and philosophical standpoint, all belong without distinction to the same family.

Malewicz's stance on the national question is clearly spelled out in his "Declaration" of February 1920. Titled "UNOM" and included in the *Unovis No. 1* miscellany, which had the force of a collective manifesto, it expressed the social and aesthetic position of the Vitebsk UNOVIS group's Suprematist ideology. Resorting to an incantatory style, Malewicz asserts openly that the artist is free to release himself from every group allegiance, including the one to a nation. All that matters for him is the universal dimension, the superior domain of Suprematism beyond any particular belonging or national reference – a position he had affirmed as early as the start of his path towards Suprematism in 1915. In contrast to Witkiewicz's exacerbated Polishness, Malewicz's detachment from any particular national feeling allowed him to roam freely along the roads of universal imagination. What a wonderful alternative to nationalisms of all kinds!

This attitude was hardly new in the artist's libertarian history, for in 1918 he had already publicly made an extremely bold declaration concerning the "rights of the artist".[28] Flaunting all social constraints, he had called for in the manner of anarchist manifestoes an absolute freedom for the artist, both in terms of his own work and in those of his moral and physical identity, a revolutionary announcement which up to this day seems to have attracted little attention. The artist's freedom from social and national limits could not have been more unconditional. To publish such a manifesto at the time – the beginning of the revolutionary terror – was no trifling thing. The boldness of the artist's statement attests to a great faith in absolute freedom and in the commanding presence of true works of art, of any work worthy of being called art, which the artist places above all laws, including those of the Revolution itself.

When one plunges into the very sources of the Suprematist revolution one realises that the term derives from the urgent need for unconditional freedom which it inevitably implies, the need for the highest kind of universality, a fundamental attitude that goes back to the year 1913, more specifically to the work on the Futurist "opera", *Victory over the Sun*. The telluric register at the origin of this subversive spectacle led to a new way of looking at things, a vision of novel non-objective forms spawned by the artist's unconscious. The artist's creation is

[28] K. Malewicz, "Deklaracija prav khudozhnika" (Declaration of the Painter's Rights), *Anarkhija* (Anarchy), no. 92, Moscow, 23 June 1918, p. 4.

situated beyond the reality of the familiar world, the "flesh-and-bone" world that Malewicz transcends, downgrades and discards as a useless burden.

Despite its universal and supranational character, the "UNOM No. 1" statement was penned at a critical moment in modern history, especially that of Russia, by then already largely Bolshevik, and Poland, only just emerging from the ashes of more that a century of having its statehood denied. This was also the period of a violent civil war in Russia when the recently resurrected Polish state found itself at war with Bolshevist Russia and as such became an enemy of the new Bolshevik state. Given the date of the daring UNOM declaration, the fact that it coincided with the turmoil of both a civil war and an international war, one cannot help being impressed by the author's freedom of spirit, a freedom that appears to take no heed at all of social considerations. It can thus be described as perfectly unconscious and, owing to its spontaneity, perfectly genuine.

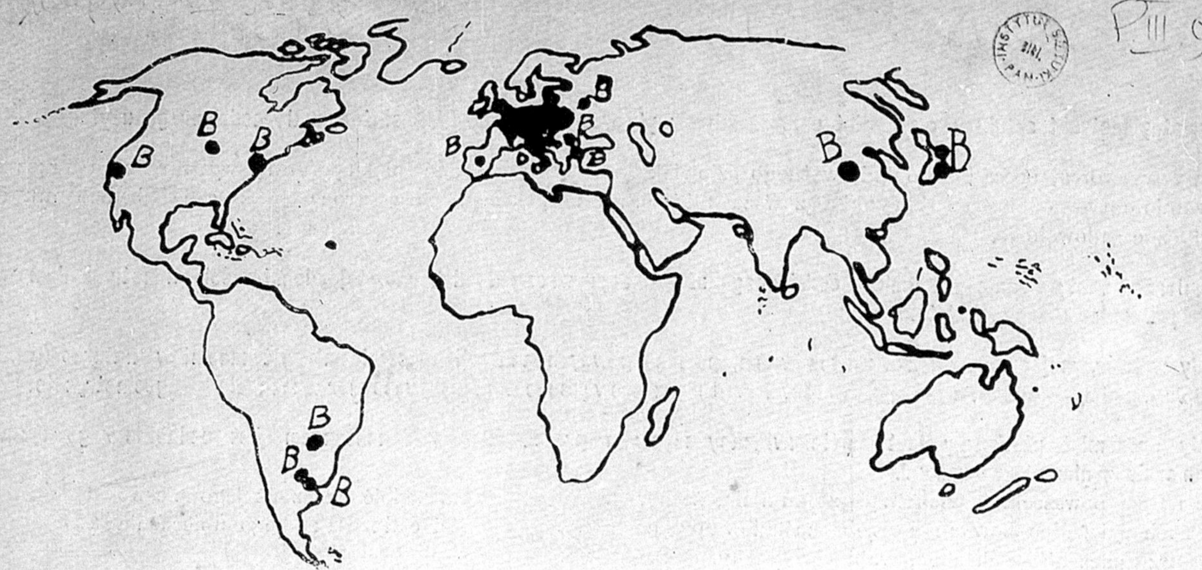

DOKĄD DOCIERA BLOK

BLOK № 10

ROK II
KWIECIEŃ
1925

VARSOVIE-POLOGNE, Wspólna 20-39

Redakcja: T. ŻARNOWER & M. SZCZUKA

NUMER POŚWIĘCONY ARCHITEKTURZE i TEATROWI

K. MALEWICZ

Nieutylitarna
dynamiczna
suprematyczna
architektura

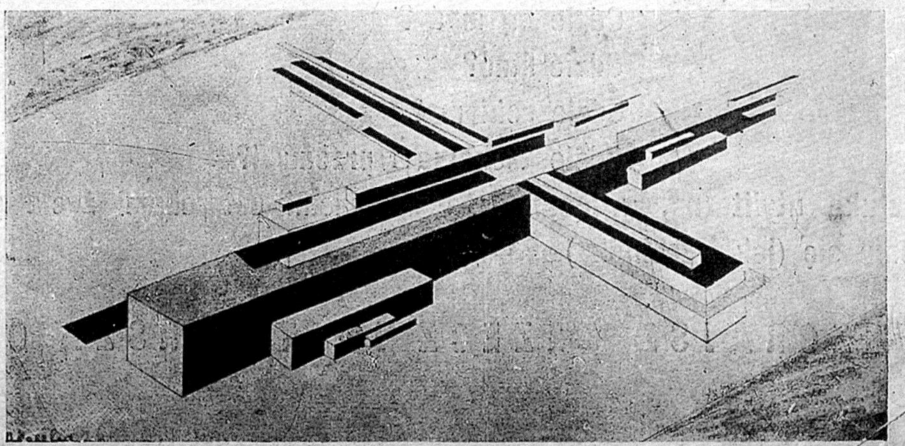

CHAPTER 4

LOOKING TO THE WEST

29 Invited by Lissitzky to teach at the Vitebsk art school in 1919 Malewicz had accepted. In the beginning Vitebsk was better supplied in agricultural produce than Moscow, but this situation deteriorated rapidly. Thus Malewicz continued to write to David Shterenberg, then in charge of the Visual Arts Section of Narkompros (People's Commissariat for Enlightenment or Ministry of Culture) that he was "waiting to return to the centre", i.e. the capital.

30 See Malewicz's letters of 20 June and 20 July 1926, which Burljuk published in his *Color and Rhyme*, no. 60, New York, 1930, pp. 114–115.

31 Katherine Dreier bought Malewicz's Cubo-Futurist oil *The Knife Grinder* (Cat. F-354) at the Van Diemen exhibition in Berlin (1922) and subsequently organised a certain promotion of Suprematism in New York – including the lectures of Louis Lozowick in February 1924. In 1925 the Société Anonyme, which she directed and sponsored, published Lozowick's *Modern Russian Art*, the first publication devoted to this topic in the United States.

12. Cover of *Blok*, no. 10, Warsaw, April 1925, with an illustration of a Suprematist architectona

O

wing to the existence of social problems facing Malewicz from the summer of 1919 on, he moved to Vitebsk in the late autumn of that year, "provisionally" he thought. In spite of his usual enthusiasm, he soon had only one desire: to leave that provincial town where he felt sidelined.[29] Rejected in Moscow, he consequently sought to establish contacts abroad. Initially he looked towards Holland, because the Neo-Plastic De Stijl movement seemed closest to his own aesthetic orientation. Later on as the social difficulties confronting him increased exponentially, he did not hesitate in 1926 to solicit the help of David Burljuk, by then living in the United States.[30] At the time Burljuk was already close to Katherine Dreier, the patroness of Société Anonyme.[31] Around the same time, Malewicz appealed to another friend from his Futurist days, Mikhail Larionov, who, he knew, had permanently settled in Paris.[32] Finally, in February 1922, in the wake of the Comintern Congress, Malewicz, sensing that the social noose was tightening around the UNOVIS group, wrote a "Letter to the Dutch artists" (who had contacted their Moscow counterparts in the summer of 1921).[33]

From Berlin, where he had been sent on a propaganda mission by the new authorities in Moscow, Lissitzky, for his

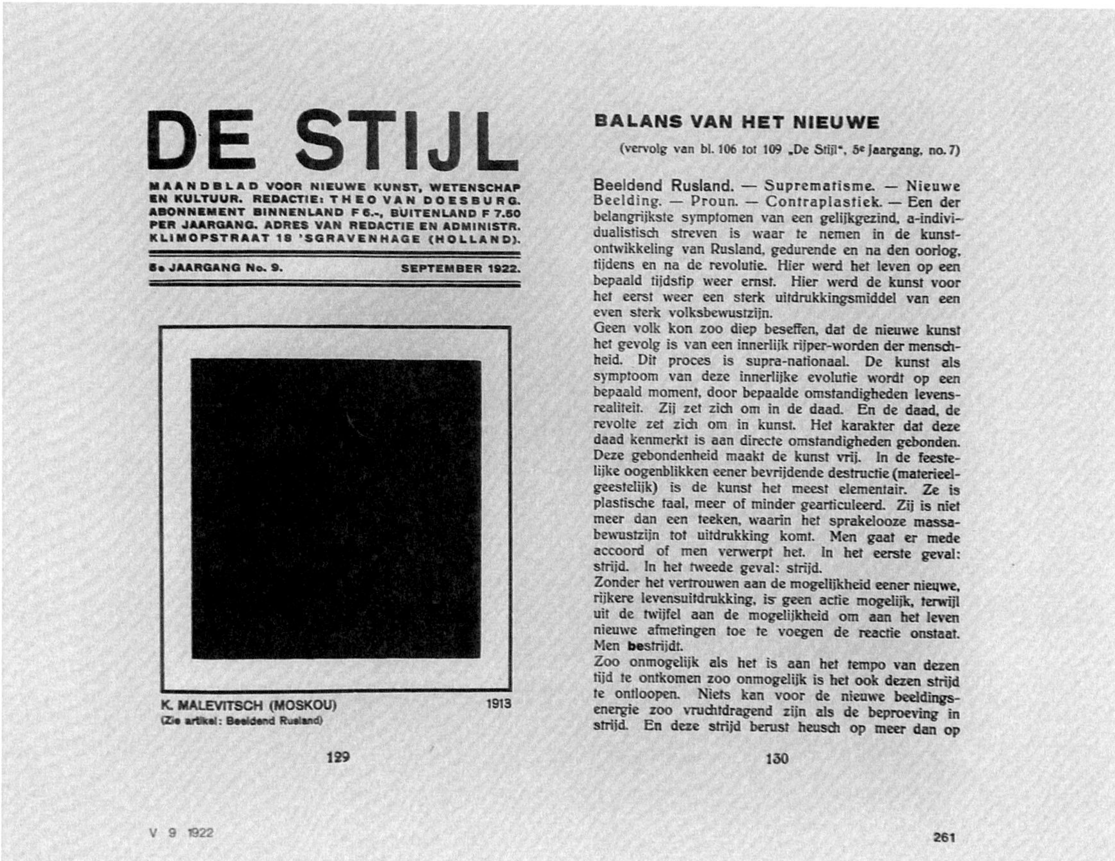

DE STIJL

MAANDBLAD VOOR NIEUWE KUNST, WETENSCHAP
EN KULTUUR. REDACTIE: THEO VAN DOESBURG.
ABONNEMENT BINNENLAND F 6.-, BUITENLAND F 7.50
PER JAARGANG. ADRES VAN REDACTIE EN ADMINISTR.
KLIMOPSTRAAT 18 'SGRAVENHAGE (HOLLAND).

5e JAARGANG No. 9.   SEPTEMBER 1922.

K. MALEVITSCH (MOSKOU)   1913
(Zie artikel: Beeldend Rusland)

129

BALANS VAN HET NIEUWE

(vervolg van bl. 106 tot 109 „De Stijl", 5e jaargang, no. 7)

Beeldend Rusland. — Suprematisme. — Nieuwe
Beelding. — Proun. — Contraplastiek. — Een der
belangrijkste symptomen van een gelijkgezind, a-indivi-
dualistisch streven is waar te nemen in de kunst-
ontwikkeling van Rusland, gedurende en na den oorlog,
tijdens en na de revolutie. Hier werd het leven op een
bepaald tijdstip weer ernst. Hier werd de kunst voor
het eerst weer een sterk uitdrukkingsmiddel van een
even sterk volksbewustzijn.
Geen volk kon zoo diep beseffen, dat de nieuwe kunst
het gevolg is van een innerlijk rijper-worden der mensch-
heid. Dit proces is supra-nationaal. De kunst als
symptoom van deze innerlijke evolutie wordt op een
bepaald moment, door bepaalde omstandigheden levens-
realiteit. Zij zet zich om in de daad. En de daad, de
revolte zet zich om in kunst. Het karakter dat deze
daad kenmerkt is aan directe omstandigheden gebonden.
Deze gebondenheid maakt de kunst vrij. In de feeste-
lijke oogenblikken eener bevrijdende destructie (materieel-
geestelijk) is de kunst het meest elementair. Ze is
plastische taal, meer of minder gearticuleerd. Zij is niet
meer dan een teeken, waarin het sprakelooze massa-
bewustzijn tot uitdrukking komt. Men gaat er mede
accoord of men verwerpt het. In het eerste geval:
strijd. In het tweede geval: strijd.
Zonder het vertrouwen aan de mogelijkheid eener nieuwe,
rijkere levensuitdrukking, is geen actie mogelijk, terwijl
uit de twijfel aan de mogelijkheid om aan het leven
nieuwe afmetingen toe te voegen de reactie onstaat.
Men bestrijdt.
Zoo onmogelijk als het is aan het tempo van dezen
tijd te ontkomen zoo onmogelijk is het ook dezen strijd
te ontloopen. Niets kan voor de nieuwe beeldings-
energie zoo vruchtdragend zijn als de beproeving in
strijd. En deze strijd berust heusch op meer dan op

130

V 9 1922   261

13.

part, was able to publicise Suprematism through his modernist journal *Veshch/Gegenstand/Objet* and even more so thanks
to the review *De Stijl*, which published an article by Theo
van Doesburg on this topic in September 1922.[34] Illustrating
this article was a modified reproduction of Malewicz's *Black
Square*, the first to cross the border into the Western press.[35]

Two years later Malewicz renewed his contacts with Poland where two of his closest adherents were now living: the
painter Władysław Strzemiński and his companion Katarzyna Kobro, a Latvian-born sculptress who became Polish by
marriage to Strzemiński and even more so by the fact that
her work fits in with the best modernist achievements of her
adoptive country. The contacts Malewicz established with
these two artists, who had opened a UNOVIS "branch" in

[32] Two letters dating to the summer of 1926, one
in Malewicz's hand, the other in that of his assistant Vera Yermolayeva (27 June 1926), attest
to the fact that Malewicz asked Larionov to help
him obtain a French visa.

[33] Under the title "Open Letter to the Dutch
Painters van 't Hoff and Chris Beekman", this text
was published in the Petersburg review *Zhizn Iskusstva* (The Life of the Arts) on 9 December 1924.

[34] T. van Doesburg, "Beelden Rusland", *De Stijl*,
September 1922.

[35] Lissitzky had published a reproduction of
Black Square in *Veshch/Gegenstand/Objet*, the
first issue of which appeared in Berlin in May
1922, but as the review was backed financially
from Moscow this publication must be viewed as
a Russian (in this case Soviet) propaganda action.

13. *De Stijl*, September 1922, cover design by Theo van Doesburg (first reproduction of *Black Square* in a Western publication)

14. *Veshch/Gegenstand/Objet*, no. 3, Berlin, May 1922, multilingual review edited by El Lissitzky and Ilya Ehrenburg. First publication of *Black Square* outside Russia

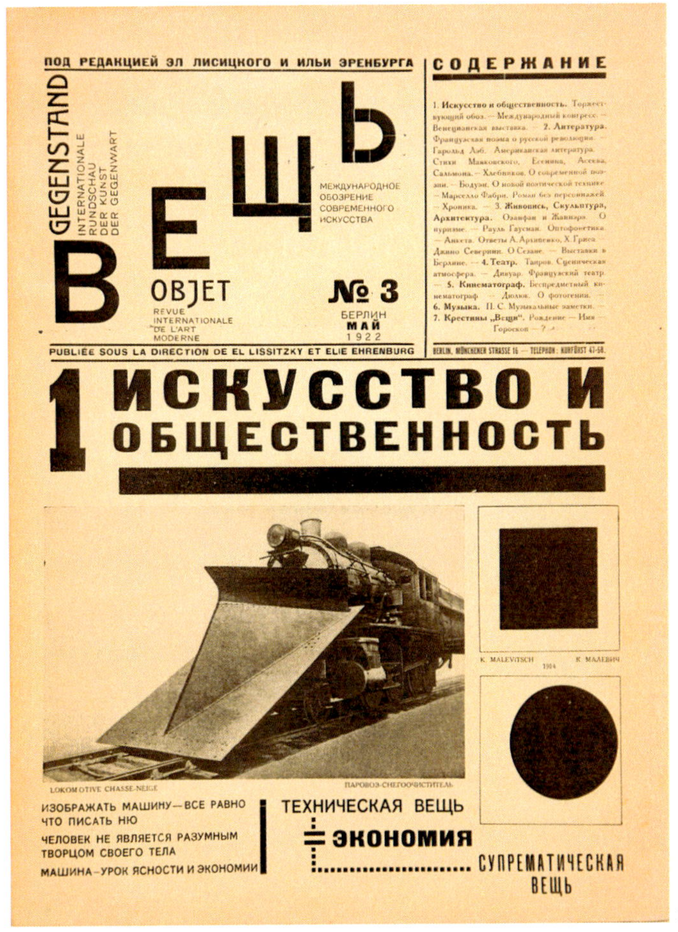

14.

Smolensk, which he visited and where he lectured at their invitation, subsequently paved the way to his presence in Poland. Thanks to Strzemiński, an abstract painter and brilliant theoretician of the then new "Unist" current, several of Malewicz's texts and illustrations of his Suprematist works (paintings and "architectonas") were published in the review *Blok* in 1924. Two years later *Praesens*, the journal of a group of modernist Polish architects, published in Warsaw, again at Strzemiński's urging, more reproductions of Suprematist works as well as translations of texts by Malewicz, this time in French as well – a first for the period.[36] The road to Paris seemed to open up for Malewicz at this point, and one can be sure that he viewed it with particular interest. But to return to

[36] Helena Syrkus-Niemirowska, the wife of the association's president, the architect Szymon Syrkus, translated Malewicz's texts. The artist subsequently generously presented the couple with a Suprematist painting and an architectona.

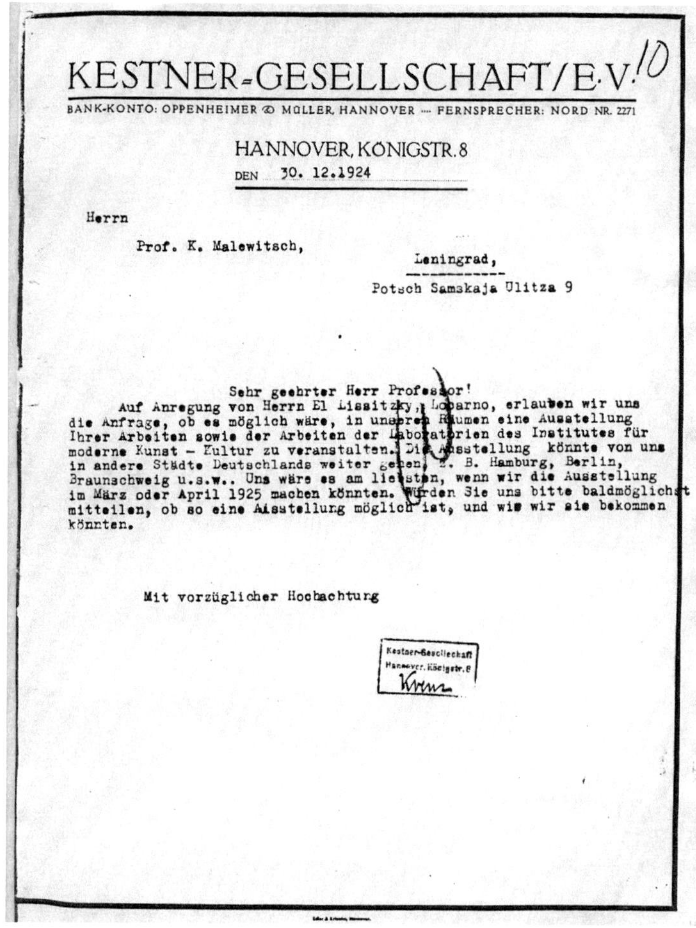

15. Letter of the Kestnergesselschaft inviting Malewicz to exhibit his works in Hanover, December 1924

15.

Poland, the Praesens group organized an exhibition of a rather representative selection of the artist's works in Warsaw and, in the last week of March 1927, Malewicz himself came to present a selection of paintings and architectonas from the extensive selection of works he had prepared for the Berlin show.

Back in 1924 a large German retrospective had been a project of Lissitzky's in Hanover. It was to be held initially in the Kestnergesellschaft in Hanover, but in the end, owing to administrative and socio-political obstacles in Russia, it opened in Berlin and ran throughout the summer of 1927 in the guise of a display of architectonas, a "utilitarian" cover to attenuate the ideological "danger" of an exhibition of a large number of Expressionist, Cubo-Futurist and especially Suprematist

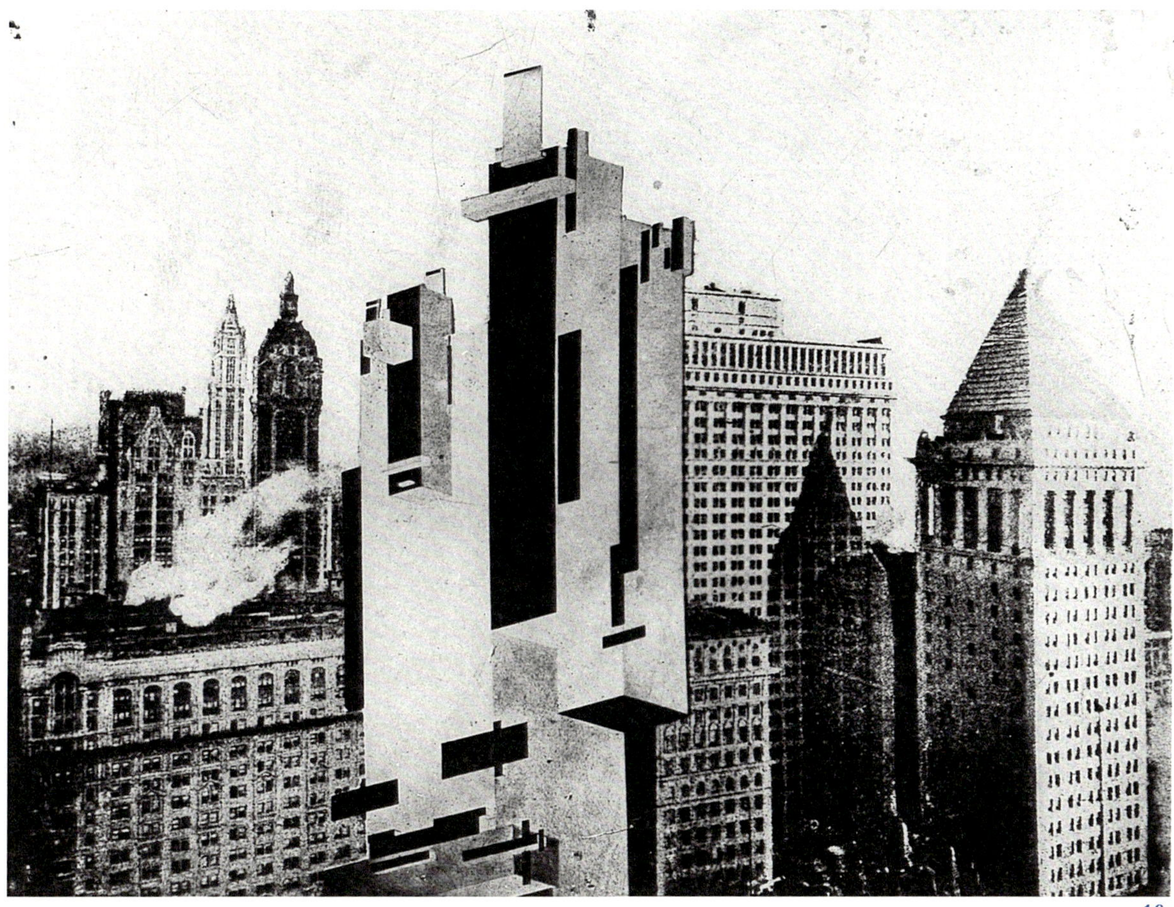

16.

16. K. Malewicz, Suprematist transformation of the City of New York, 1926, collage (lost) published in *Praesens*, no. 1, Warsaw

37 Peiper later accompanied Malewicz to Berlin. He facilitated the latter's visits in Germany and served from time to time as his translator.

38 In the language of Polish cultural constructions, "Sarmatian" is often used to designate the mythical character of the national panache.

paintings, including several "white" compositions that attracted particular attention in Germany. Warsaw being situated on the way to Berlin, Malewicz stopped there for a week. His visit, a veritable event for the Polish avant-garde, was well prepared thanks to several rhapsodic announcements, in particular ones published by the writer Tadeusz Peiper in his journal *Zwrotnica* (The Switch).[37] In Warsaw Malewicz exhibited a limited selection of paintings alongside his architectonic models. Warmly received in the Polish avant-garde milieu, he was not only fêted with a banquet (on 25 March) but was also invited to give a couple of lectures, which he delivered in a somewhat "peculiar" Polish (according to the press). His ideas were no less strange. True to its spirit of "Sarmatian"[38]

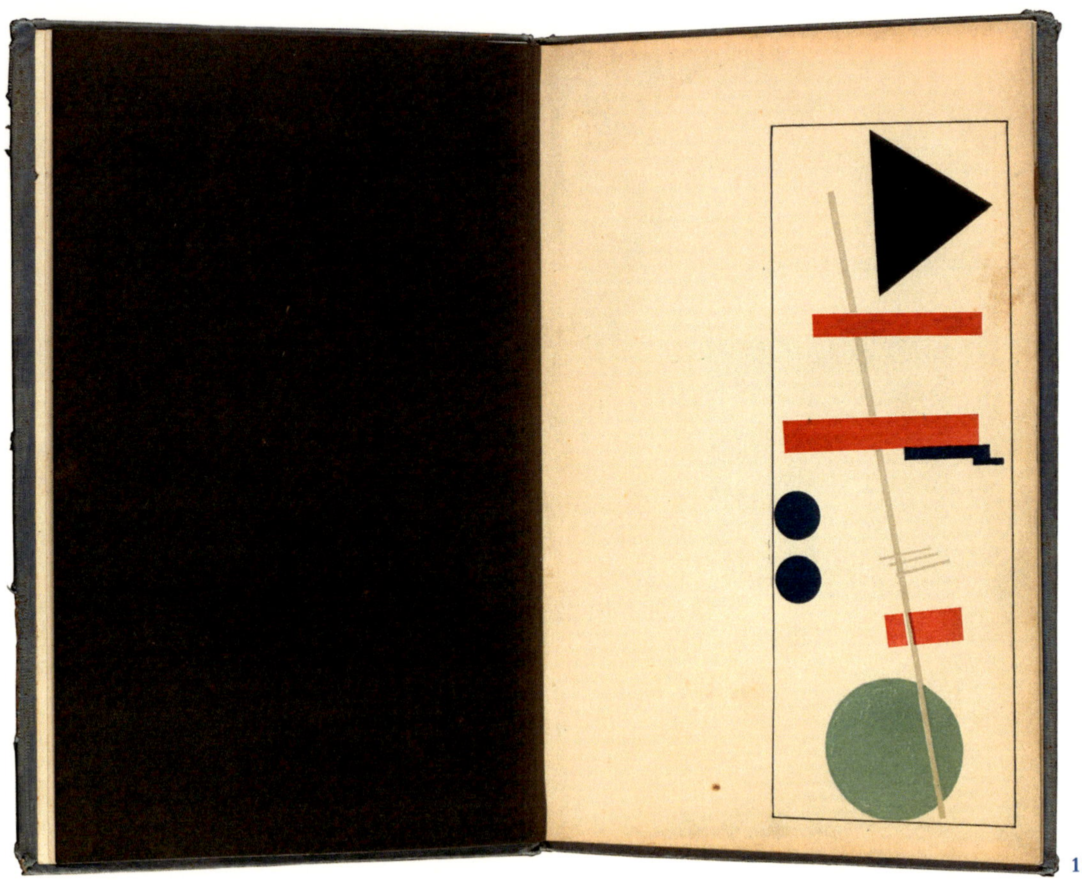

17.

extravagance, the modernist Warsaw audience greeted Suprematism with its usual panache – only to forget it shortly afterwards.

This visit was the occasion of a rather unusual initiative. The time for modernist optimism was fast coming to an end; as early as the summer of 1926 Malewicz was openly attacked in the Soviet press and the very original Leningrad art institute of "artistic culture" (GINKhUK) he had been directing since 1923 was threatened with being closed down permanently after the exhibition of Suprematist architectonas in June 1926 met with a violently anti-modernist response in the local press. Openings for his work in Russia were rapidly shrinking. As a result the artist decided to apply for a Polish passport. Two of his brothers having chosen to obtain Polish

17. Suprematist composition by Władysław Strzemiński, reworked (1921?) as a lithograph (28.5 × 18.3 cm), in the album *Kazimierz Malewicz 1876–1935* (sic!) that Strzemiński produced in 1936, MoMA, New York•

• Two versions of this album are known to exist, the second is in Muzeum Sztuki, Łódź, Poland.

[39] As one of the consequences of the peace treaty ending the Russo-Polish War Poles residing in Russia were allowed in 1921 to settle in Poland. Malewicz's brothers Antoni and Bolesław chose to do so while Kazimir and his youngest brother, Mieczysław, opted to remain in the Soviet Union. The history of the Polish branch of the family came to light only after the fall of the Berlin Wall.

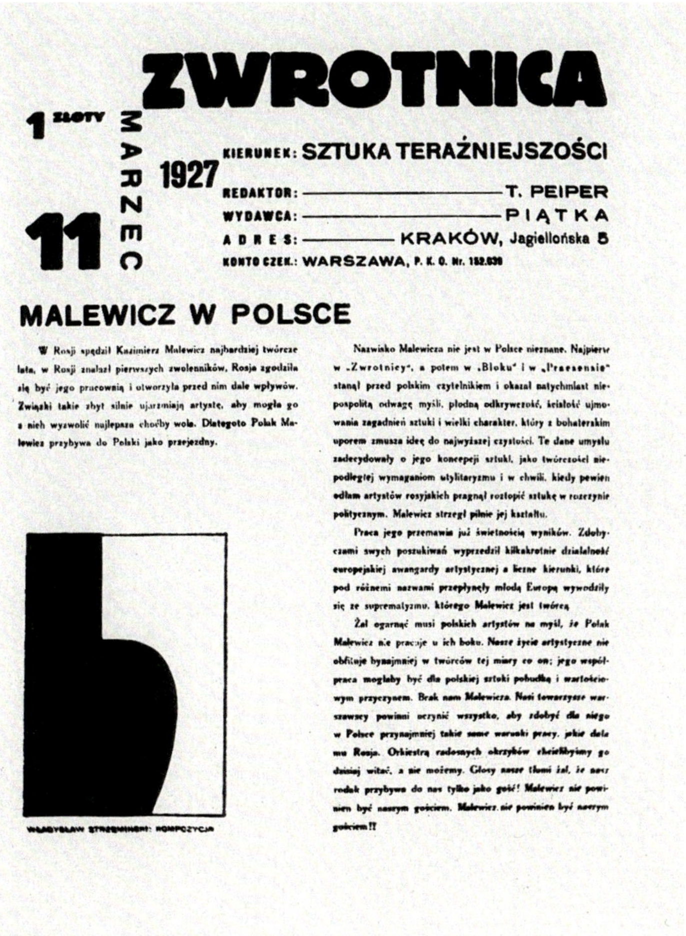

ZWROTNICA

1 ZŁOTY · MARZEC 1927 · 11

KIERUNEK: SZTUKA TERAŹNIEJSZOŚCI

REDAKTOR: ——————————— T. PEIPER
WYDAWCA: ——————————— PIĄTKA
ADRES: ——————— KRAKÓW, Jagiellońska 5
KONTO CZEK.: WARSZAWA, P. K. O. Nr. 152.636

MALEWICZ W POLSCE

W Rosji spędził Kazimierz Malewicz najbardziej twórcze lata, w Rosji znalazł pierwszych zwolenników, Rosja zgodziła się być jego pracownią i otworzyła przed nim dale wpływów. Związki takie zbyt silnie ujarzmiają artystę, aby mogła go z nich wyzwolić najlepsza choćby wola. Dlategoto Polak Malewicz przybywa do Polski jako przejezdny.

Nazwisko Malewicza nie jest w Polsce nieznane. Najpierw w „Zwrotnicy", a potem w „Bloku" i w „Praesensie" stanął przed polskim czytelnikiem i okazał natychmiast niepospolitą odwagę myśli, płodną odkrywczość, ścisłość ujmowania zagadnień sztuki i wielki charakter, który z bohaterskim uporem zmusza ideę do najwyższej czystości. Te dane umysłu zadecydowały o jego koncepcji sztuki, jako twórczości niepodległej wymaganiom utylitaryzmu i w chwili, kiedy pewien odłam artystów rosyjskich pragnął roztopić sztukę w roszczynie politycznym. Malewicz strzegł pilnie jej kształtu.

Praca jego przemawia już świetnością wyników. Zdobyczami swych poszukiwań wyprzedził kilkakrotnie działalność europejskiej awangardy artystycznej a liczne kierunki, które pod różnemi nazwami przepłynęły młodą Europę wywodziły się ze supremalizmu, którego Malewicz jest twórcą.

Żal ogarnąć musi polskich artystów na myśl, że Polak Malewicz nie pracuje u ich boku. Nasze życie artystyczne nie obfituje bynajmniej w twórców tej miary co on; jego współpraca mogłaby być dla polskiej sztuki pobudką i wartościowym przyczynkiem. Brak nam Malewicza. Nasi towarzysze warszawscy powinni uczynić wszystko, aby zdobyć dla niego w Polsce przynajmniej takie same warunki pracy, jakie dała mu Rosja. Orkiestrą radosnych okrzyków chcielibyśmy go dzisiaj witać, a nie możemy. Głosy nasze tłumi żal, że nasz rodak przybywa do nas tylko jako gość! Malewicz nie powinien być naszym gościem. Malewicz nie powinien być naszym gościem!!

WŁADYSŁAW STRZEMIŃSKI: KOMPOZYCJA

18.

Having the good fortune to encounter the artist's youngest sister, Victoria Zaitseva, in 1974, I was gradually able to piece together the family history. The first book on Kazimir Malewicz to be issued in Poland appeared in 2004 (A. Turowski, *Malewicz w Warszawie: rekonstrukcje i symulacje* [Malewicz in Warsaw: Reconstructions and Simulations], Kraków: Universitas, 2003, actually published in 2004). Based on information I had already published in 2002, this volume did not shed any new light on the subject. According to information gathered in Warsaw National Museum (*Muzeum Narodowe*) in the late 1970s, Kazimir Malewicz appears to have left one (or possibly two) paintings with Antoni. I was unable to establish the veracity of this fact.

[40] The Canadian art historian Maria Kosinska researched this topic meticulously in Warsaw in the mid-1980s. I am grateful to her and to my colleague professor Juliusz Chrościcki for kindly communicating her findings to me.

passports in 1921, he arranged for a discreet meeting with one of them, Antoni (at the time the powerful Soviet police were especially vigilant regarding "international" contacts).[39] Surrounding himself with every precaution, the artist applied for a Polish passport through friends connected with the Praesens group.[40] But his request was rejected due to his reputation as a "revolutionary" artist – which in the language of the period meant a "dangerous Bolshevik". It was thus that the modernist metaphors of Malewicz's disordered language were interpreted.

A deliberately slanted reading of a lengthy interview the artist gave earlier in Warsaw to *Segodnia*, the journal of

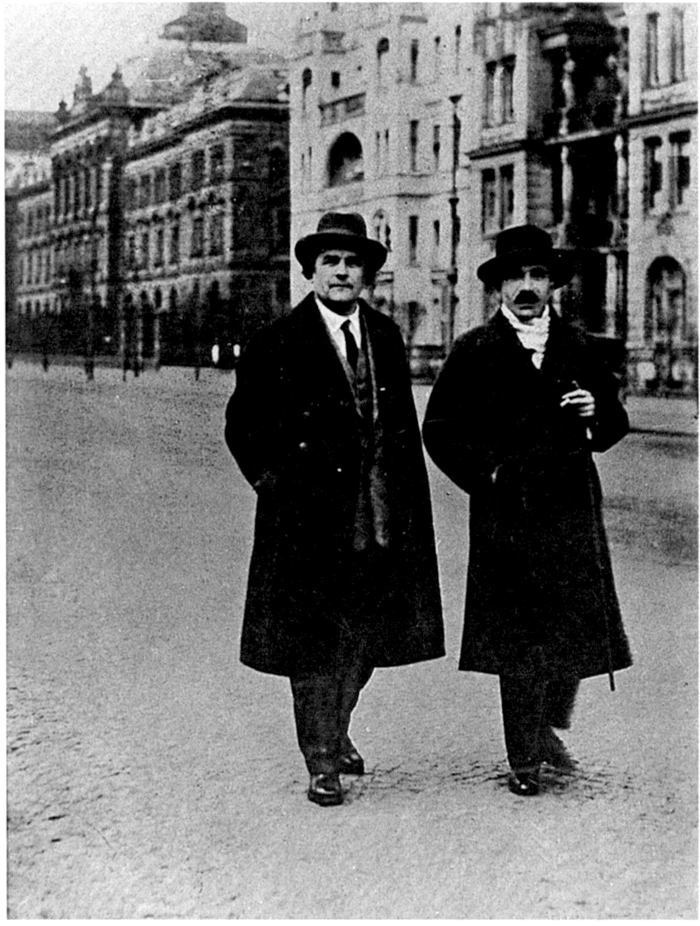

19.

19. Kazimir Malewicz and Tadeusz Peiper in Berlin, 1927

Russian émigrés in Riga, had the sudden effect of placing him unwillingly but no less openly in the camp of untrustworthy citizens. Upon his return to Leningrad this got him into serious trouble. Straddling national and political divisions had already become unthinkable. The police repression in Russia was beginning to show that the time for cultural and social nuances was gone. For Malewicz the bugle calls of terror were soon to sound as well. Yet in the months before this era of terror was to become established, he experienced, if only briefly, a moment of freedom and warm welcome in Germany. Prior to the salvo of sinister police warnings awaiting him in Leningrad, a sort of rainbow of recognition greeted his art.

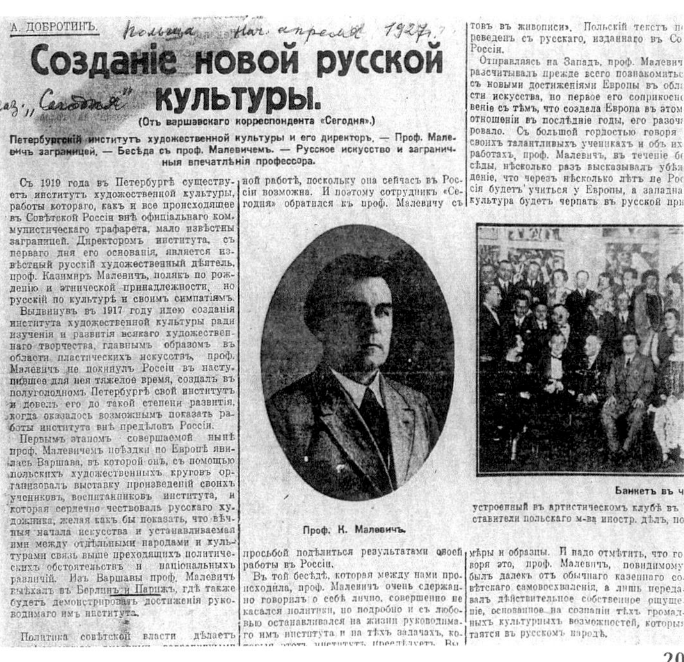

20.

Malewicz's name was first heard a few years ago among the hodge-podge of news about the arts in revolutionary Russia… He was reported to have pared down painting to its essential components, planes and color, and was said to have ended up painting white on white. It was even said that what he was accomplishing in his paintings was, as it were, a gradual self-disintegration of painting. By being rendered flat again thanks to his white [compositions] he was said to have returned painting to the lap from which it sprang, so to speak. Further, Malewicz was said to have drawn all the practical conclusions from this disappearance of art and to have given up painting. The reports of his subsequent career were very strange and had an almost legendary flavor: Malewicz appeared to be a second Moses, a Moses of art who was said to have freed his disciples from the shackles of painting and to have conducted them to the confines of a new artistic territory filled with promise; beyond the blurry outlines of easel painting, the [pictorial] surface had become a clean slate, space had opened up.

Ernst Kallai, 1927

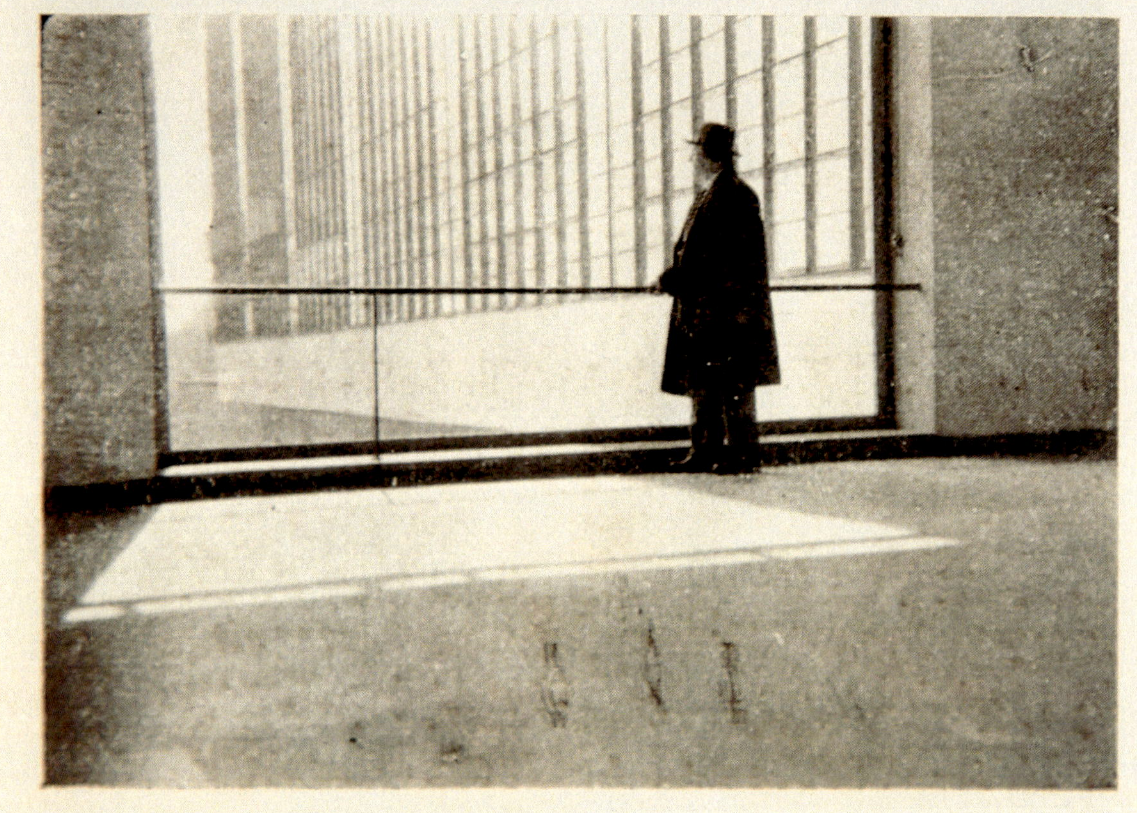

21.

From June to September the retrospective that included his paintings, architectonas and didactic panels was held at the Grosse Kunstausstellung in Berlin under the aegis of the local Society of Modernist Architects. Almost immediately after his arrival Malewicz lost no time in visiting the humanist architect Mies van der Rohe, who was deeply impressed by his personality.[41] In the days that followed, Malewicz travelled to the Bauhaus in Dessau, where he was received with open arms by its director, Walter Gropius. A future filled with

21. Malewicz visiting the Bauhaus (view of the main stairs), April 1927, photograph. Nakov Archives, Paris

[41] Malewicz's visit to Mies van der Rohe in the very first days of his stay in Berlin is known to us through the account of Tadeusz Peiper, who accompanied him on this occasion. The Polish writer was also present as Malewicz's translator during other visits in Germany, notably to the Bauhaus (see T. Peiper, "W Bauhausie" [At the Bauhaus], in

hope suddenly seemed open to him.[42] The project of a German edition of his writings was immediately set into motion and teaching plans were discussed. In the modernist oasis of the Bauhaus school, which had recently moved into new buildings at Dessau, Malewicz finally felt at home in a "promised land".

A few weeks later this brief, optimism-filled German reprieve was cut short with a brutal call to order. Not foreseeing the gravity of the reprisals by the Soviet authorities – how could he? – Malewicz returned precipitously to Leningrad in mid-June in the hope that he would be able to save his "Institute" and then return to Germany. These illusions dissolved soon after when in mid-September he was detained for two weeks at the "Big House" (the headquarters of the Leningrad police). This, he believed, was for the purposes of a simple though particularly thorough "verification". Released a couple of weeks later, he told his friends that his "conversations" with the inspector who had interrogated him had been "interesting"… Not without a substantial dose of naiveté, this modernist optimism vanished completely three years later when the artist had a distinctly more bitter taste of incarceration. Arrested in the final days of September 1930, he only walked out of the same police building two and a half months later, this time deeply traumatized. The experience of prison frightened him so badly he did not even dare to speak about it to his closest friends. He sought to leave Leningrad at any price but this proved impossible. The most basic material means needed for his survival began to grow scarce. Both he and his wife experienced hunger. All contacts with other countries were forbidden, depriving him of correspondence with his new Polish and German friends. His immediate family was equally traumatized: during his second detention his wife and mother resigned themselves to burning most of his papers as the latter contained references to the artist's correspondents abroad, especially his particularly dangerous contacts in Poland, then an openly anti-Bolshevist country. The noose of police oppression was tightening relentlessly.

Zwrotnica, no. 12, June 1927, pp. 25–26, reprinted in *Tędy, nowe usta*, Kraków, 1972; French translation in *Cahiers du Musée National d'Art Moderne*, no. 3, Paris, 1980, pp. 125–129).

[42] In a letter sent from Berlin to Lev Yudin on 7 May 1927, Malewicz urged his students to learn German (did he believe then that he would get a permanent position at the Bauhaus?), as he himself had begun to do in Berlin.

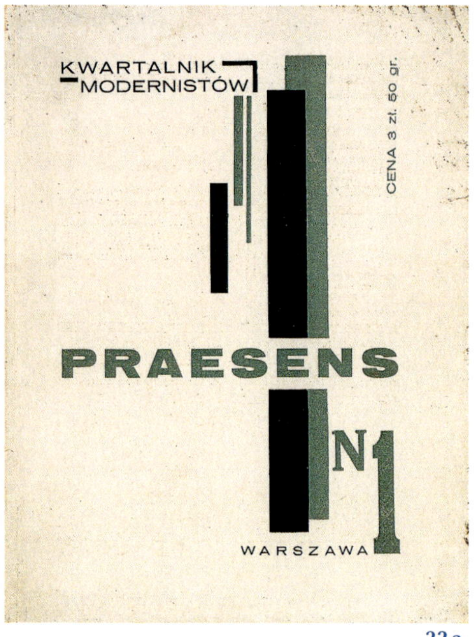

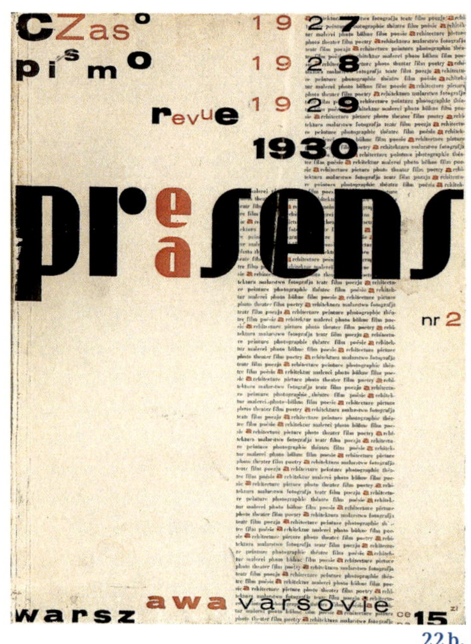

22 a.   22 b.

* * *

The last four years of Malewicz's life were a gradual descent into hell. His situation became all the more critical in the autumn of 1933 when it was discovered that he was suffering from cancer of the prostate. Completely ignorant of the police surveillance he was being subjected to, his Polish friends wondered why they were not receiving answers to their letters, and in Paris, at the moment when the Abstraction – Création association was being founded (1931), the question of whether "he was still alive" began to be asked.[43]

A moving funeral ceremony followed the artist's death in May 1935, but none of his friends and correspondents abroad was informed of his demise. In late September 1935 his friends or at least his modernist "fellow travellers" flocked to the Soviet Union, if only to the International Congress of Writers in Kharkov.[44] Social and artistic modernity evolved so fast (even brutally) that no one even bothered to find out whether he was still alive. Erasing all traces of Suprematism, the dark totalitarian night lasted long after World War II.

22 a and b.
a. *Praesens*, no. 1, Warsaw, June 1926.
Cover by Henryk Stażewski.
Issue containing the first French
translation of writings by Malewicz
b. *Praesens*, no. 2, Warsaw, 1930.
Cover by Henryk Stażewski

[43] The first *Abstraction – Création* miscellany (Paris, 1932) contains the brief notice: "We have not been able to reach Malewicz, Tatlin or Lissitzky".

[44] The list of visitors to this event would be too long to detail here; it included André Breton and André Malraux, followed by André Gide, H. G. Wells and many others. At the time, a certain curiosity about the young "land of the Soviets" existed in modernist and already anti-fascist circles. Among other figures the philosopher Ludwig Wittgenstein even briefly envisaged settling there permanently. (His trip to the USSR during the summer of 1936 put him off and he soon backtracked.) By mid-1936 this vogue was dying rapidly.

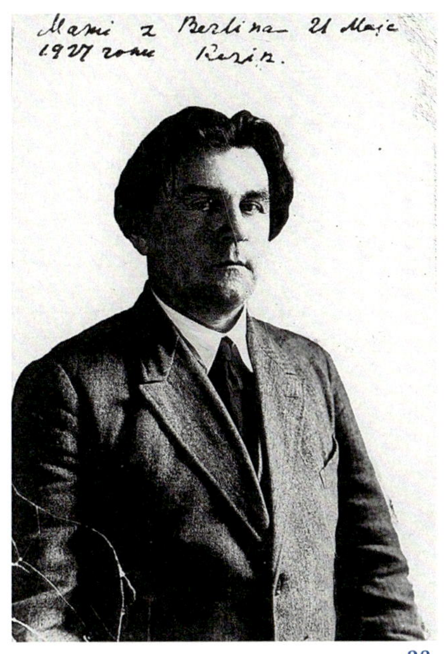

23.

23. Postcard sent by Malewicz from Berlin
to his mother, May 1927 ("To my dear
mother..." in Polish). Former archives
of the family of Natalia Andréeva
(Malewicz's wife). Whereabouts unknown

In the post-war decades the *fortuna critica* of Malewicz's
work followed the bumpy evolution of Russian society. Just as
the Nazi period relegated modern art to the category of "de-
generation" for long years, Soviet censorship ruled in Russia,
and it was only after the Chernobyl tragedy and the fall of
the Berlin Wall that Malewicz's art began to be displayed in
Russian museums. The rediscovery of his writings and of the
Suprematist aesthetic took even more time. To this day it suf-
fers from ideological residues lingering from anti-modernist
purges. Whether conscious or unconscious, these filters often
still persist. The remainder of this essay will be devoted to
identifying and refuting them.

They will use our names
to oppress generations to come.
That is how one makes preserves.

Viktor Shklovsky, *Knight's Move*,
Berlin, 1923

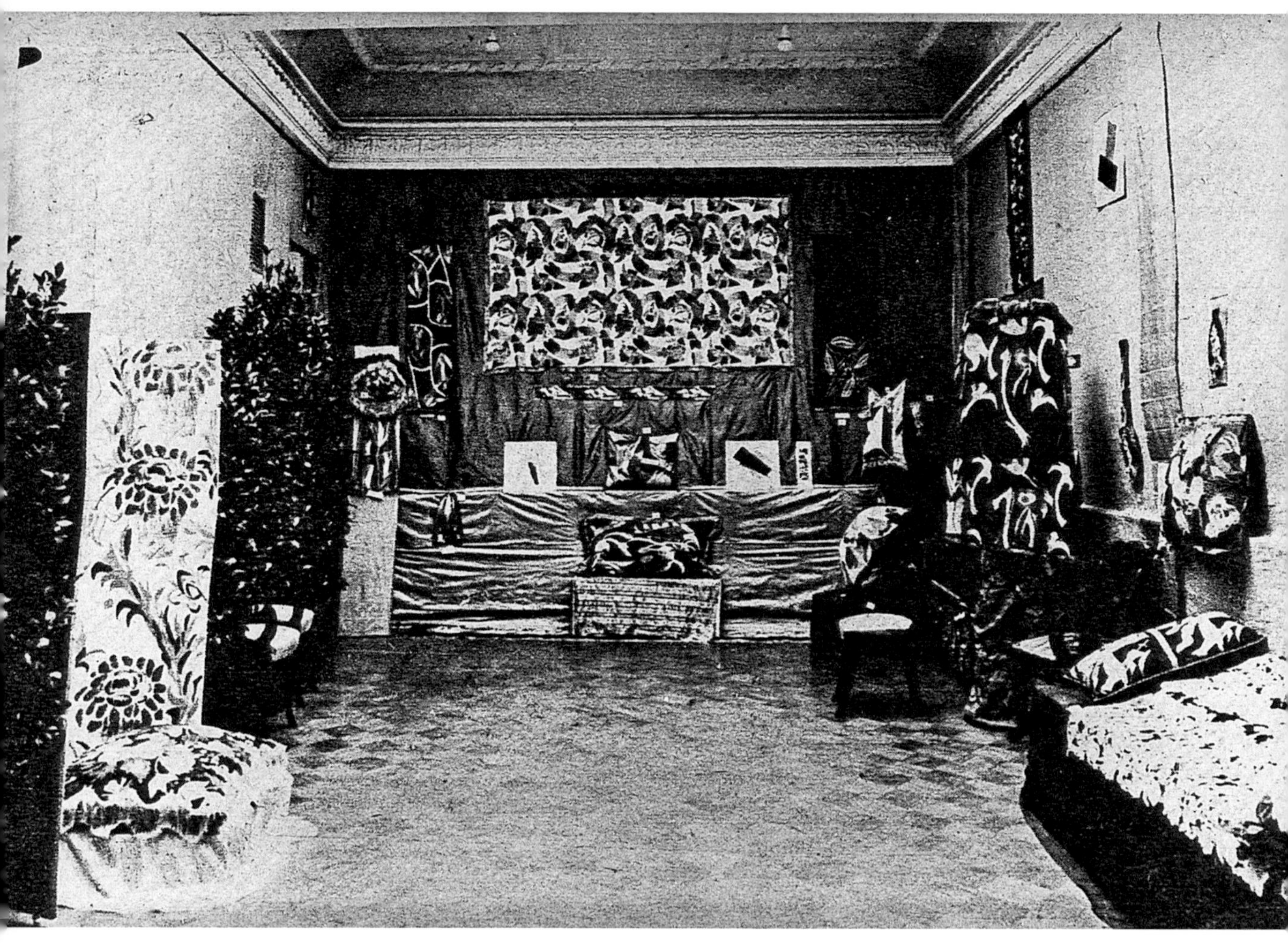

CHAPTER 5

RAISING THE FLAG:
SUPREMATISM, A "STRANGE WORD"[45]

The abstraction to which Malewicz's Cubo-Futurism and later his Alogism led, emerged in December 1915 under the banner of Suprematism. Though this word did not exist previously in the Russian language, it was not a Futurist neologism like those that Kruchenykh, Khlebnikov and Burljuk coined after 1910. As early as the spring on 1915 Non-Objective artworks, still regarded as outgrowths of Cubo-Futurism, were realised by some of Malewicz's comrades (Tatlin, Rozanova, Exter), but were not grouped in the new, clearly identified stylistic category and were not considered to belong to a specific category. In the course of the summer of 1915 the critic Yakov Tugendhold began using the term "Non-Objective" to designate them – one of the first (perhaps the first?) to do so.[46] This is the term that Malewicz used sparingly a few months later. As he wrote to his friend and at that time mentor Mikhail Matyushin in late September 1915, he had as yet not found his own term for "christening" the new current of art.

Without the usual Futurist fanfare and mainly without a specific designation – which did not yet exist in his vocabulary – the artist contributed several paintings of this type to

24. *The First Exhibition of Modern Decorative Art*, Lemercié Gallery, Moscow, November 1915. Three Suprematist paintings by Malewicz are visible among the works of decorative art. One of them hangs at the top of the right wall

[45] A reference to Giuliano Briganti's well-known essay "Barocco, strana parola", *Paragone*, no. 1, 1950, pp. 19–24.

[46] See my remarks on Tugendhold and the appearance of the term "Non-Objective" in *Kandinsky, the Enigma of the First Abstract Painting*, Kraków: IRSA, 2015 (hereinafter Nakov, *Kandinsky*, 2015) and in Nakov, *Tatlin*, 2020.

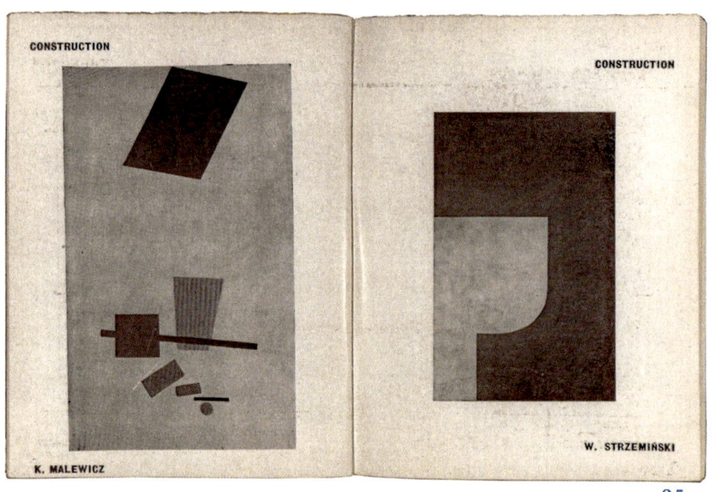

25 a.

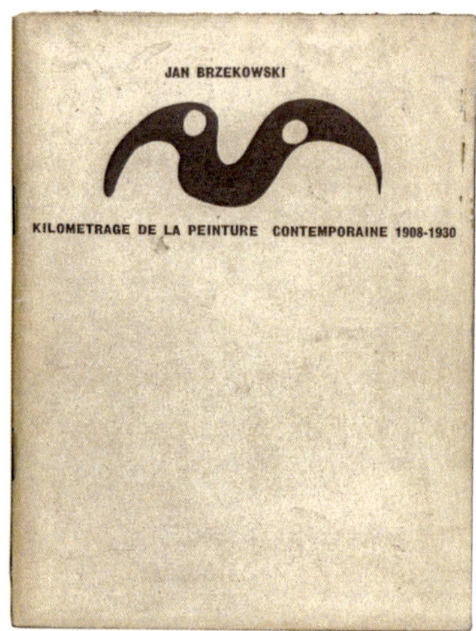

25 b.

a group show at Moscow's Lemercié Gallery in November 1915. The event was called *The First Exhibition of Modern Decorative Art* – hardly an alluring heading and an extremely modest one compared to Malewicz's philosophic ambitions.[47] Chosen by Alexandra Exter, one of the very few artists to have access to Malewicz's studio before the announcement of Suprematism, the works on display in this show of "decorative art", included a few paintings, three of them by Malewicz, as well as items of his decorative art. The strictly abstract canvases by Malewicz were so remarkable that one easily imagines they were last-minute additions, all the more so that they were not identified as paintings in the catalogue, though they are definitely present on a contemporary photograph of the event. The artist was probably still pondering their content and hesitating about how to "christen" (as he called it) the new creations. The notion of a title that would express their "domination" over the other currents was uppermost in his mind but as yet he lacked a word to translate the idea.[48] To his mind the new level he had attained in his art was an indisputable transcendence over the entire chain of (Cubo-Futurist) stylistic variations preceding it.

This development not only transcended everything that had gone before it, for Malewicz it was also a synthesis and a new departure for the art of painting. Viewed in the light of his absoluteness it represented the culmination of the artistic

25 a and b. Jan Brzękowski, *Kilométrage de la peinture contemporaine*, Paris: Librairie Fischbacher, 1931, 16 × 12 cm, private collection. Cover and double page with works by Malewicz and Władysław Strzemiński. Nakov Archives, Paris

[47] See my article "Ce 'galimatias non-objectif' du futurisme...': un épisode méconnu des origines du suprématisme", in the exh. cat. *Europe 1910–1939: quand l'art habillait le vêtement*, Paris: Musée Galliera, 1997, pp. 56–63. The essence of my comments is repeated in Nakov, *Malewicz*, 2007/2010, vol. 2, chap. 14. Recently various authors have repeated this information, as usual without attribution.

[48] Writing to Matyushin on 24 September 1915, Malewicz uses the term *gospodstvo* signifying (royal) domination. See E. F. Kovtun, in *Ezhegodnik rukopisnogo otdela Pushkinskogo doma na 1974 god* (Register of the Manuscript Section in the Pushkin House for the Year 1974), Leningrad, 1976, pp. 177–195, in particular p. 187.

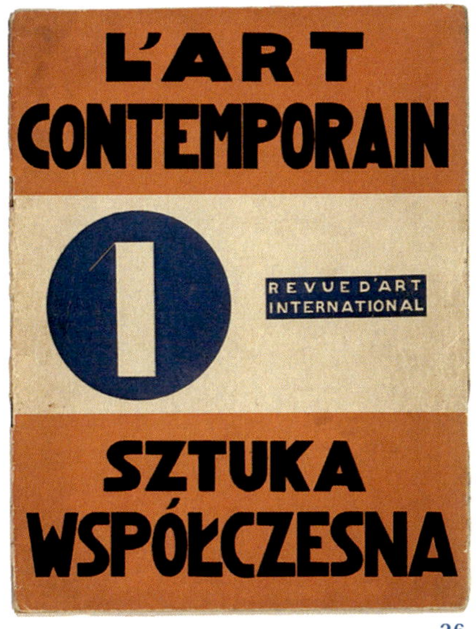

26.

26. Cover of *Sztuka Współczesna/L'art contemporain*, no. 1, Paris, 1931. Bilingual review published in Paris by a group of Polish modernists

[49] Nakov, *Malévitch. Écrits*, 1975. The note concerning the term "Suprematism" is reprinted without a change in the 1986 and 1996 editions, pp. 173–177. See the *Appendix* below.

evolution that had led up to it. The leap into the yonder of abstraction meant "non-objectivity" (*bespredmetnost*) for him and was the equivalent of a qualitative vault into a hitherto untouched spiritual, hence existential, dimension, a conceptual move definitely superior to a simple "stylistic" change. Quite simply, it was a new birth, the affirmation of a new being. This is why the new art required a baptism to mark its new identity. A symbolic act of the highest importance, the baptism was intended to signal the entrance into a new religion. Given these considerations the word "Suprematism" seemed ideally suited to expressing the nature of the new, "superior" art. As Malewicz puts it, it had been produced by "intuitive reason" and calling it by that name would assert its place in the universe. The "baptism" (the term that the artist used) was a decisive moment in the modernist evolution of the new art, an act of affirmation that was also an act of revelation, for it proclaimed that the artist's modernist strivings had at last reached maturity. "Suprematism", then. But where did the roots of its baptismal name lie?

In 1975, in the remarks I added to my first publication in French translation of the artist's writings, I included a short etymological explanation of the term "Suprematism".[49] With linguistic evidence to support my statements, I indicated that Malewicz had not only drawn inspiration from Catholic canon law as practised in the Polish Church of the time; he had actually borrowed from its vocabulary. Was "Suprematism" a memory, a scrap of something heard in childhood? It is difficult to imagine another source, all the more so that Malewicz, a highly intuitive artist, almost never, if ever, gave references for his borrowings. That his discovery of the term was a revelation (in the Biblical sense) seems unlikely, for in that case it would have had little significance for him, and his role would have been merely that of a finder. Once propelled into the sphere of modernist currents, the term "Suprematism" designated the sole production of Malewicz and at most his closest students, unconditional followers of his aesthetic, i.e. his philosophical system (as was also the case for Strzemiński who was to follow the same classification model in naming his "Unistic" compositions a few years later).

From the word "Suprematism", the artist soon derived another typically Polish-sounding heading, *Supremus*, sugges-

27 a.

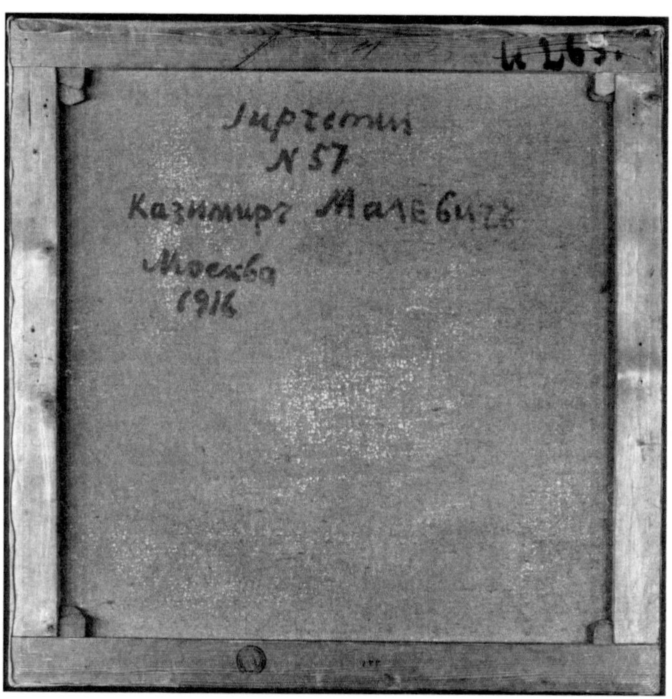

27 b.

tive of a collective identity and seemingly designating a warrior in some future Non-Objective battalion.[50] *Supremus* is usually accompanied by a number to create the impression that it belongs to a kind of Suprematist legion of works. From the spring of 1916 on Malewicz used these military-like titles for his different Non-Objective compositions. Written almost always in Latin characters (at least at first and long afterwards) on the back of several of these Non-Objective works (and in some cases on the drawings accompanying them), these titles are like battle cries. Conducting our etymological investigations still further, we note that the term *architectona*, which Malewicz used for his architectonic projects in the early 1920s, is feminine, whereas in Russian it is masculine. And yet another detail – but is it really a detail? – that reveals the psychological depth of the artist's imagination, the title *tors* (correct in both Russian and Polish) which Malewicz used in the last stage of his post-Suprematist work, is contemporary with the title *torso*,[51] which he also employed despite its foreign (probably also Polish) consonance.

27 a and b. Versos of paintings inscribed "Supremus"
a. Supremus-57 (Cat. S-434, Tate Gallery, London)
b. Supremus-50 (Cat. S-297, Stedelijk Museum, Amsterdam, photographed before relining)

[50] The sound of this word, derived from its Latin root, recalls that of the Polish *servus*, originally a military salutation (from the Austrian "K. und K." monarchic tradition) used widely in civil society. *Servus* was especially popular in Poland during the 19th century and was still in use in the late 1930s and even after World War II. Recall that the ancient-style chivalrous tradition, particularly alive during the 19th century, left deep traces in Malewicz's family (the first name of his officer-uncle was Tytus and his father's was Seweryn, derived from the Roman Severus, both evocative of an extremely ancient lineage).

[51] Cat. PS-180 in the *Catalogue raisonné*.

54

The artist relied on the same system of Latin letters (and Arabic numerals) in the mid-1920s to classify his Suprematist production. In all likelihood, he worked out this method in late autumn 1919 or even earlier (the winter of 1918–1919, when he started teaching at the Moscow Free Studios, "SVO-MAS"). El Lissitzky used a similar system (Latin characters indicating series) around the same time to designate his *Proun* constructions, which stemmed directly from Malewicz's example. In the mid-1920s Strzemiński would adopt the same system of references for his "Unist" compositions.[52] These are subtle differences but, beyond the private nature of these artists' respective visual imagination, they nevertheless indicate an unavoidable cultural attachment that must be taken into account.

[52] Strzemiński was active in the first abstract period and he too was marked by Malewicz's example (and this from the very beginning of his abstract production).

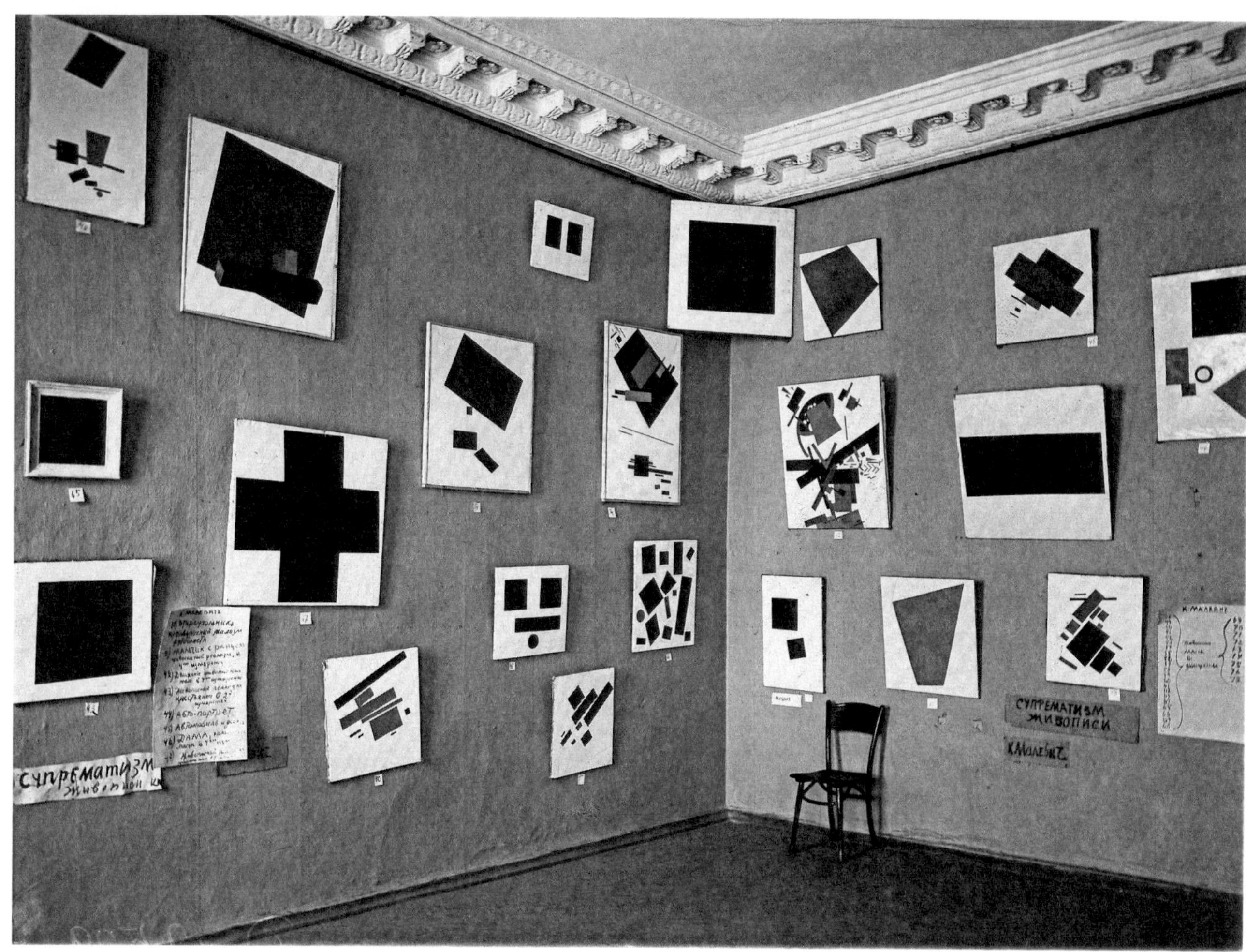

28.

CHAPTER 6

"I HAVE TRANSFORMED MYSELF
IN THE ZERO OF FORM"[53]

*At first Suprematism possesses a purely
philosophical movement [...]
passing through colour.*

K. Malewicz,
"Suprematism, 34 Drawings", 1919[54]

28. Some suprematist works shown at the
0,10 exhibition in 1915, gelatin silver print.
Nakov Archives, Paris

[53] K. Malewicz, *From Cubism and Futurism to
Suprematism*, Moscow, 1916. At least two English-language translations of this text are available: T. Andersen (ed.), *K. S. Malevich, Essays
on Art, 1915–33* (trans. by X. Glowacki-Prus and
A. McMillin), New York: George Wittenborn
and Company (The Documents of Modern Art),
1968, and J. E. Bolt (ed. and trans.), *Russian
Art of the Avant-Garde*, London: Thames and
Hudson, 1988. See also the French Translation by Nakov, *Malévitch. Écrits*, 1975/1986, pp.
180–183/173–177.

[54] Artist's statement included in the catalogue of
the 10th State Exhibition *Non-Objective Creation
and Suprematism*.

Suprematism appeared for the first time publicly in St Petersburg in December 1915 on the occasion of the *0,10* exhibition
subtitled "The Last Futurist Exhibition". The artist having up
until then given no explanation for this choice, both he and
the word "Suprematism" were viewed with an identical degree
of astonishment, if not derision. For the most part, the Russian
press of the period and many of Malewicz's friends simply
ignored it. In the then prevailing atmosphere of avant-garde
competitiveness the show's heading was probably regarded
as yet another "Futurist" extravagance that popped up at the
time like mushrooms after a shower, only to disappear even
more rapidly. Much later on the other hand, when Suprematism was rediscovered, a multitude of explanations flour-
ished in the 1960s and early '70s. Certain misunderstandings
persist to this day. In the absence of any comprehension of
the particular aesthetic context surrounding the birth of Suprematism – not to mention the exhibition itself – the cipher
0,10 remained somewhat enigmatic. For years it was misunderstood. Worse still, it was transformed without explanation
into a sort of mathematical cryptogram. The zero followed by

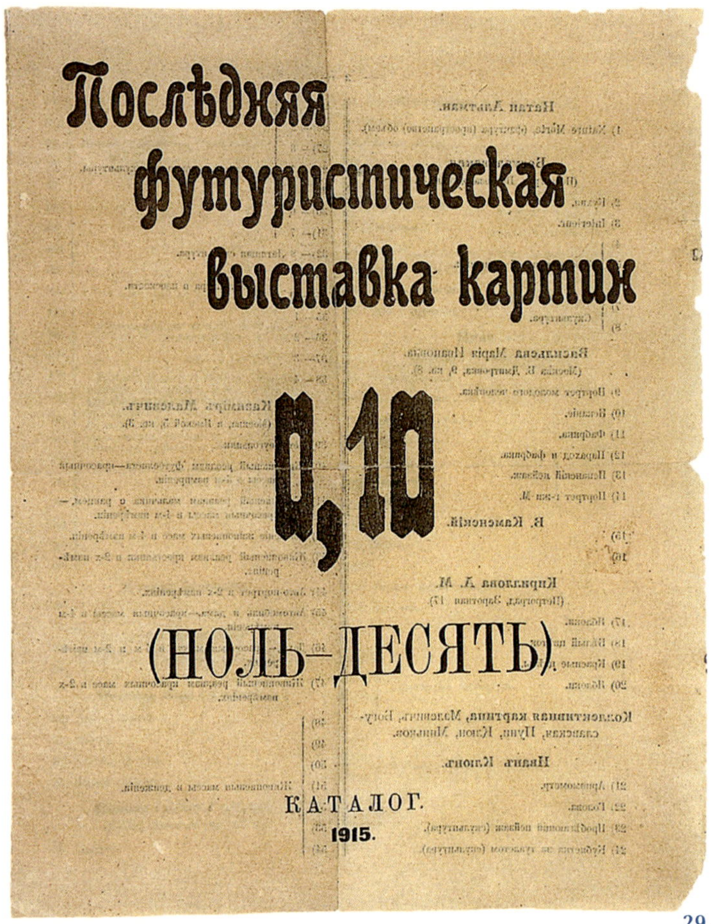

29. *0,10* exhibition, Dobychina Gallery, Petrograd, December 1915, cover of the catalogue. Nakov Archives, Paris

29.

a comma and placed before the number 10 was even said to have no other justification than that of a typographic mistake! It was probably intended to be 0.10, the tenth part of… something (but what?).[55] That is why for decades commentators preferred to use the subheading "The Last Suprematist Exhibition" and leave the main heading 0,10 outside the event's semantic field.

Yet the symbol zero does in fact occur on the very first page of the 1915 manifesto. More importantly still, it figures with undeniable frequency in several paintings and texts that punctuate the artist's progress along the path to Suprematism. Understood as a symbol in the chain of Futurist signs, the point of departure for Transrational and, later, Alogist

[55] Another invented version of the heading appeared in the catalogue of an exhibition in the Hutton Gallery in New York, where it is written "0-10" (see S. Bodine, "Suprematism: the Zero Point", in *Malevich, Suetin, Chashnik. Watercolors, Drawings, Porcelain*, New York, 1983, pp. 5–7).

30. Invitation card to the *0,10* exhibition, Petrograd, December 1915

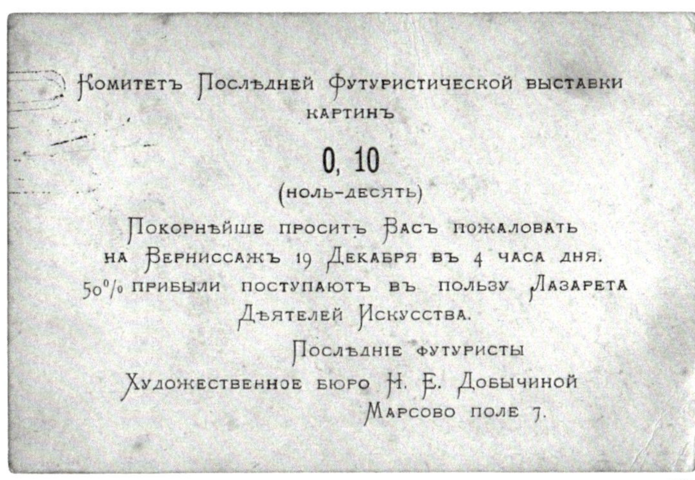

30.

⁵⁶ See Kovtun's comments and introduction in *op. cit.*, 1976, pp. 177–195.

⁵⁷ The catalogue of the *0,10* exhibition lists more than ten artists; as for reasons of avant-garde diplomacy, and particularly for financial reasons (Puni financed the exhibition), Malewicz must have accepted the presence of certain participants (Marie Vassilieva) who did not correspond to the aesthetic positions of his Suprematist Non-Objectivity. As a matter of fact, we know that before the opening of the exhibition he vetoed the participation of David Burljuk, whose latest paintings (those of 1915) he did not esteem compatible with his own avant-garde requirements.

⁵⁸ An inheritance from the Marxist ideology that was essentially anti-modernist, the accusation of nihilism levelled against Suprematism goes back to the first anti-Suprematist attacks of 1916 (I refer in particular to the ultra-conservative criticism of Alexandre Benois). In the 1930s and later, materialist detractors of Malewicz's aesthetics repeated this imputation blatantly. This type of interpretation lingered on for a long time and even today nihilist readings are unconsciously (or not?) reflected in the work of some scholars (see, for example, some of Aleksandra Shatskikh's comments of 2017, not to mention those of other less well-informed writers).

developments, zero reveals the deep meaning of what Malewicz called the "philosophical movement" underlying his conceptual advance during the period running from summer 1913 to the autumn of 1915.

The heading *0,10* thus actually consists of three elements: zero, the number 10 and the comma in between. One of the first plausible interpretations was suggested in 1976 by Evgueny Kovtun. A friend of mine, Kovtun was a Russian art historian fascinated by the Petersburg avant-garde in general and by Malewicz's St Petersburg followers in particular.[56] In his comments on the correspondence between Malewicz and Matyushin in the months preceding the advent of Suprematism, Kovtun rightly listed the title *0,10* not as a kind of mathematical reference but as an Alogist symbol and pointed out that the presence of the comma reveals this plainly. As for the number 10, Kovtun thought that it indicated the number of artists, argonauts of the new world of Non-Objectivity, initially chosen to participate in the show.[57] The zero stands both symbolically and explicitly for the stage of purification preceding the "Promised Land" of the new creation. Like the Hebrews' mythical crossing of the desert Malewicz's zero is thus by no means a symbol for the absence of something, still less a "nihilistic" affirmation,[58] but, Kovtun believed and I agree, the sign for an unknown dimension full of mystery, one charged with fascinating possibilities from which the richness of the future art was to emerge.

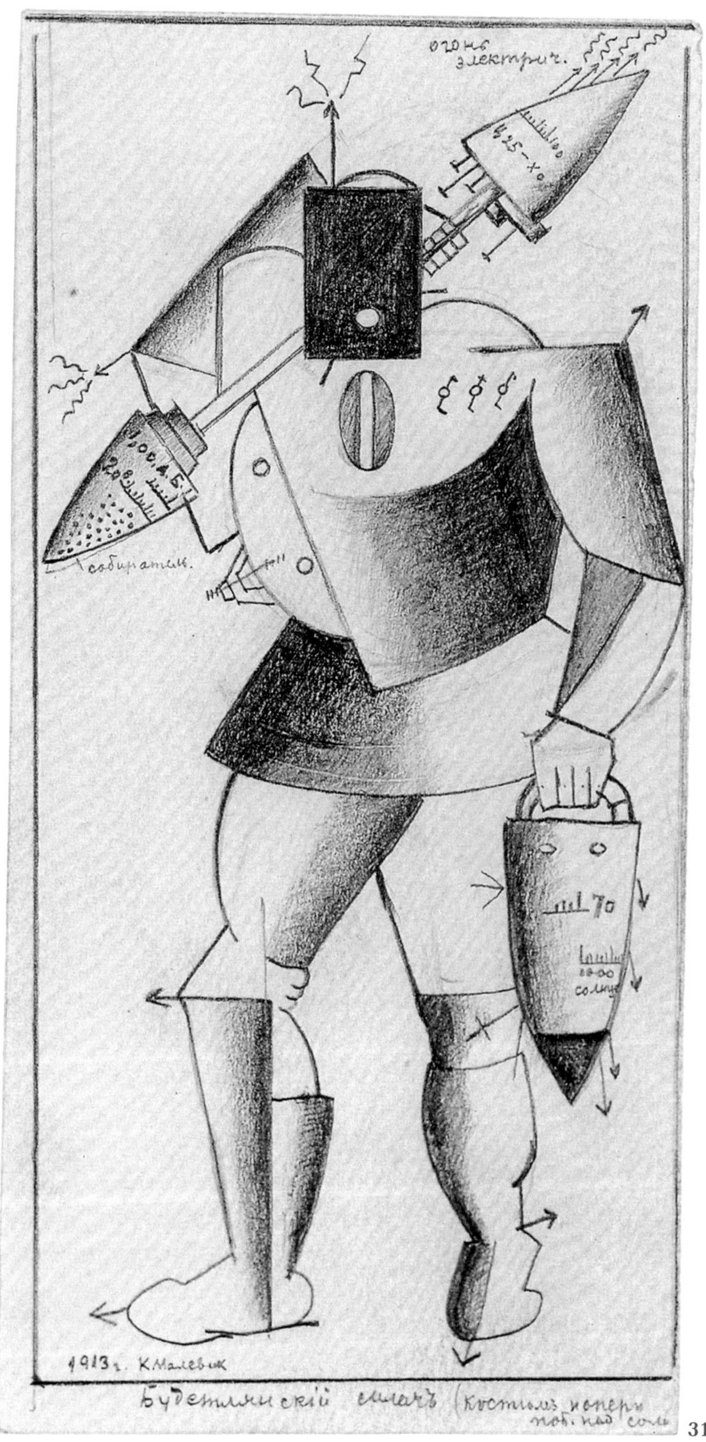

31. *(Futurist) Strongman*, motif of 1913
reworked in spring 1915 (Cat. F-408),
pencil on paper, 16.2 × 8 cm, State
31.   Museum of Literature, Moscow

32. (Futurist) Strongman, motif of 1913 reworked in spring 1915 (Cat. F-475), pencil on paper, 10.2 × 11.5 cm, Khardzhiev-Chaga Cultural Foundation, Amsterdam (on deposit at the Stedelijk Museum, Amsterdam)

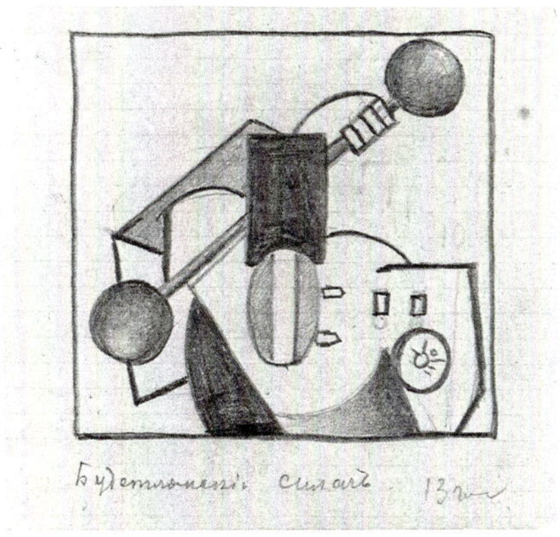

32.

And, in fact, when one examines the array of "Transrational" symbols in the artist's work surrounding the staging of *Victory over the Sun*, a Futurist performance that can be viewed as a reservoir of pre-Suprematist themes, one is struck by the presence of zeros, perhaps already then a key element for Malewicz. We know that in the first months of 1915 the artist returned to his cogitations of 1913 surrounding that production, and that he subsequently insisted that the Ubuesque "opera" was the principal inspiration for his invention of Suprematism. What was the meaning of zero at this point? It was an unknown quantity filled with promise, a secret receptacle brimming with the possibilities of a "future" that lay close at hand, a continent where Non-Objective creativity would blossom.[59] Thus a zero features prominently in *Aviator* of 1914,[60] where it is placed on the hat worn by the aviator, one of the leading characters in *Victory over the Sun*, which had been staged the previous December. In that position zero stands for both the concept of intriguing, i.e. creative "nothingness" and the dimension of the imagination, two central components of the Alogist revolution.

Another zero, magnified to the point of becoming as large as the figure's head, occupies the centre of the composition known as *(Futurist) Strongman* (F-475). Like the Aviator, the Strongman is a key figure in the "opera". The zero is further emphasized, very emphatically, in yet another representation, this one actually based on the spectacle, a meticulously rendered drawing of 1915 (F-408) where it features prominently

[59] Secrecy is one of the recurring themes of the 1913 "opera", suggesting an almost cabbalistic level of hidden meaning – another major theme of the Symbolist epic, a theme calling for explanations that would take us slightly beyond our present subject.

[60] *Cf.* Cat. F-444.

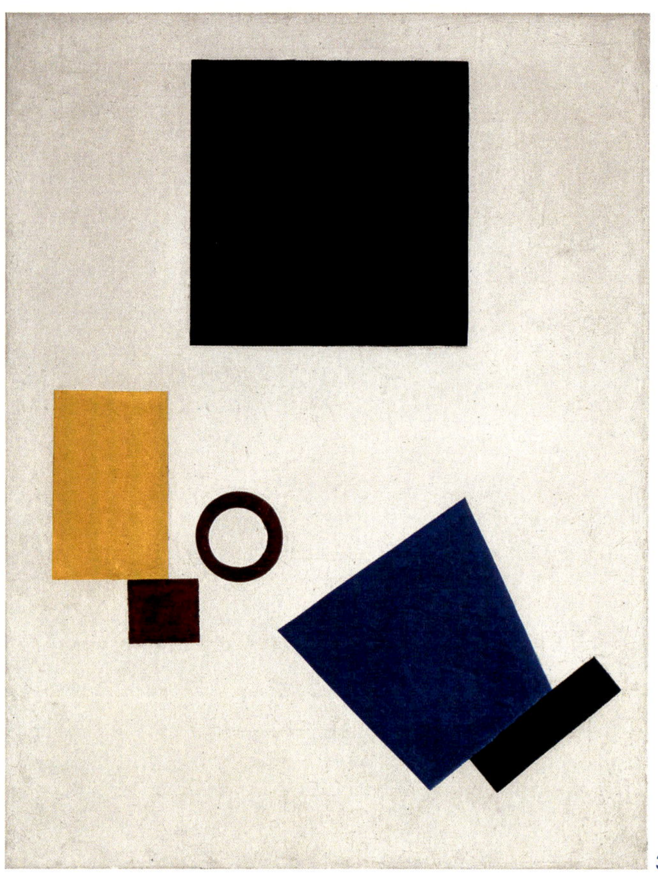

33 a.

on the character's chest. One gets the feeling that the artist's work on *Aviator* has come to fruition. There is yet another zero, also in a major project, a stage design for *Victory over the Sun,* a drawing noteworthy for the form of the zero, which is thickened into a kind of wheel so that it is no longer just a thematic symbol but now belongs to the category of pictorial signs. A year and a half early, this image announces the formal transformations of the first Suprematist compositions of the summer of 1915 (S-21, S-23 and S-24). The zero also appears in the background of the centre of *Lady at an Advertising Column* (F-455), a painting that very closely precedes the appearance of the first Suprematist planes. Adhering to a line of thought that propelled each narrative detail into a form (as was the case initially with Suprematism), Malewicz would rapidly transform the Alogist zero into a visual zero. We find

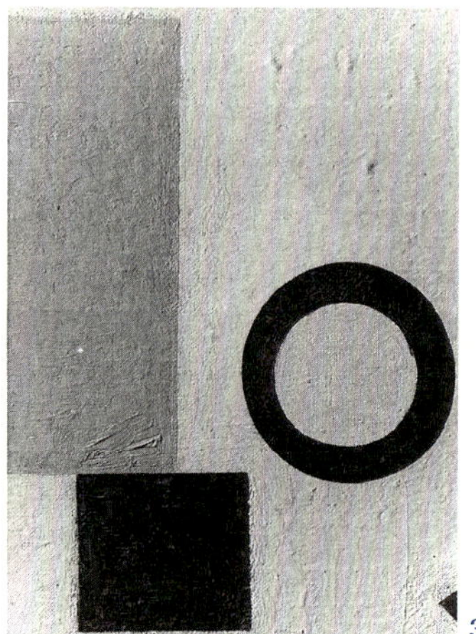

33 b.

34. *Aviator*, 1914 (Cat. F-444), oil on canvas, 125 × 65 cm, State Museum of Russia, St Petersburg. Inscription on the back: *"Awiator"* (in Polish). On the frame: *"Aviator no. 82"*

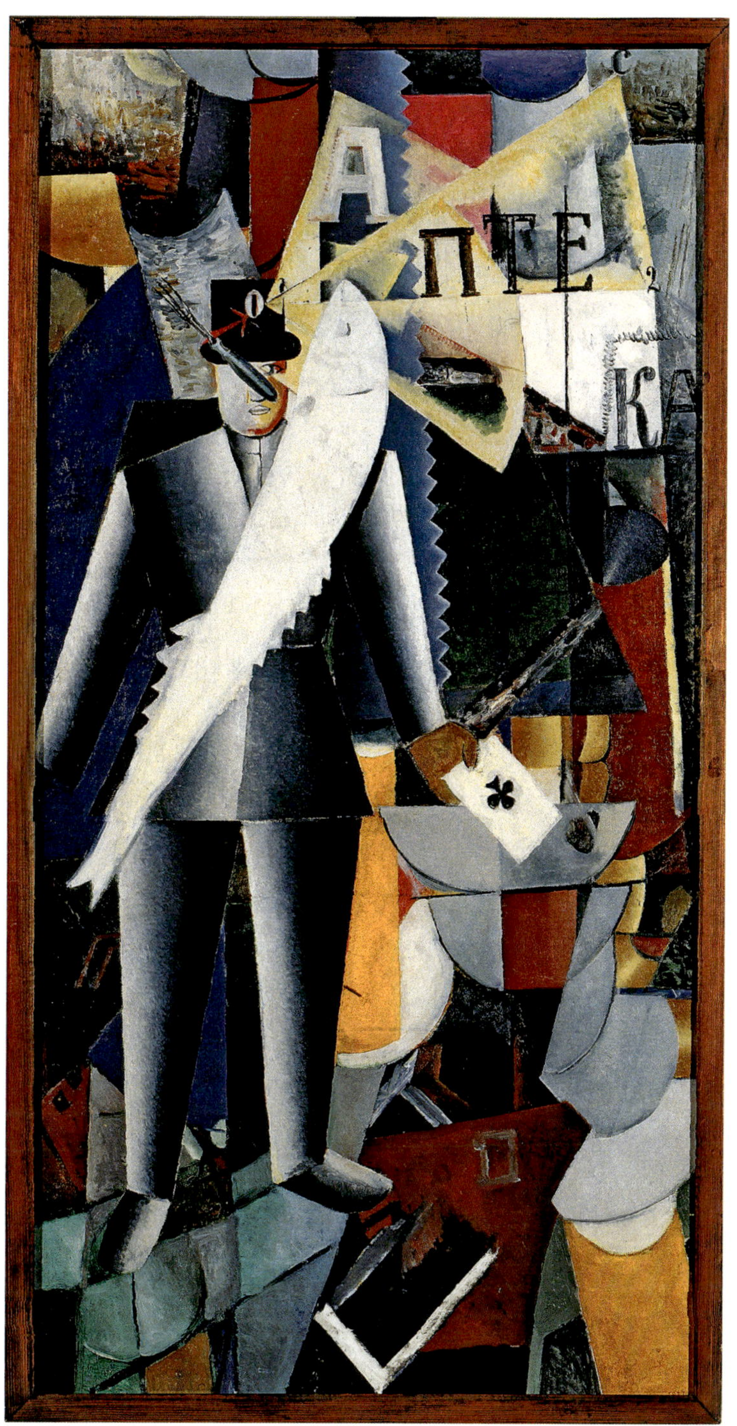

34.

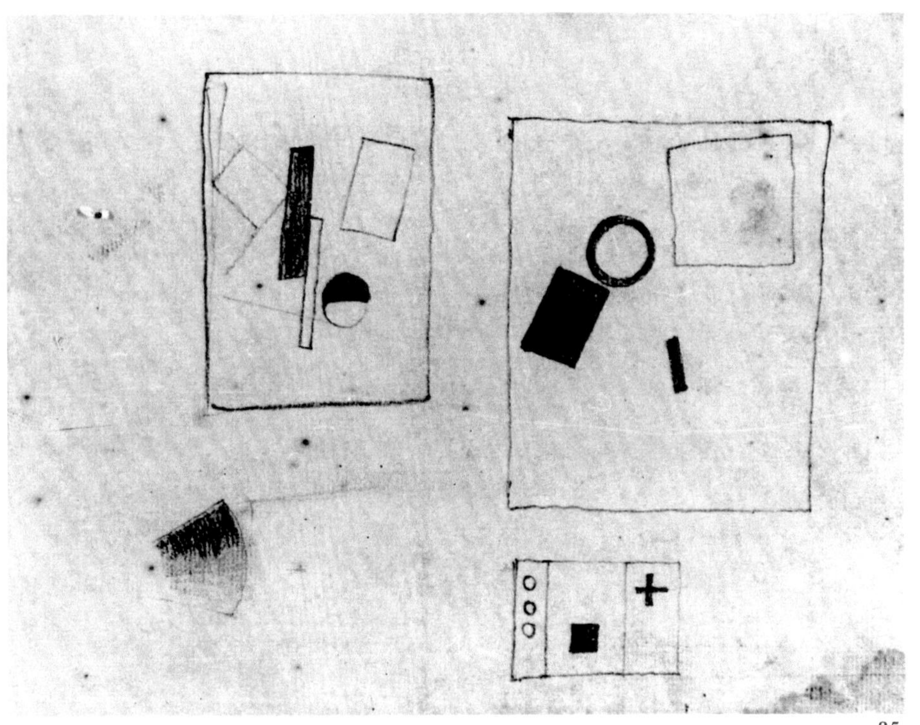

35.

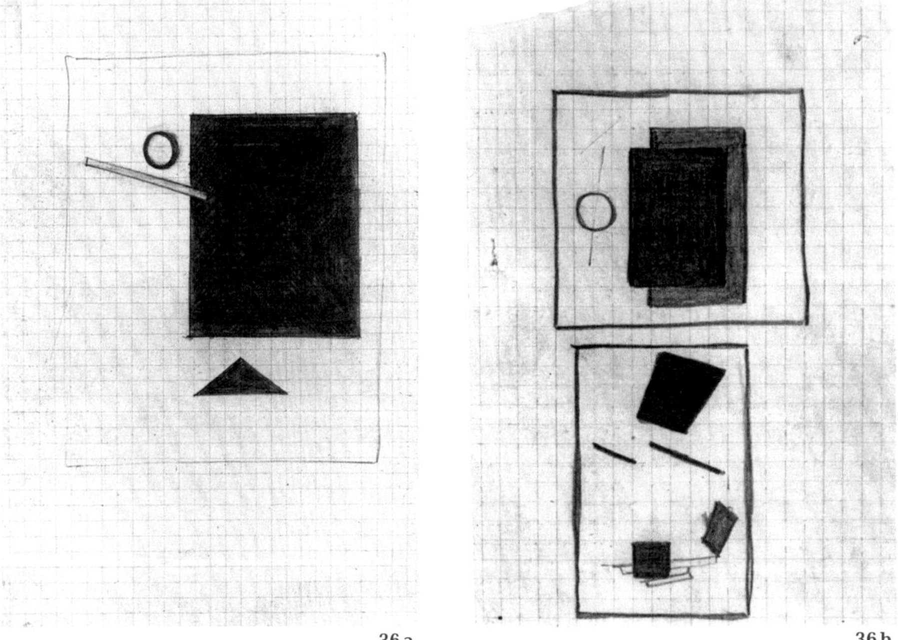

36 a.   36 b.

35. (Suprematist composition), 1915
(Cat. S-22), pencil on paper, 20 × 25 cm,
private collection

36 a and b.
a. (Suprematist composition), 1915
(Cat. S-24), pencil on paper, 21 × 14 cm,
present whereabouts unknown
b. Two Suprematist compositions, 1915
(Cat. S-10), pencil on paper, 16.2 × 12.2 cm,
private collection

37 a and b.
a. *Lady at an Advertising Column*, 1914
(Cat. F-455), oil and papier collé on canvas,
71 × 64 cm, Stedelijk Museum, Amsterdam
b. *Lady at an Advertising Column* (detail)

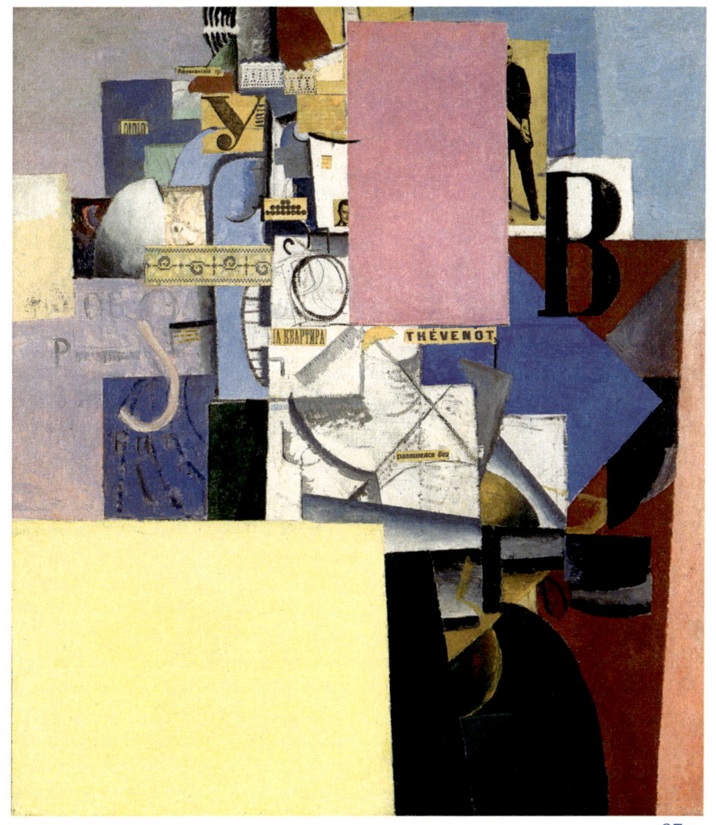

37 a.

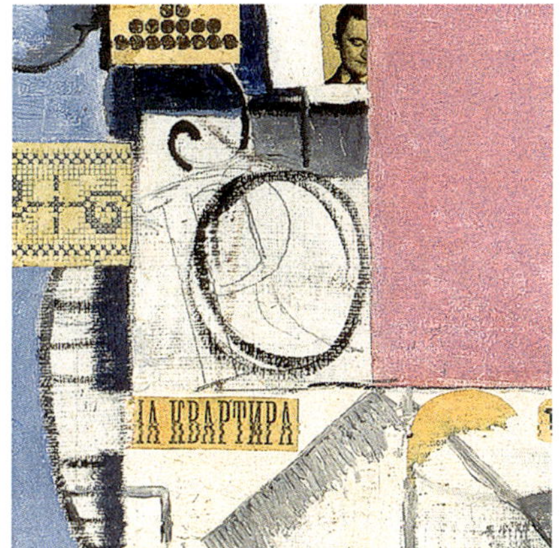

37 b.

this zero transmuted almost imperceptibly into a Non-Objective form. In the early Suprematist compositions it coagulates,
so to speak, into a full-blown plastic form. It appears as a thick
circle in the series of Suprematist "portraits" that are still
dependent on the "narrative" approach, *Self-Portrait in Two
Dimensions* (S-21), *Lady* (S-170), *Airplane in Flight* (S-48),
Automobile and Lady (S-52) and *Sable and Cat* (S-18). Other
compositions in which the narrative reference is just as clearly
indicated can also be directly related stylistically to this first
sequence of Non-Objective constructions.[61]

I have repeatedly explained
our collective position in De Stijl:
it was a matter of attaining 0 as a neutral axis,
as a moment of absolute harmony.

Theo van Doesburg,
De Stijl, January 1932

[61] See S-23, S-24 and S-29 verso.

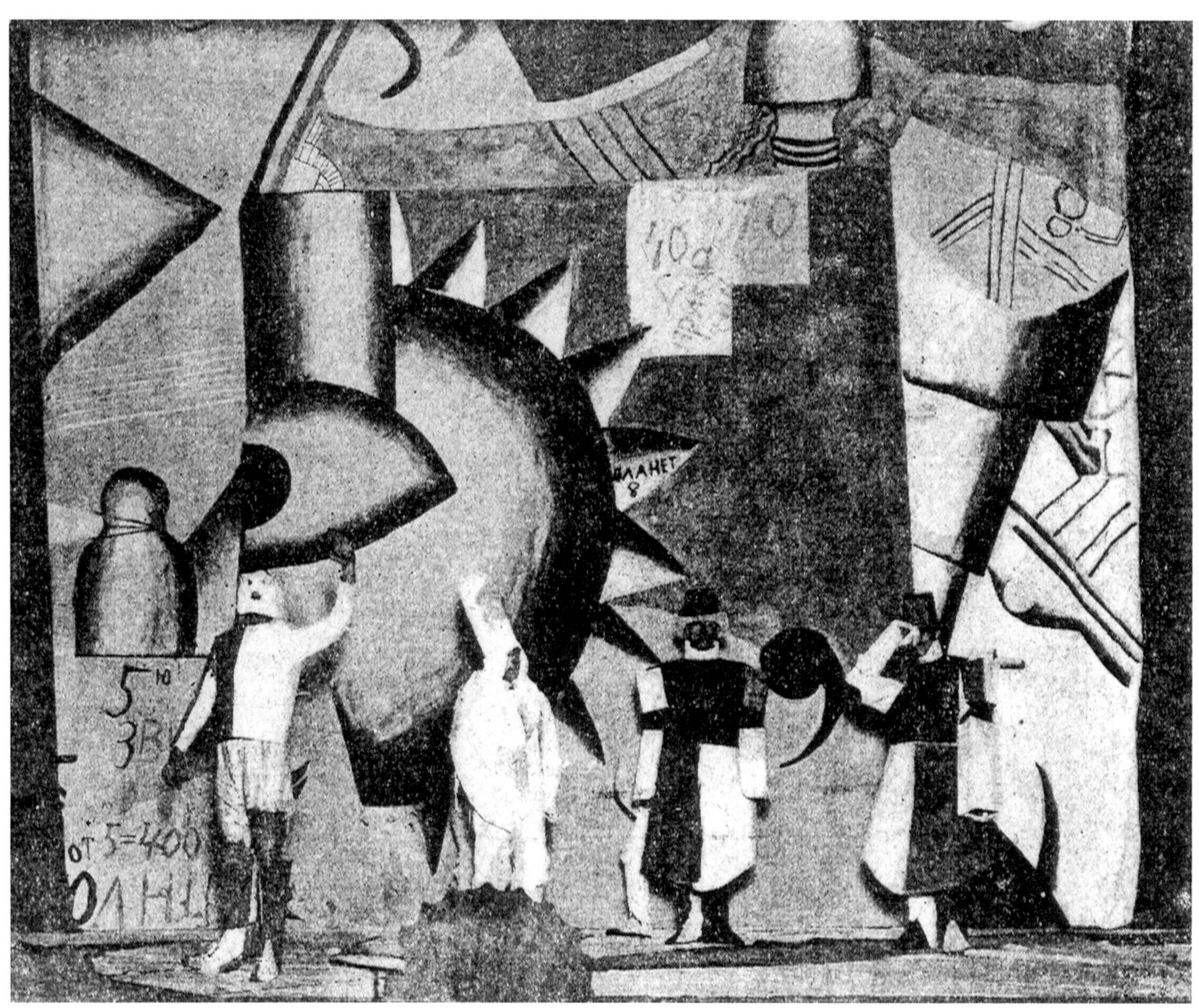

38.

COMMAS, ALOGIST LEVERS OF MEANING

We have broken up grammar and syntax.

Aleksei Kruchenykh,
New Ways of the Word, 1913

We have destroyed punctuation.
Only exclamation marks are left…
an authentic primitiveness…

Aleksei Kruchenykh,
Bukh Liesinnyi, 1913

The most original element of the indubitably symbolic heading *0,10* is the inclusion of a comma. It too refers to the Transrational revolution of 1913 which, as I have said, comprises the staging of *Victory over the Sun*. Elevated to the level of a pictorial sign, in other words treated as a full-blown figurative entity, it asserts its autonomous figural presence. It appears as such in several compositions which occur in conjunction with Malewicz's stage designs for the "opera" and in some cases even precede them very slightly. Thus one can follow the evolution of the comma, treated at the time as a major motif, in several lithographs from the summer of 1913: *Grammar* (F-353), *Arithmetics* (F-351 and F-352), *Noises* (F-350) and *Universal Landscape* (F-390). The last composition looks directly forwards to certain themes in the libretto of *Victory over the Sun*, such as the windows "of the houses that all face inside", a *quasi*-Freudian thematic invention.

As an element possessing a cardinal authority of its own, the comma at this point transcends the linear logic of the sentence (Kruchenykh describes it as an "added" element)[62] in order to signify the obsolescence of the semantic order and the fact that it is being surpassed. The sequences of linear thought,

38. *Victory over the Sun*, Futurist "opera" by A. Kruchenykh, K. Malewicz and M. Matyushin, performances of 3 and 4 December 1913 at the Luna Park Theatre, St Petersburg. Sets and costumes by Malewicz

[62] The Futurist poet refers to a "drop by drop" (*kapleobraznaya*) order (Kruchenykh, *op. cit.*, 1913).

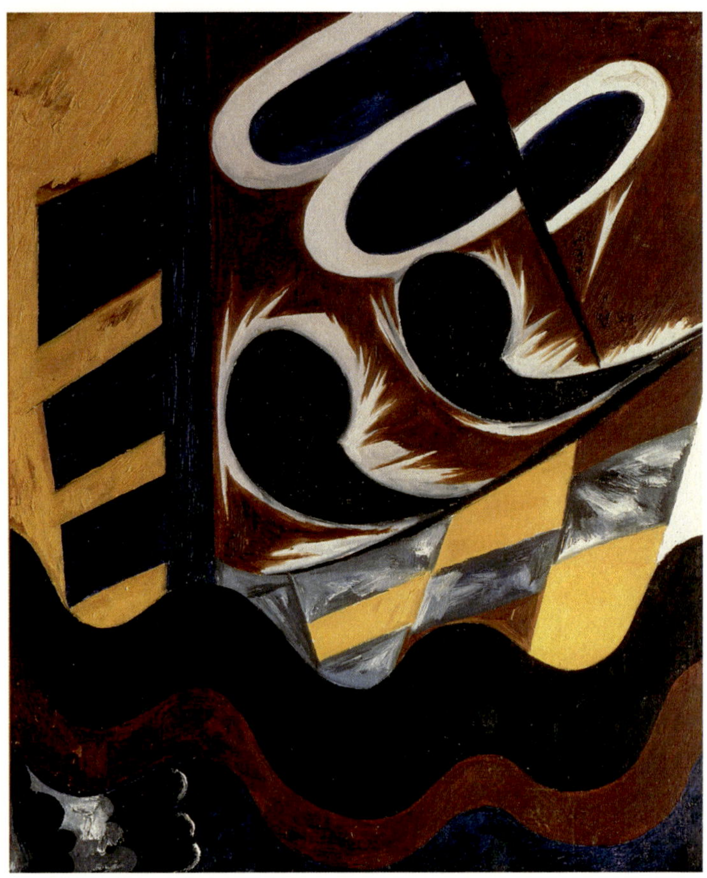

39.

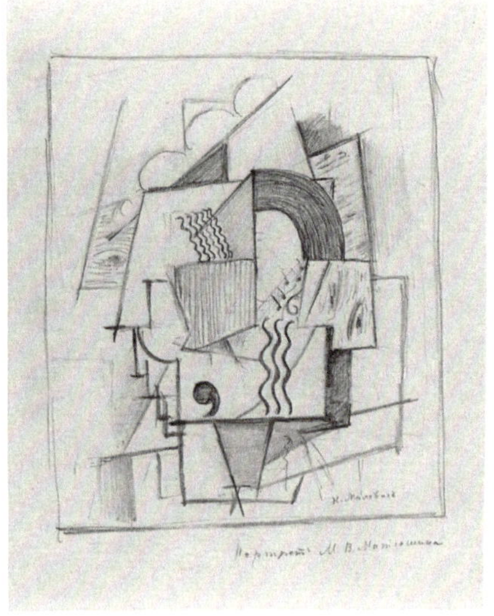

40.

39. Natalia Goncharova, *Elektricheskii ornament* (Electrical Ornament), *c.* 1914, oil on canvas, 90.5 × 40.77 cm, Tretyakov State Gallery, Moscow

40. *Portrait of M. V. Matyushin*, preparatory drawing, autumn 1913 (Cat. F-398), pencil on paper, 18.4 × 14.5 cm, Khardzhiev-Chaga Cultural Foundation, Amsterdam (on deposit at the Stedelijk Museum, Amsterdam)

in which commas are raised to the rank of a "master of cere-monies" imperiously abolishing authority, are clearly identi-fied in *Victory over the Sun* as belonging to the "old world". Based on the reflection that commas, unquestionably signs of major semantic importance, govern the logical order of sen-tences authoritatively, they determine quite simply the way in which each discursive component is to be understood. Thanks to the "transrational" logic of the Futurists commas are sud-denly transformed into major pictorial figures. They change their level of existence and thus anticipate the future Non-Ob-jective forms. Arising in Malewicz's Cubo-Futurist repertoire they are soon transmuted into Natalya Goncharova's "pure signs", as we can see in her *Electrical Ornament*, an unusu-al and even exceptional abstract composition assigned to the

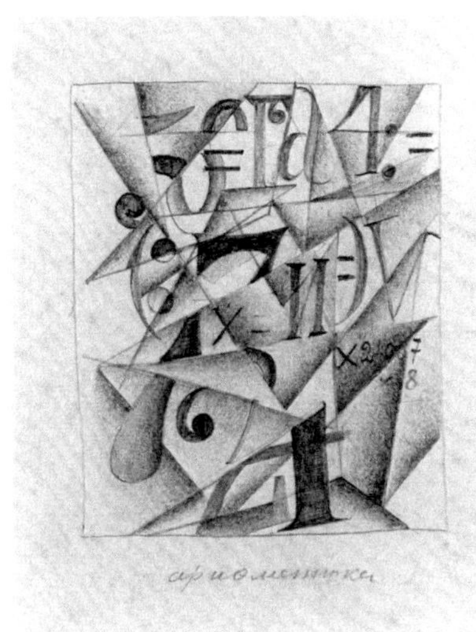

41.

41. *Arithmetic*, summer 1913 (Cat. F-351),
pencil on paper, 11.7 × 9.7 cm,
Khardzhiev-Chaga Cultural Foundation,
Amsterdam (on deposit at the Stedelijk
Museum, Amsterdam)

42. *Grammar*, summer 1913 (Cat. F-353),
pencil on paper, 11.8 × 9.4 cm,
Khardzhiev-Chaga Cultural Foundation,
Amsterdam (on deposit at the Stedelijk
Museum, Amsterdam)

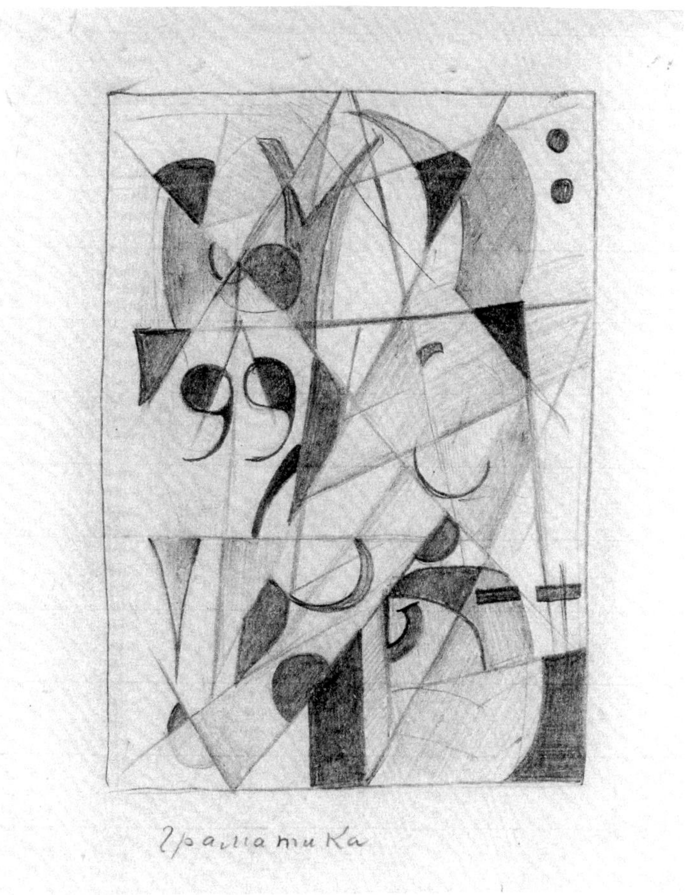

42.

[63] The title of this work could be apocryphal and
has as yet to be confirmed if not elucidated.

[64] Cat. F-403-e.

[65] Cat. F-403-e bis.

[66] See the preliminary drawing F-398.

first half of the year 1914, i.e. painted immediately after the
Troe miscellany and *Victory over the Sun*.[63]

Rendered as a figurative element in a new language of
sorts, the Futurist (and more precisely Transrational) comma
figures prominently in the visual repertoire of *Victory over
the Sun*; it is clearly discernible at the centre of Malewicz's
design for the setting of Act I.[64] This image was considered
significant enough for the artist to repeat on the cover of the libretto, a booklet issued on the occasion of the St Petersburg
performance of the "opera" in December 1913.[65] From there
the comma migrated to the array of thematic elements initially used for the portrait of Mikhail Matyushin, who composed
the music for *Victory over the Sun*.[66] Significantly, it vanishes

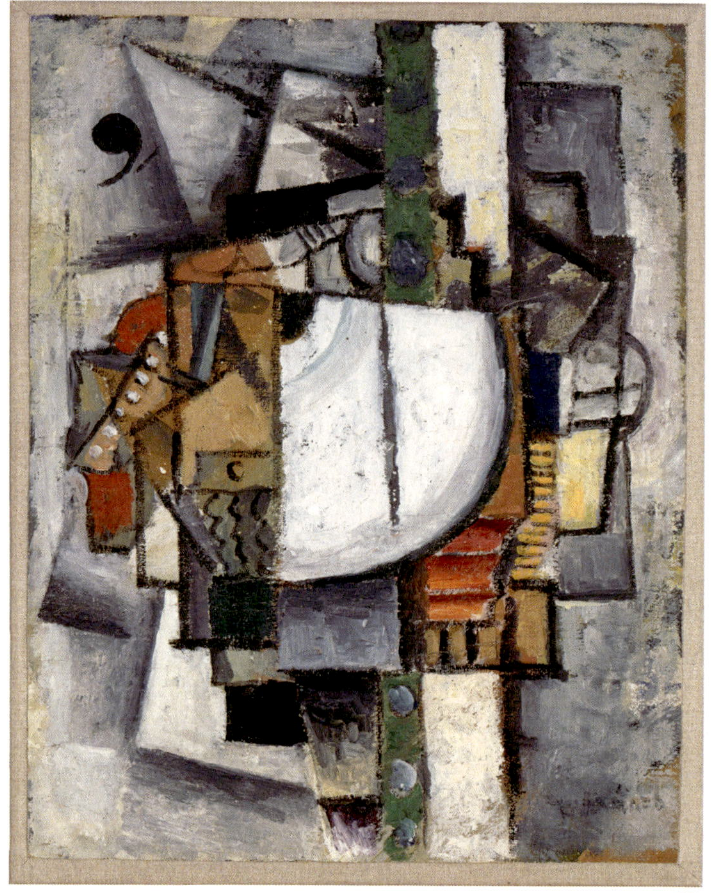

43.

43. *Cubo-Futurist composition with piano,* autumn 1913 (Cat. F-387), oil on canvas, 39.5 × 31.3 cm. Back signed "K Malewicz, 1913", Khardzhiev-Chaga Cultural Foundation, Amsterdam (on deposit at the Stedelijk Museum, Amsterdam)

in the final version of the portrait, the oil painting (F-401) that Malewicz executed just after designing the set for *Victory over the Sun* – as if the comma's range of action were limited to the "opera".

The most interesting image in this brief sequence of Trans-rational commas is without question the one on the cover of the Futurist *Troe* (The Three) miscellany.[67] Published in July 1913, it grouped the "collective" work that went into producing the futurist performance.[68] *Troe* can be seen as a record of this work: apart from information concerning the artists' manner of working it also includes an important theoretical text by the poet Aleksei Kruchenykh, "New Ways of the Word".[69] The cover includes a large, conspicuous comma placed at the

[67] See the drawing Cat. F-350-bis.

[68] In the "logbook" of the work on the show as given in the *Troe* miscellany Kruchenykh writes that the spectacle was elaborated together i.e. "collectively", each of the authors departing from his specialty in order to encroach on his neighbour's particular field.

[69] A. Kruchenykh, "Novye Puti Slova. Jazyk Budushchego, smert' Simvolizmu" (New Ways of the Word. The Language of the Future, Death to Symbolism), *Troe*, St Petersburg, 1912, pp. 22–41.

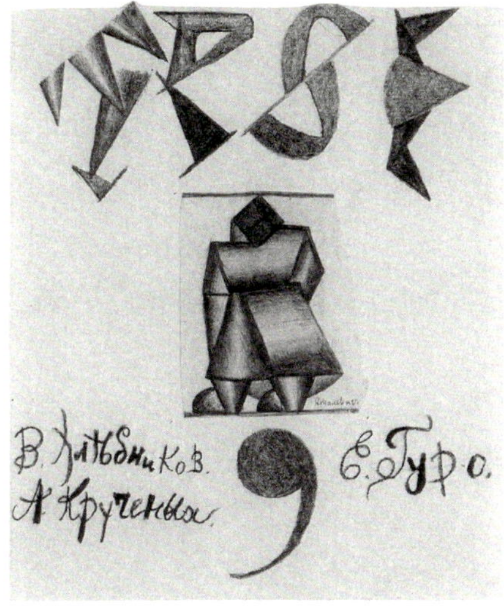

44.

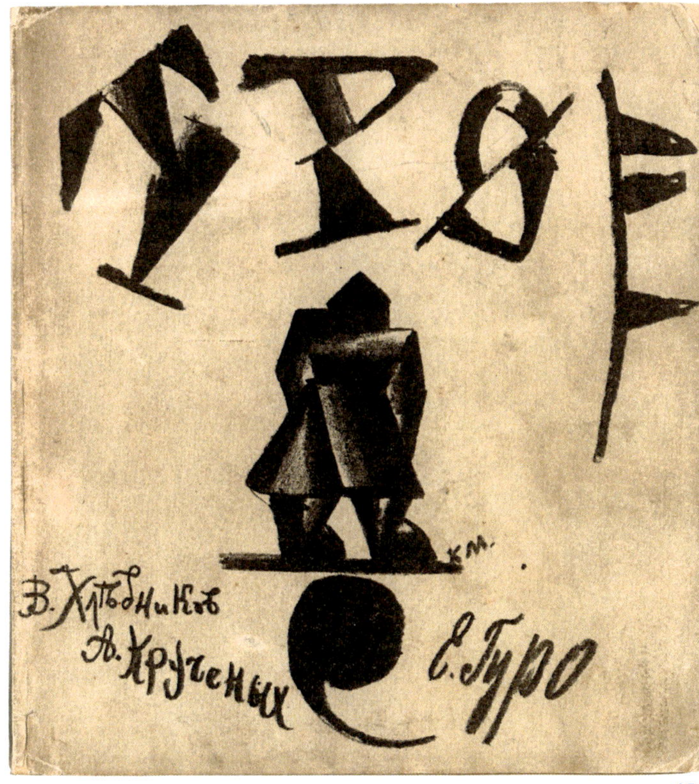

45.

44. *Troe*, sketch for the cover, summer 1913 (Cat. F-350-a), drawing and collage, 18 × 15.4 cm, Khardzhiev-Chaga Cultural Foundation, Amsterdam (on deposit at the Stedelijk Museum, Amsterdam)

45. *Troe*, Futurist miscellany, autumn 1913, lithograph, 19.6 × 17.8 cm

bottom centre of the composition, like a main character elevated to the rank of a full-blown pictorial form. Contrary to convention, however, this figure inverts the "foot", normally a stroke descending from right to left, to a slash sweeping from left to right. We are therefore in the presence of a new type of sign; though initially based on a comma thanks to the artist it now has a different semantic function. Yet in the preliminary pencil drawing (F-350-a) it is positioned in the standard way with a rightwards curving "foot". The inescapable conclusion is that between the moment of choosing the comma as a traditional language symbol and settling on the final cover design (several days or at most weeks later?), Malewicz – and Malewicz alone – altered the comma's status by transferring it from the field of literary discourse – the discourse of written language – to that of a Futurist *visual* symbol. This change of status reveals the extent to which the work of giving a visual presence to the opera proved decisive in Malewicz's conceptual

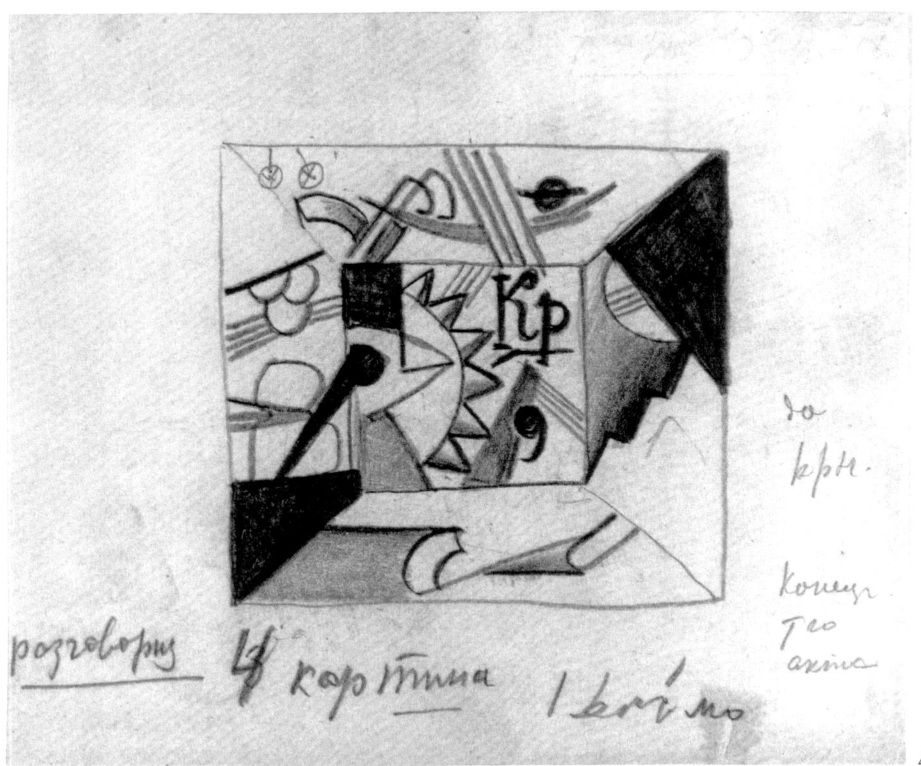

46.

evolution. The qualitative transformation represented by this shift continued to progress until the appearance of the artist's first Suprematist compositions in the summer of 1915.

* * *

Refined culture has incinerated the reason of art.

K. Malewicz, "Declaration"
("White" Manifesto), 15 June 1918

In his key essay in *Troe* Kruchenykh advocates "grammatical casualness (*proizvol*)", "unexpected sounds" and the "irrational". He declares that "the irrational [in his case the 'transrational'] is given as directly as is the rational". This pro-

46. *Victory over the Sun*, preliminary drawing for the 4th tableau of Act I, 1913 (Cat. F-403-e), cover of the libretto, pencil on paper, 16.8 × 20.6 cm. Khardzhiev-Chaga Cultural Foundation, Amsterdam (on deposit at the Stedelijk Museum, Amsterdam)

47. *Aviator*, Alogist composition, 1914 (Cat. F-441), preliminary sketch, pencil on paper, 16.2 × 10.1 cm. Inscriptions in Russian ("pharmacy, errands, general staff") and, beneath the composition, in Polish "pękła sprężyna" (the spring broke). Khardzhiev-Chaga Cultural Foundation, Amsterdam (on deposit at the Stedelijk Museum, Amsterdam)

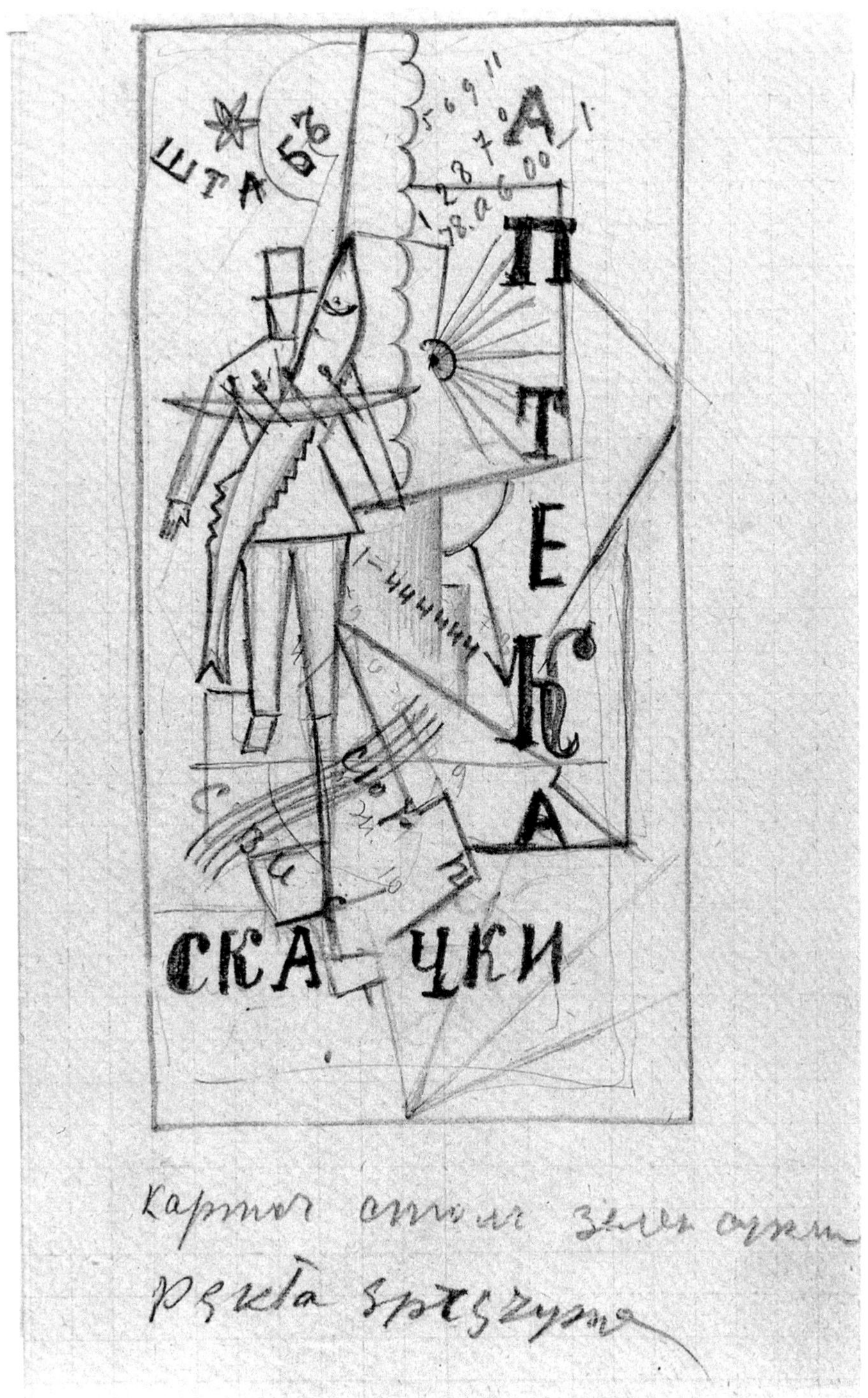

47.

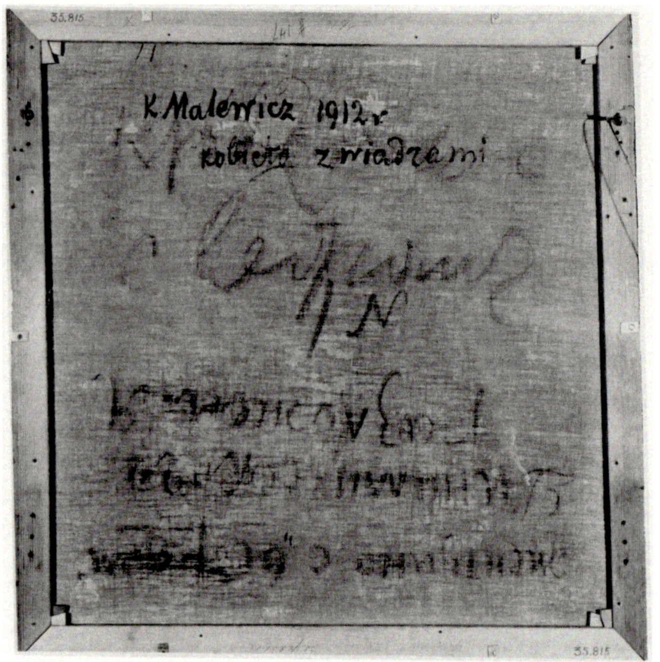

48 a.

48 b.

48 c.

48 a, b and c.
Versos of paintings with inscriptions in
Polish:
a. *Peasant Woman with Pails* (1912,
Cat. F-332, oil on canvas, 80.3 × 80.3 cm,
MoMA, NY), verso: "K.Malewicz, 1912 r.
kobieta z wiadrami"
b. *An Englishman in Moscow* (1914,
Cat. F-440, oil on canvas, 88 × 57 cm,
Stedelijk Museum, Amsterdam), verso:
"Młody Anglik" (young Englishman)
c. *Desk and Room* (1913–1914, Cat. F-438,
oil on canvas, 79.5 × 79.5 cm, Stedelijk
Museum, Amsterdam), verso: the artist's
signature in Polish

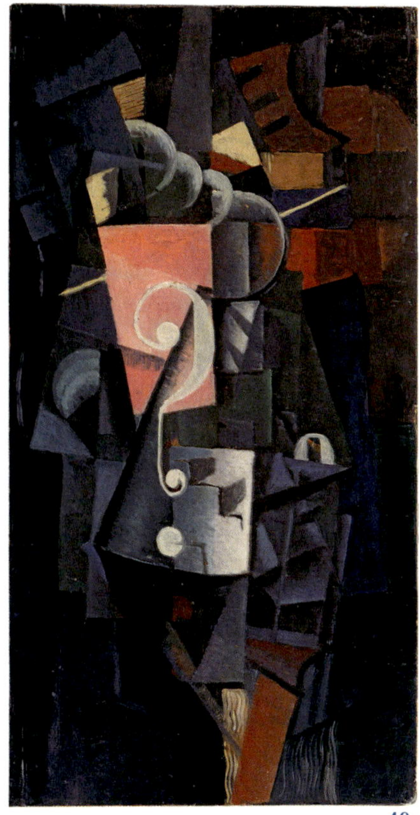

49. *Through Station Kuntsevo*, 1914
(Cat. F-421), oil on wood panel,
49 × 25.5 cm, Tretyakov State Gallery,
Moscow

[70] As startling as it may seem the artist would
again use the choice of this image years later in
his pedagogic discourse. In 1928, analysing the
work of one of his young students in Leningrad,
Malewicz remarked "the spring can be used as
a counter form [for] it possesses life, which by itself is sufficient to create a painting" (quoted by
Karasik in "Po radusu osnovy" in the anthology
V kruge Malevicha [In Malewicz's Circle], St Petersburg: Palace Editions, 2000, pp. 7–11 [Eng-
lish-language edition]).

nouncement followed the Futurist manifestoes proclaiming "the liberty of the word" and even of the "letter", yet not only, for the summons to the irrational opened a breach in the traditional order of the "logical" rigidity underpinning "normal" language (the language of the past). It was at this point that Malewicz, highly sensitive to new forms of verbal expression, crossed over into the unconscious.

Some of the artist's very few Transrational drawings from this period are extraordinary testimonies of this sudden liberation of the unconscious Futurist imagination. In addition to letters released from the context of words in the manner of Cubist collages to become fully-fledged visual elements of their own, one now and then comes across odd inscriptions. In the dialogue between textual elements and forms freed from their narrative context flashes from the artist's subconscious occasionally burst forth. One of the most startling and significant examples of this occurs in the margin of a drawing unquestionably connected yet again with the thematic sequence of the Futurist opera, as it is linked to the portrait of the *Aviator* (F-444). The drawing in question (F-441) contains motifs that one encounters in *Aviator*: the fish, the saw blade and the word *Apteka* (pharmacy) in Cyrillic characters. Accompanying this Rimbaud-like inventory is an extremely unusual utterance under the solid line surrounding this complex composition (from the compositional standpoint a highly concentrated arrangement of disparate elements): the phrase "Pękła sprężyna" (the spring broke), this time in… Polish. Can a better demonstration of the incursion of the artist's subconscious be conceived of than these Polish words in a work belonging to the Alogist tradition of Russian Futurism? For the unconscious acts in two ways here: first though the choice of symbols – a spring, the mainspring[70] of this creation being suddenly released – and, secondly, through the unexpected recourse to the Polish language referring to a cultural and above all an emotional, profoundly personal background. Startlingly and abruptly present in the creative process, the artist's use of Polish, the innermost language of his childhood, seems to have been muffled for years in – and by? – his art. If such is the case, what is involved here is not just a dialogue or discursive incursion but the savage irruption of a very private level of expression that seems as fundamental as it is uncontrolled.

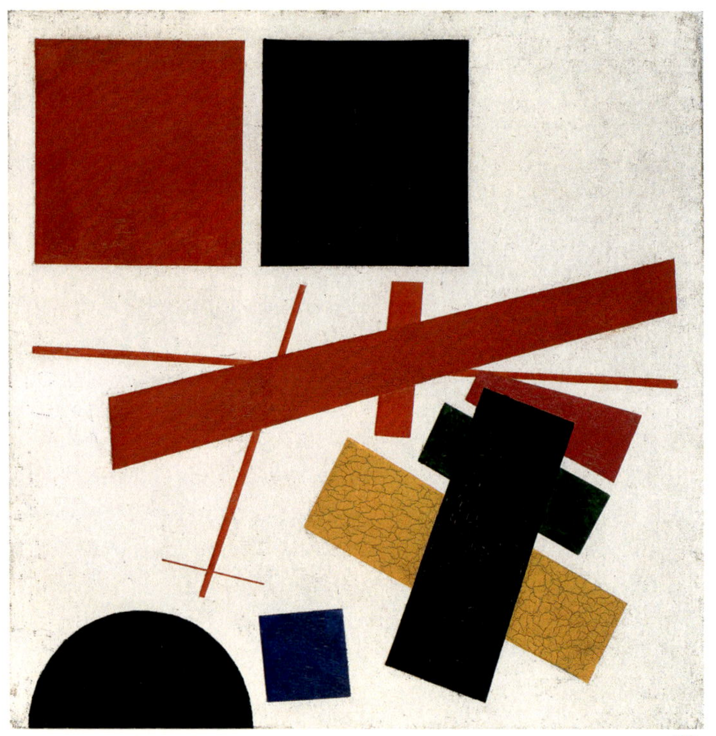

50. (Suprematism), 1916 (Cat. S-420), oil on canvas, 74 × 76 cm, Ekaterinburg Museum of Fine Arts

A few years later, reflecting on the logic of Cubist collages in their Dadaist extension, Tristan Tzara published an inspired interpretation of the coupling of extravagant elements with an unexpected delivery. In a brief but extremely intense text which lends an aura of nobility to this process, Tzara elevates the collage's specific character – the unexpected, astonishing pairing of utterly different, even contradictory, poetic realities – to a Dionysian level: "Language has become very different to its model, speech [...], in grammar we encounter the supreme attempt to wrest words from their too solid carapace. [...] Through a secret and totally uncontrollable association, a word placed next to another word may produce a shock, a strange process [...] an emotion of a poetic order".[71] Here in a nutshell is the logic of the title *0,10* summed up retrospectively by one of Dada's leading theorists.

[71] T. Tzara, "Le papier collé ou le proverbe en peinture" (The Pasted Paper or the Proverb in Painting), *Cahiers d'art*, no. 1, Paris, 1931, pp. 61–64.

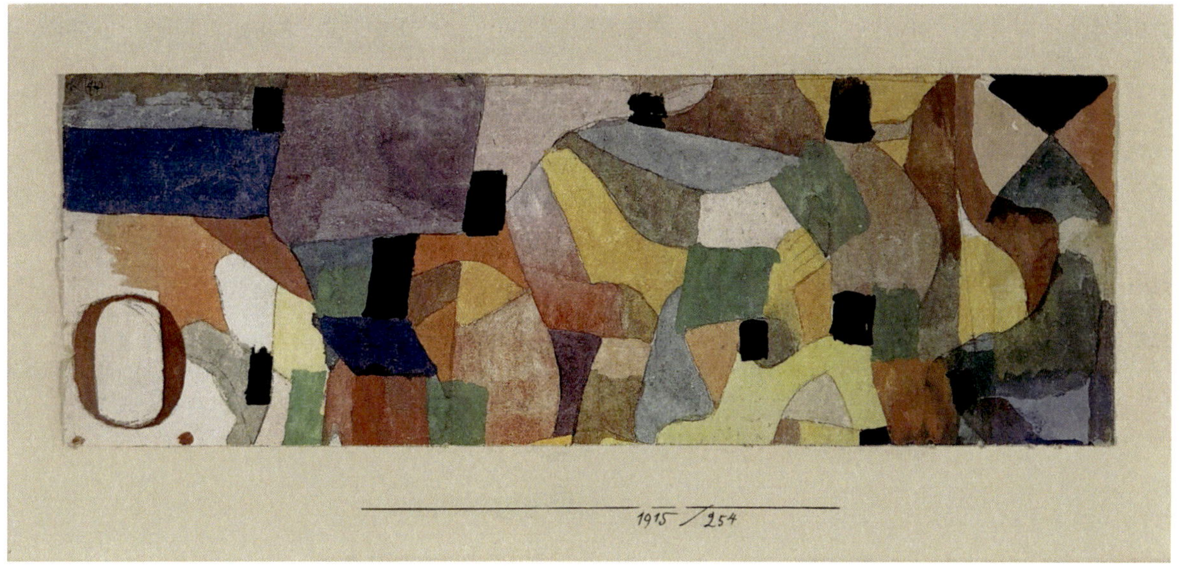

51.

* * *

[72] So far the topic has been little explored. We know of a first letter of Klee's to Tristan Tzara, dated 23 January 1916, preserved in the Tzara papers at the Bibliothèque Doucet in Paris. Tzara's reply is dated the same day (Zentrum Paul Klee archives, Bern, Switzerland).

[73] See the catalogue of the *Bulletin D* exhibition in Cologne, which lists two works by Klee. (However, we must bear in mind that this highly original event was censored by the British occupation authorities.) The connection between Klee and Dadaism, in particular the artist's participation in crucial exhibitions like *Bulletin D*, appears to this day to have been up insufficiently investigated (see Klee's drawing *Automat* [1922/28, Zentrum Paul Klee] with its striking resemblance to the female figure in George Grosz's 1920 collage *Daum…* (Berlinische Galerie, Berlin), later reproduced as well in Grosz's book *Mit Pinsel und Schere*, Berlin: Malik Verlag, 1922).

[74] See Malewicz's Alogist paintings of 1914, such as *Cow and Violin* (F-418), *Partial Eclipse* (F-459), *An Englishman in Moscow* (F-440) and several other works from the series F-440 to F-463.

Not unsurprisingly, the comma as an autonomous visual symbol makes another appearance around the same time, quite independently of the Russian context, in the work of a Western artist: Paul Klee. Between 1915 and 1917 the painter-poet was directly in touch with the Dadaist revolution, which he was able not only to witness at the Cabaret Voltaire in Zurich but also to take part of it. As early as 1916 he exchanged letters with Tristan Tzara[72] and participated personally in Dada exhibitions in Zurich and Cologne.[73] After detaching himself from the exacerbated stridency of Expressionism (see his interest in Alfred Kubin) and experiencing Cubism at first hand, first in Paris in 1912, then in Munich (1913) and Berlin, Klee began to work with newly "liberated" visual symbols in a highly original way, which recalls indirectly the logic of certain Malewicz compositions of 1913–1915.[74] At first sight this radical manipulation of visual elements looks simply like a gleeful game of fragmenting images, but was actually part of a vertiginous transformation of visible reality. Thanks to the post-Cubist disintegration of figures, signs and letters engaged a new

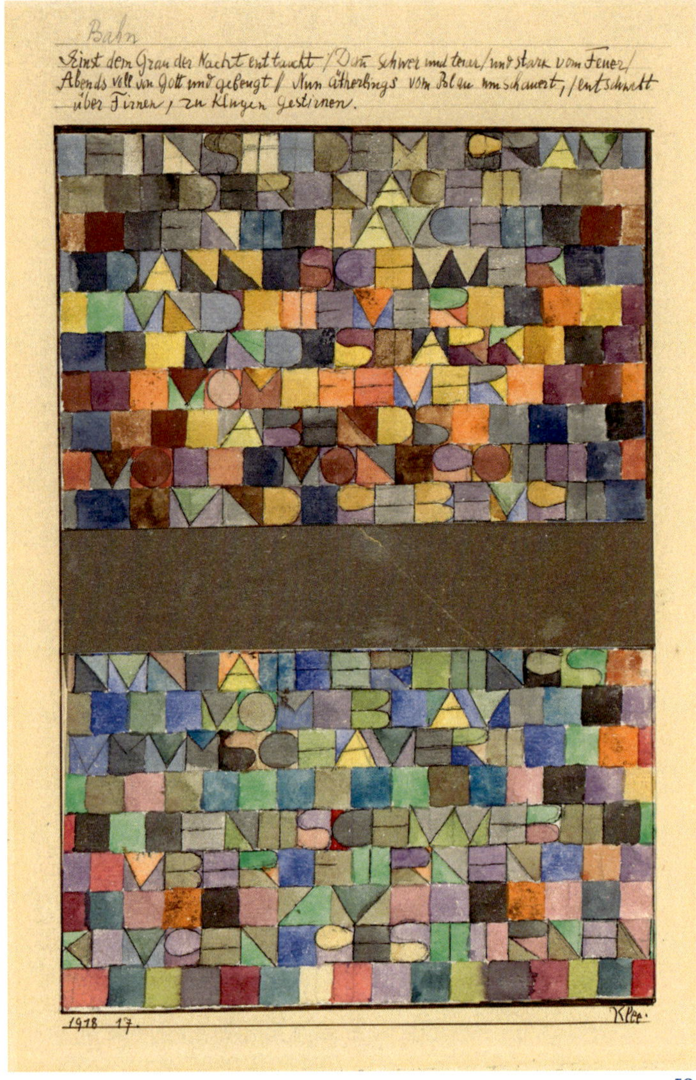

52.

52. Paul Klee, *Einst dem Grau der Nacht enttaucht…* (Once Emerged from the Grey of the Night…), 1918/17, watercolour, 22.6 × 15.8 cm, Zentrum Paul Klee, Bern

dialogue in Klee's work, proclaiming the interconnectedness of visual and verbal symbols. The resulting language, similar to Malewicz's Alogist practice, was like an extension of the Transrational discourse of Russian Cubo-Futurism. Thus the path towards abstract art lay open for Paul Klee.

In this new order of visual narration commas appear suddenly like the waving flag of a magician signalling a fresh challenge. Letters, arrows and… a comma combine startlingly

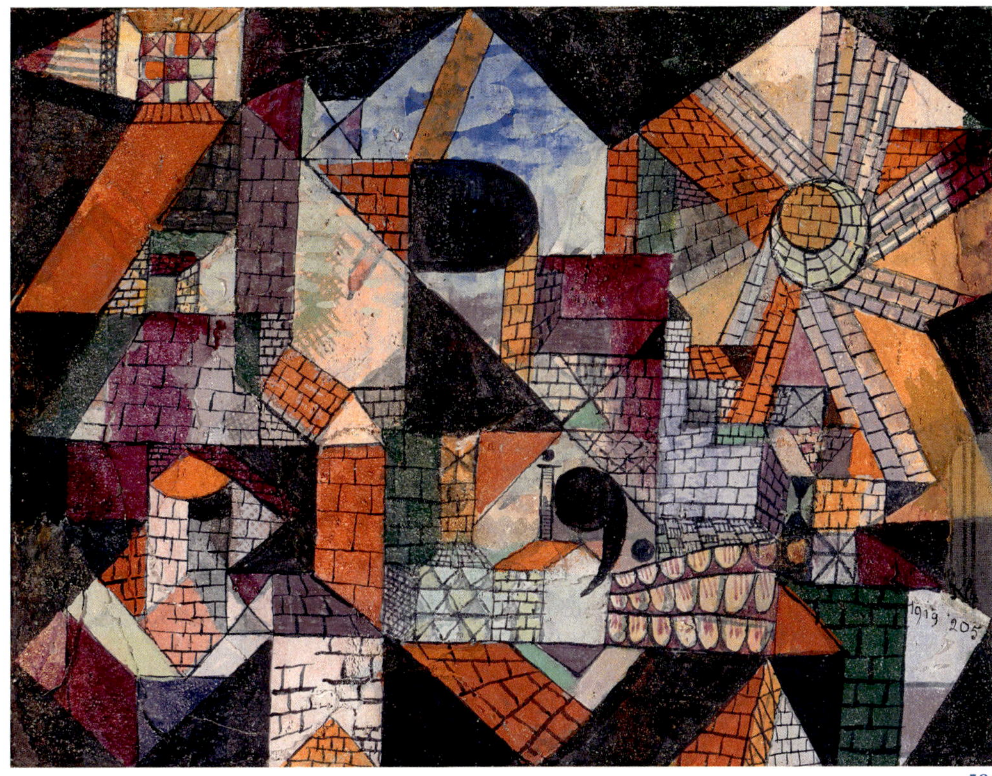

53.

53. Paul Klee, *Stadt R* (City R), 1919/205, watercolour on cardboard, 16.5 × 22 cm, Städtische Galerie im Lenbachhaus, Munich

in a poetic disquisition governed by new rules. In the lyrical explosion of Paul Klee's subconscious, as unbridled as it was surprising, the comma is suddenly there, in the middle of the 1919 composition *Stadt R*.[75] Here the multi-directional character of the urban fragments translates into a pure (albeit extraordinarily lyrical!) post-Cubist geometrical mosaic dominated by a large comma. Rendered in black and positioned ostentatiously in the centre of the composition, it stands out imperiously against a variegated background of richly coloured forms. It is followed by a black full stop almost as large as it. In Klee's composition the two elements have the same role as the comma in Malewicz's *Troe* design; they gave an authoritative presence that contrasts sharply with the miscellaneous collection of flat fragments behind them. These two signs wrested from the domain of written language and shifted to that of pictorial entities introduce a distance, hence a difference of meaning. A major interrogation results from this. Such

[75] *Stadt R*, 1919/205. This work belongs to the same series as *Villa R*, 1919/153, Kunstsammlung, Basel. See W. Grohmann, *Paul Klee*, Geneva, 1954, fig. on p. 138.

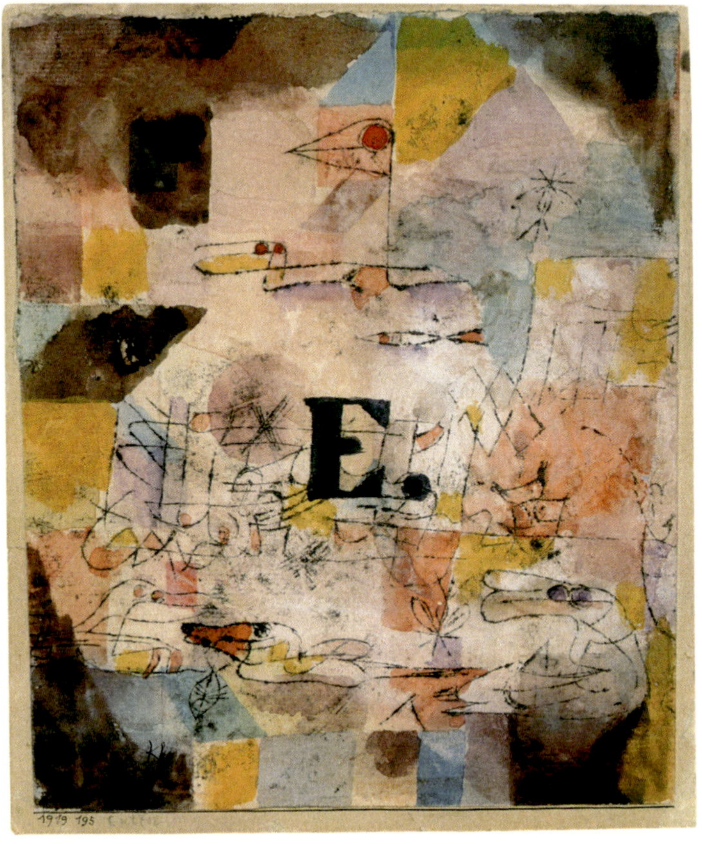

54. Paul Klee, *Enten* (Ducks), 1919/195,
oil and watercolour on prepared paper
mounted on cardboard, 23.1 × 19.9/19.2 cm,
Museum Heinz Berggruen Nationalgalerie,
Staatliche Museen zu Berlin

54.

too was the primary function of Malewicz's comma. Much as
in the figurative questioning of the Russian artist's work between autumn 1914 and early 1915, Klee's compositions of
the same period, especially the 1918 *Zoologischer Garten* (Zo-
ological Garden),[76] juxtapose disparate, seemingly conflicting
images (a goat, a bird, several houses and a large eye placed
conspicuously at the top of the composition), thereby staging
the arbitrariness of figurative alignments organised by "traditional" logic. As in Malewicz's Alogist compositions, this juxtaposition quite simply eliminates the old logic of figurative
narration.

During the years 1917–1919, a period of great "alphabetical" invention, Klee produced a number of groundbreaking
compositions in which verbal language in the form of straight-
forward alphabetical units functioned as totally independent

[76] Or *Tiergarten* (Zoo), watercolour, Paul Klee
Stiftung, Zentrum Paul Klee, Bern. Reproduced
in Wilhelm Hausenstein's monograph *Kairuan
oder eine Geschichte von Maler Paul Klee*, Munich, 1921, which had a definite influence on
Joan Miró's development (Miró was familiar with
Hausenstein's book by the early 1920s).

55. Paul Klee, *Landschaft bei E* (Landscape near E), 1921/182, oil, watercolour and India ink on paper, 49.8 × 35.2 cm, Zentrum Paul Klee, Bern

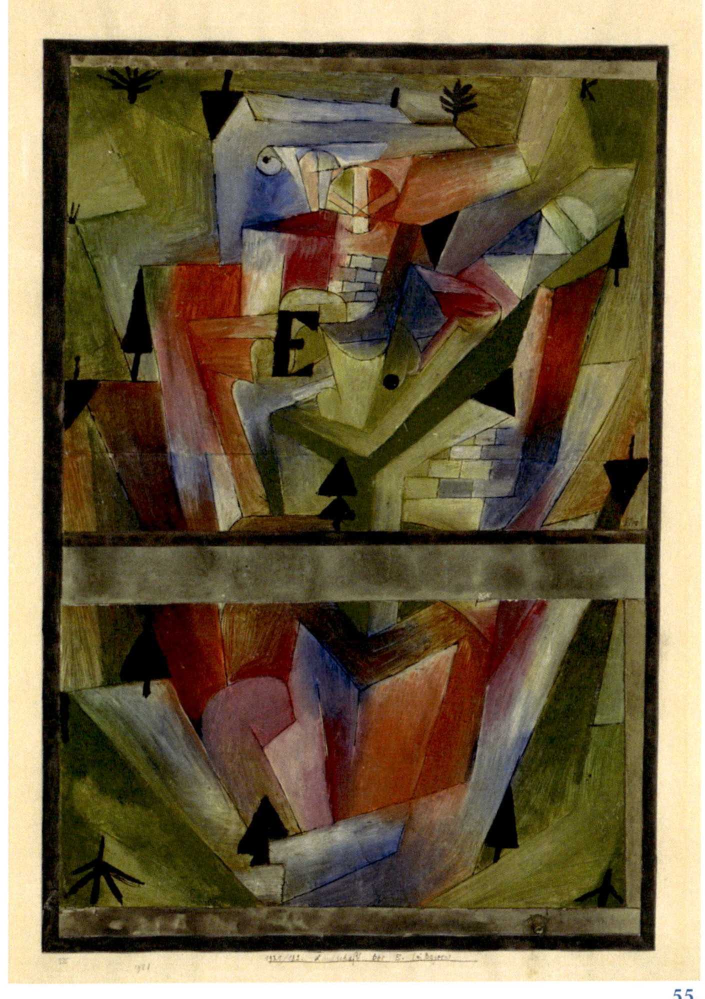

55.

visual elements that were perfectly integrated in the composition's pictorial tissue. Such is the logic behind the highly original composition *Einst dem Grau der Nacht enttaucht…* (Once Emerged from the Grey of the Night…) of 1918.[77] It so happened that it was precisely at this time that Raoul Hausmann and Kurt Schwitters invented sound poetry, an abstract language that remains a moment of particular intensity in the area of letters and sounds thanks to which individual characters attain the auditory dimension, that other conquest of Futurist poetry known as "phonetic" poetry.

[77] Klee 1918/17.

In 1919 Klee confirmed the practice of reducing a single word, that is to say a single concept, to a single visual sign – concomitantly contracting a visual sign to a figure reduced to the extreme (or minimalist figure, as it would later be called) – in his composition *Enten* (Ducks).[78] Here, pared down to its initial letter, E, the title predominates, like Malewicz's square among the first Suprematist works, at the very centre of a complex mosaic of forms that mesh in a subtly fanciful way recalling the poetic delicacy of the dishevelled drawings in the *Candide* series (1912–1920). The detail of the letter E is especially significant: it is shaped like a typographic character and creates the impression it was produced with a stencil (as were the letters in Picasso's Cubist compositions of 1912). An equally explicit and powerful black dot follows it. (Thus both Klee and Malewicz [1913–1915] elevate that punctuation mark to a new semantic position.) The poetic dialogue between the eye and the background surrounding the letter E, where ones makes out duck-like elements combined with abstract planes like those in Klee's abstract phase of 1915,[79] are reminiscent of the simplifying tendency in the first Suprematist works from the same year. In the latter case the reduction of figures culminates radically in the hyper-elementary visual signs observable in the sequence gravitating around *Self-Portrait in 2 Dimensions* of 1915.[80]

Klee continued to the last to reflect on the sound (therefore musical) independence of the phonetic units of speech and their relationship to the visual field, witness his 1938 "alphabetical" composition *Alphabet Aioek*.[81] Paul Klee the musician played simultaneously on several levels of expression.

Malewicz's approach in *Cow and Violin* is no different. Except that in his case the juxtaposition of two disparate elements, semantically far removed from each other but remaining in the visual order alone, is particularly violent. As provocative as can be, their confrontation has the force of a didactic demonstration. It is like a manifesto – a logical announcement that opens the poetic way to future developments.

Not unexpectedly, during the 1920s the use of whole or fragmentary figurative elements considered as splinters of independent geometrical forms constituted the substance of Klee's figurative language. In the early years of that decade (the 1920s) this manner of viewing figurative elements passed

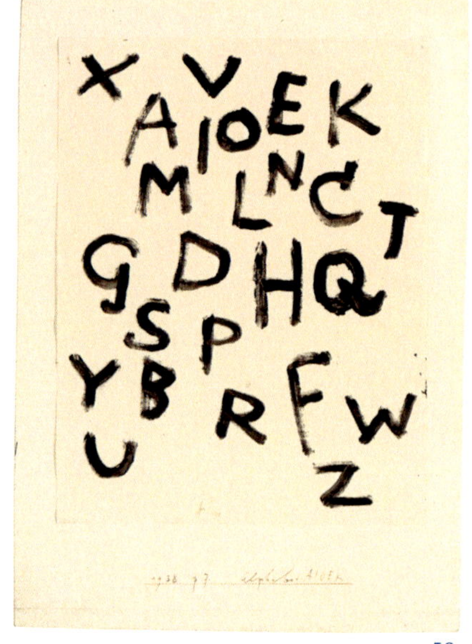

56.

56. Paul Klee, *AIOEK*, 1938/227, black paste on paper, 27.3 × 21 cm (support 35.1 × 25.4 cm), private collection

[78] Klee 1919/195.

[79] See for example the watercolour *Anatomie der Aphrodite*, 1915/45. Klee repeats the same title contraction in *Landschaft bei E*, 1921/182.

[80] See the series Cat. S-18 to S-31.

[81] A large watercolour consisting solely of written characters, Klee 1938/227, private collection, Canada. See another, even larger, composition of the same type, *So fang es heimlich an*, watercolour, 48.3 × 62.8 cm, 1938/189. Works in the same series, by no means exceptional though relatively scarce, punctuate Klee's production throughout the 1930s.

from Klee to Miró. It opened the way to the lyric abstraction that the Spanish artist subsequently practised with ever increasing exuberance until his dying day (the large canvases of the 1960s).

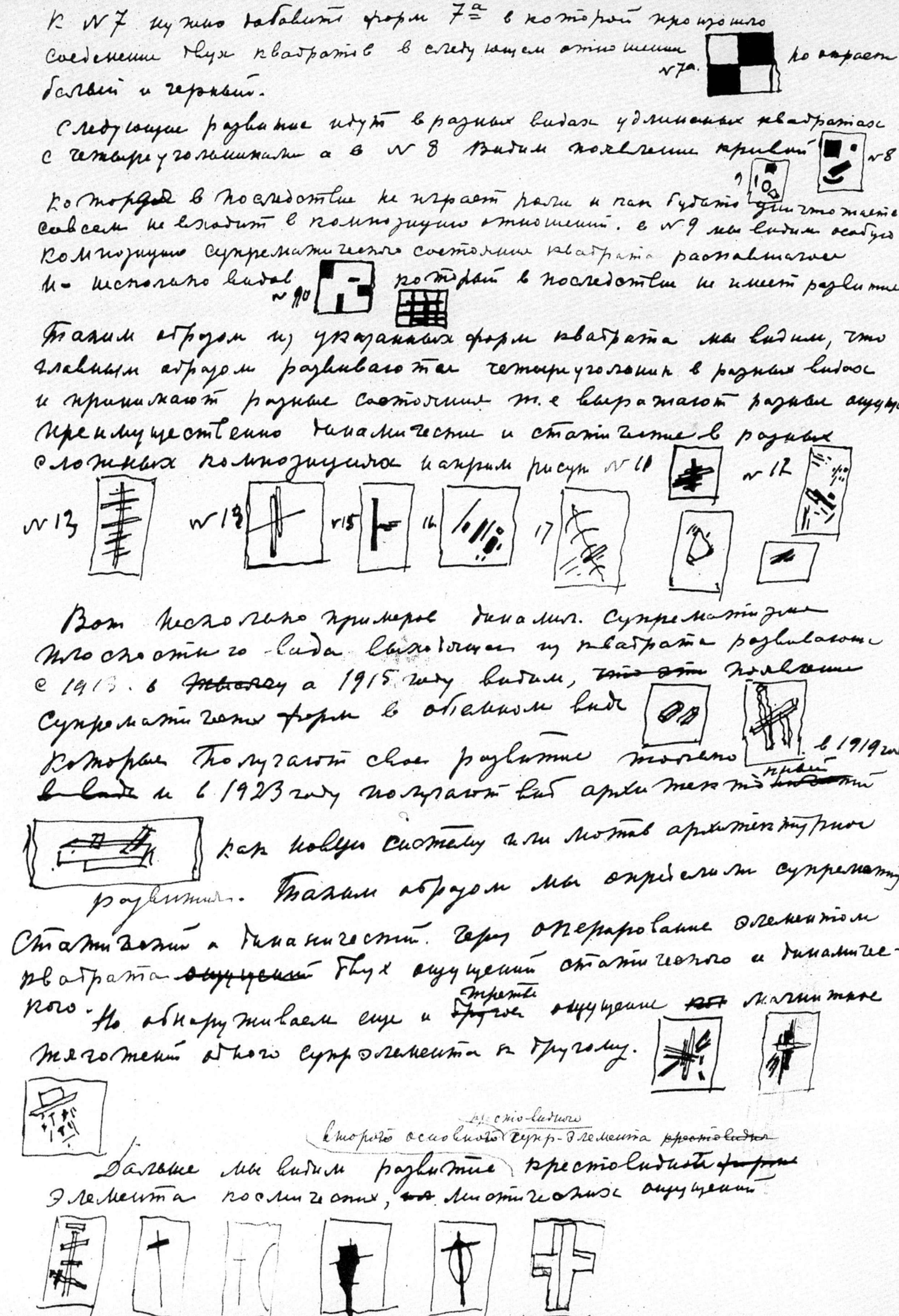

К №7 нужно добавить форм 7ᵃ в которой произошло
соединение двух квадратов в следующем отношении №7ᵃ по окрасе
белый и черный.

Следующие развития идут в разных видах удлиненных квадратах
с четыреугольниками а в №8 видим появление крылаи №8
которая в последствии не играет роли и как будет что ...
совсем не входит в композицию отношений. в №9 мы видим особую
композицию супрематического состояния квадрата расположен
на несколько видов №10 которой в последствии не имеет развитие

Таким образом из указанных форм квадрата мы видим, что
главным образом развиваются четыреугольник в разных видах
и принимают разные состояния т. е выражают разные ощущения
преимущественно динамические и статические в разных
сложных композициях например рисун №11 №12
№13 №14 №15 16. 17.

Вот несколько примеров динамич. супрематиз
ного скоростного вида выходящих из квадрата развивалось
с 1913. в ноябре а 1915 году видим, что эти появление
супрематических форм в объемном виде
которые получают свое развитие только в 1919 году
в виде и в 1923 году получают вид архитектон прав

как новую систему или мотив архитектурного
развития. Таким образом мы определили супремат
статический и динамический через оперирование элементом
квадрата ощущении двух ощущении статического и динамиче-
кого. Но обнаруживаем еще и третье ощущение магнитное
тяготений одного супр элемента к другому.

второго основного супр-элемента крестовидного
Дальше мы видим развитие крестовидного форм
элемента послизаний, магнитное ощущении

CHAPTER 8

REJECTION AND CENSORSHIP

*The best names that men bear are those
given by their enemies.*

J. Barbey d'Aurevilly,
Les Quarante Médallions de l'Académie,
1864

The first presentation of Suprematist works in December 1915 met with an immediate rejection among traditionalist visitors, a response as violent as it was unpremeditated, almost a gut reaction. In a vibrant tirade, the backward-looking critic Alexander Benois, already a confirmed adversary of the Cubo-Futurist movement, gave free vent to his feelings of horror at Malewicz's new work. "Everything we held sacred and holy, everything we loved and lived for, has vanished", he wrote in January 1916.[82] Castigating the new Non-Objective art, Benois went on to describe with unconcealed scorn Malewicz's *Quadrilateral* as an "icon of the Square". Taken up by anti-modernist critics, the description of the painting as an "icon" was only too understandably a sarcastic metaphor. It had the power of journalistic clichés and caught on owing to its evocation of sacrilege. Was not art after all not only a "superior" value but a "sacred" one as well, and was it not the role of criticism to defend its "higher" content at all costs? Buttressed in his anti-modernist convictions, Benois attacked the new abstract painting with the most powerful weapon available to him: the sacrilegious argument. Within the province of sacredness, a fundamental concern for the Symbolist

57. Kazimir Malewicz, "Suprematism. Moments of its development", 1927, manuscript, 33 × 21 cm, former Hans von Riesen coll., present whereabouts unknown

[82] A. Benua (Benois), "Poslednaya futuristitcheskaya vystavka" (Last Futurist Exhibition), in *Rech'* (Speech), Petrograd, 9 January 1916. See my commentary in Nakov, *Malewicz, 2007/2010,* vol. 2, chap. 13.

generation, Benois focussed on Malewicz's approach – with the crucial difference that the two men were defending diametrically opposite positions. Malewicz was not about to let this attack go unanswered. Since "the doors of the press were closed to me" (as he puts it) he addressed a personal "open letter" to the critic, which he circulated actively in May 1916.[83]

* * *

Innovators have always been ridiculed.

Théodore Duret, 1885, an avant-garde critic
and a major exponent of French Impressionism

The term "square" that Benois used to describe Malewicz's *Quadrilateral*, undoubtedly the most shocking of the Suprematist paintings in the show, encountered an immediate success. So successful was it that the artist quickly resigned himself to calling it by the same name, despite the fact that it was brutally reductive with respect to the real content of a work that was a manifesto expressing the essence of his new creative approach, a purely existential and lyrical one. With the remarkable dialectical skill characterising Malewicz's talent for public speaking, he repeated his adversary's argument and, like an expert in judo, used it to his own advantage. Benois having referred to the "icon of the Square", he retorted in like manner. Yes, he said in essence, I have an icon in my pocket – a symbolic one! (meaning that it was concealed in his pocket) – and I will show you what it is and what it is capable of. In the early weeks of 1916 this difference turned into a shouting match. But was the painting really an "icon", a sacred Orthodox image, or was it merely a strong, cultural metaphor? What was the artist's relation to the tradition of Byzantine icons kept alive by the Russian Orthodox Church since the late Middle Ages?

From the 1950s and '60s on, the period when Suprematism was rediscovered in the West, the supposed connection between Malewicz's aesthetic system and the pictorial tradition of Byzantine icons was taken up enthusiastically by a broad

[83] "A Letter from Malevich to Benois", in *K. S. Malevich, Essays, op. cit.*, 1971, pp. 42–48.

84 It would be fastidious to list all the variations of this approach in the aesthetic output and/or the literature of the last three or four decades. A bibliography would be as extensive as it would be useless. The climax of the "Byzantinophile" craze was Andrew Spira's *The Avant-Garde Icon: Russian Avant-Garde Art and the Icon Painting Tradition*, London: Lund Humphries, 2008. Far from being regarded as an eccentric exercise this publication was reviewed positively in *The Burlington Magazine* (vol. 151, December 2009, pp. 851–852), yet another proof of the lack of specific knowledge in the field of modern art among most tradition-minded art historians. A peak of absurdity was reached in an article in *The Art Newspaper* ("Radicals Go Back to the Future", no. 198, January 2009) in which the author explains the choice of a "Byzantine source" peculiar to the Russian avant-garde in contrast to the "primitive influences" ("Negro and Oceanic art") that characterised the path of the Cubists in Western Europe. One can only conclude that the name of V. Matvejs (Markov), the first and most remarkable theorist of Black African art as early as 1914 (hence before Carl Einstein) and an art critic for the Union of Youth group, was unknown to the editors of *The Art Newspaper.*

majority of "cultural" commentators of Suprematism. Thus what was at first (in 1916) merely an anti-modernist metaphor, a sarcastic one at that, suddenly became a substitute for the visual content of Suprematist painting. Viewed uncritically, without questioning its origin or that of the principles guiding its realisation, the theme of the "sacred icon" became a kind of cultural if not nationalistic leitmotif. Counterbalancing the sarcastic reduction of *Quadrilateral* to a banal square the increasingly widespread explanation that it was an "icon" pre-empted all other attempts at understanding the picture, primarily pictorial explanations.[84] Yet Malewicz speaks of nothing other than modern art in his texts of the winter of 1915/1916, from Cubism to Futurism as indicated in the subtitle of his first booklet. As the new painting was difficult to conceptualise from the strictly pictorial viewpoint culture exegetes were eager to come up with cultural explanations, and so the argument of the so-called Byzantine tradition was immediately adopted. But the triumph of the latter, it must be said, was of the stifling kind, for it neutralised every other explanation, especially pictorial ones. Scholars scrambled to examine, in a rather haphazard fashion, sources that would support the theory of this "iconic" influence. Were not the artist's texts permeated with religious metaphors? Did not the title of a short treatise he published in 1922 contain the word "God"? And mainly did he not borrow towards the end of his life from different religious images for his own pictures? The confusion of themes, widely repeated as we know, proved to be highly instrumental in the process of dissimulation.

But of course the fact that the artist and his entourage were subjected to police persecution from the 1920s on was disregarded. Commentators were unaware, or feigned to be unaware, of the impact of the family history on the young Malewicz, the fate of the martyr uncle Lucjan, the Catholic priest hung in Kiev in the wake of the "January Insurrection" (1863). The emergence of religious topics towards the end of Malewicz's life attests to the presence in his discourse of a genuine criticism of the social oppression surrounding his family and friends. In the artist's capacity as a metaphysical thinker it was not just to the aesthetics of religious art that he turned but to an even greater extent to the anti-materialist message of the religious discourse (rather than to the tradition of Byzantine icons). Several of the compositions he painted in this period indicate this clearly.

Nor should one overlook the violent anticlerical persecution of the late 1920s, the hunting down of Catholic priests and worshippers, Protestant ministers and so forth. This was a highly topical concern at the time and Malewicz reacted to it with his usual forthrightness, oblivious to the massive oppression that only increased during the 1930s, reaching peaks of horror such as the savage assassination of the stage director Vsevolod Meyerhold's wife, the actress Zinaida Reich.

During the rediscovery of Malewiczian abstraction, his pictorial language, which seemed shocking because of the unusual radicalness of its abstract figures, was at first assimilated with the apodictic system of Byzantine painting. A facile proof of this appeared to be a contemporary photograph showing the manner in which the Suprematist works were presented in December 1915 at the *0,10* exhibition. For lack of a better explanation, the two walls against which they were hung were quickly but without any real ground viewed as an iconostasis, the arrangement of icons on a screen separating the nave from the altar in Orthodox churches. Had Malewicz not hung his *Quadrilateral* in such a way that, perched at the very top of the grouping, it blocked quite irrevocably what would have been the crucial centre, the imagined, indeed more than imaginary altar that was as invisible as it was idealised?

Malewicz did indeed hang *Quadrilateral*, that primordially important painting – a work of capital importance in the advent of Suprematism[85] – at the top of the display of his compositions, which were placed above each other in rows as was the custom at the time. Unquestionably he chose a strategic place where two walls met at right angles in a corner. Accustomed to the "perspectival construction", a "normal" viewer might have assumed that he was looking at an illusionist construction of the type that in the Western tradition had governed spatial representations for centuries. The fact that *Quadrilateral* was positioned athwart two walls gave it an extraordinary importance; its corner hanging put an end to what could have passed for, in the "illusionist" system, a perspectival mono-focal construction with a traditional "vanishing point". Was this really a reminder of iconostases? Surely not, for no iconostasis is ever a perspectival, especially not an

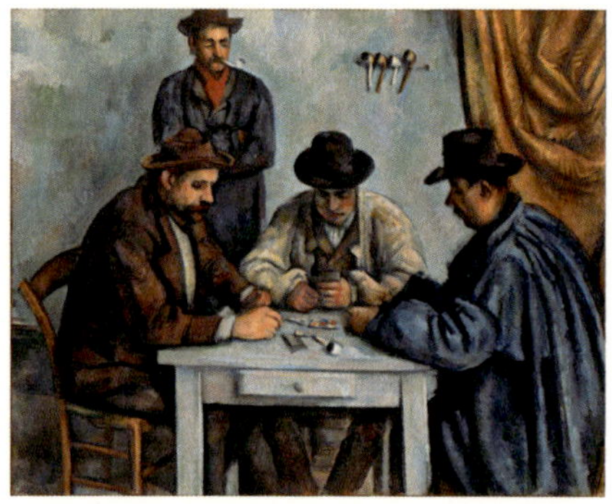

58.

58. Paul Cézanne, *La partie de cartes* (The Card Game), 1890–1892, oil on canvas, 65 × 81 cm, The Metropolitan Museum of Art, New York

[85] The list of Malewicz's works in the catalogue to the *0,10* exhibition begins with *Quadrilateral*, indicating its prime position among the other Suprematist paintings.

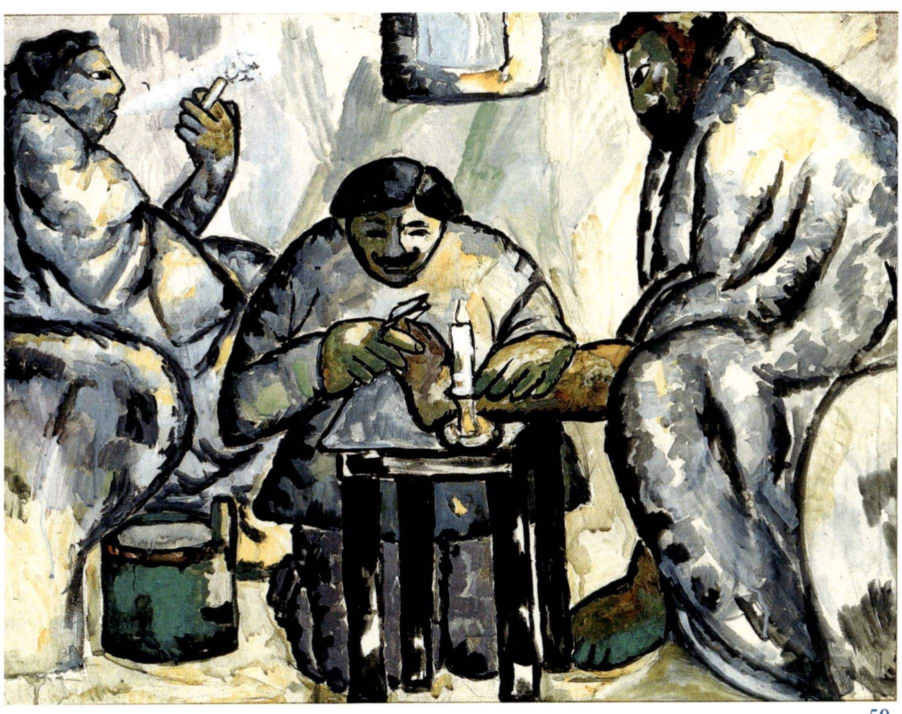

59.

"angular", construction. And, for that matter, why an iconostasis at all?

To begin with, what was Malewicz's relation to Orthodoxy, the tradition of icons and to iconostases? Scholars who saw *Quadrilateral* as a traditional icon simply forgot, or pretended they had never known, that Malewicz was raised in a Catholic environment, moreover a Polish one, and that this tradition was firmly anchored in his family roots (which included his uncle Lucjan but also the fact that the future artist's father destined his oldest son – Kazimir – to become a priest as well). What is more, Kazimir married a Polish woman in a Polish church in the town of Kursk. So what, one wonders, *was* the link between iconostases and abstract art?

Such a link did indeed exist, only it was not pictorial. It was eminently cultural and is not to be found in Malewicz's biography but in that of his Russian and, in his case, perfectly Orthodox rival, Wassily Kandinsky. In 1913 Kandinsky, who had made his own way to abstract art, published his reminiscences of the path that had led from Expressionism (and bear in mind that he was always unreservedly opposed to Cubism) to abstraction as early as summer 1911. In *Rückblicke*, a text issued in conjunction with his first retrospective at Der Sturm gallery in Berlin, Kandinsky, an Orthodox believer, recalled in 1913 a particularly moving experience he had had formerly encountering an instance of folk religious spirituality.[86] Speaking of his explorations as a young ethnologist, he remembered stopping unexpectedly one day in the home of poor peasants. In the depth of the shadowy room he entered, he spotted a weak red light illuminating an icon placed on a sort of altar or private iconostasis. The atmosphere of spirituality emanating from it suddenly gripped Kandinsky. Recall that this memory was described by a deeply Russian painter in Germany shortly after he had taken the step to abstraction, and that it was surrounded with its own intense spiritual excitement, as one gathers from the title of the aesthetic treatise he had published only a few months earlier in Munich, *On the Spiritual in Art*.[87]

The details of this transposition of Kandinskian spirituality to the *ad hoc* interpretation of Suprematism have yet to be defined, but it unquestionably did occur and, probably (but not emphatically) in a Slavic mind. It should not be forgotten that Kandinsky remained fiercely opposed to Malewicz all his life, not for religious reasons but mainly from a strictly painterly, even professional, standpoint.[88] Recall that in the field of artistic practices quite natural antagonisms, whether openly expressed or subliminal, confirm the existence of far more fundamental differences, in particular where certain deep-seated, profoundly cultural aesthetic choices are concerned.

Yet in the texts he wrote in 1915 and 1916 Malewicz had already clearly explained his own exertions to reach Non-Objective art, his struggle towards Suprematism. In the booklet *From Cubism and Futurism to Suprematism* and in the letter to Benois he refers in 1916 specifically to the precursors of Non-Objective art – Impressionism, Cubism, Futurism, Gauguin, Monet, Cézanne, Matisse and Picasso. These sources are indisputable. Nowhere does the artist speak of Byzantine art or of the aesthetic of icons. True, he does mention ancient art later on but mainly for a didactic purpose, and there is never any question at all of the Byzantine tradition coming first. At most, Malewicz refers to medieval painting, only Western

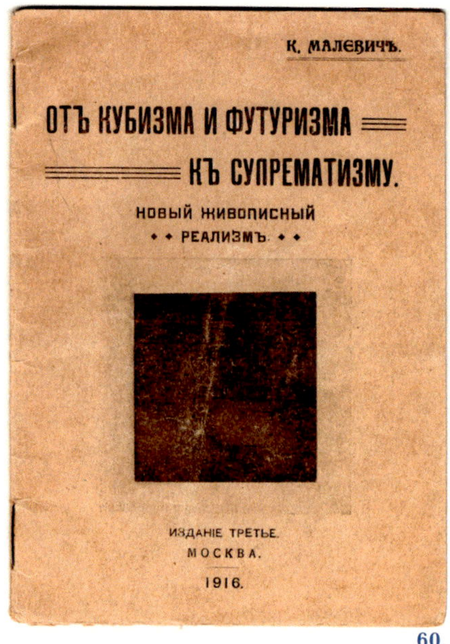

60.

60. K. Malewicz, cover of *From Cubism and Futurism to Suprematism*, Moscow, 1916, 3rd edition*

* In fact this is the second, much expanded version of the booklet initially published in December 1915 in Petrograd under the title *From Cubism to Suprematism*. At the artist's request two printings were issued during the *0,10* exhibition.

86 W. Kandinsky, *Rückblicke*, Berlin, 1913. English-language translation in K. C. Lindsay, P. Vergo (eds.), *Kandinsky: Complete Writings on Art*, Boston: G. K. Hall, 2 vols., 1982. Reprinted as a single volume by Da Capo Press (New York), 1994.

87 W. Kandinsky, *Über das Geistige in der Kunst*, 1912. English-language translation in Lindsay, Vergo, *op. cit.*

88 See Nakov, *Kandinsky*, 2015, especially the *Appendix*, pp. 193–214.

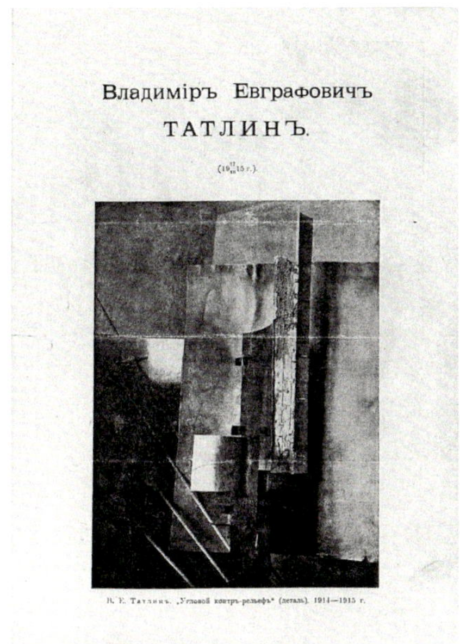

61.

61. Cover of the brochure *Vladimir Efgrafovitch Tatlin*, Petrograd, December 1915. Typographic characters, brochure printed by the *Novyi zhurnal dlia vsekh* (New Gazette for All) on the occasion of the first presentation of Tatlin's reliefs at the *0,10* show. Nakov Archives, Paris

[89] This photograph was published for the first time in 1975 (Nakov, *Malévitch. Écrits*). It appeared in the Leningrad archives thanks to the efforts of Evgueny Kovtun, a friend of mine who shared his discovery with me in 1974.

[90] The photograph is reproduced on p. 107, vol. 2 of my monograph (Nakov, *Malewicz*, 2007/2010). Malewicz's painting is displayed by itself at the top of the wall on the right. See here p. 50.

(Cimabue) rather than Eastern. His ascension to the Suprematist aesthetic is explained by Cubism and Futurism; it is these movements that document his path.

The "Byzantine" theory that surfaced with increasing frequency in interpretations of Suprematism squeezed out a pictorial explanation of vital importance. In December 1915 Malewicz positioned *Quadrilateral* for the *0,10* show in a strategic location just under the ceiling moulding. In this position the picture dominated the corner of the artist's presentation of Suprematist compositions and seemed to be at the "vanishing point" of a space known to us solely through a single photograph.[89] To speak of "iconostases" in the face of this hanging seems specious, to say the least.

In fact, a few weeks earlier, on 6 November to be exact, on the occasion of the *Modern Decorative Arts* exhibition in Moscow, Malewicz used a similar exhibition strategy for displaying one of his first Non-Objective works, without any need to save space (as we can see from an archive photograph of that event).[90] Had he done so in order to stress the difference between this new composition and the other works on show? By placing it well away from the other purely decorative works we see surrounding it, the artist was undoubtedly "staging" the Non-Objective nature of his new painting.

It would be far more relevant to consider the general context of the *0,10* show. The preparations for this event were marked by a fierce and, in the end, even violent competition between Malewicz and Vladimir Tatlin, to the point that the exhibition's opening only took place after endless negotiations were undertaken the evening before the *vernissage* thanks to the mediation of Alexandra Exter, then one of the few members of the Cubo-Futurist avant-garde to entertain friendly relations with both Tatlin and Malewicz. In the room adjoining the one in which the Suprematist paintings were being presented Tatlin, it so happened, showed his Non-Objective reliefs. One of his main three-dimensional constructions was titled *Corner Relief*. To ignore the existence of this major element in the presentation of Malewicz's chief – and perhaps only – competitor's installation would be a grave oversight. That the placing of *Quadrilateral* in a corner was a response to Tatlin is obvious.

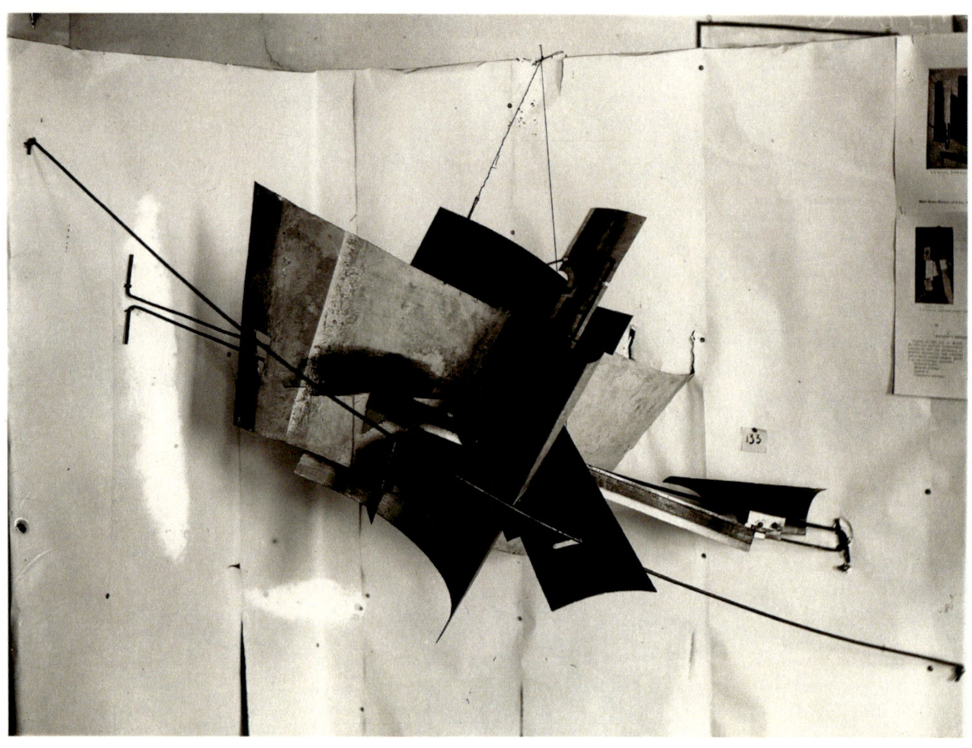

62 a.

* * *

Malewicz showed Black Square
as an old-style icon but it was an icon of art
and was therefore non-objective.

Hans Belting, 1998[91]

This being the case, references to Byzantine art seem extravagant and duck the real issue. (The excerpt from Belting is a good indication of the prevailing state of confusion.) For lack of being able to analyse the specific components of the formal Cubist system and, to an even greater degree, Alogist aesthetic, which was simply ignored by art critics as unsure of themselves as they were ill-informed, the latter travestied Suprematism, garbing it in the ecclesiastical robes of the Byzantine tradition

[91] "Malewitsch zeigte das 'Schwarze Quadrat' [...] *als eine Ikone in altem Sinne*, aber es war eine Ikone der Kunst und daher Gegenstandslos" (H. Belting, *Das unsichtbare Meisterwerk. Die modernen Mythen der Kunst*, Munich: Beck, 1998; my italics).

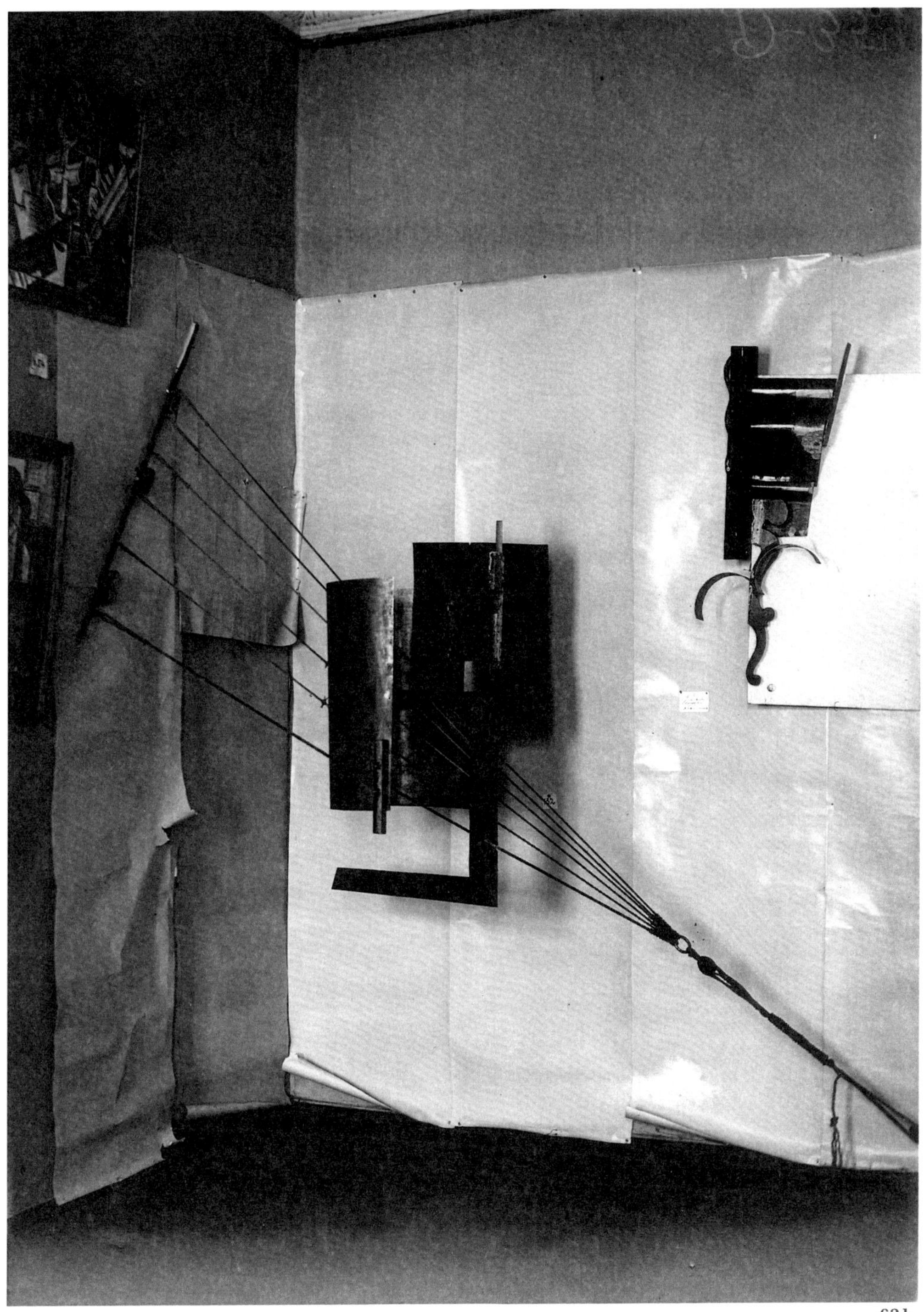

62 b.

despite the fact that this was utterly foreign to Malewicz's creative approach. In his essays, as we have said, the artist is quite explicit about the immediate forerunners of his aesthetic position: Symbolism (Gauguin), Impressionism (Monet) and Cubism (Picasso). For scholars poorly versed in the ins and outs of modern art it seemed both exotic and easier to explain Malewicz's Expressionist work (like *Pedicure*) in terms of Rublev's *Holy Trinity*[92] than as a reply to Cézanne's *Card Players* or to one of Picasso's *Violins*. Yet the artist himself made this amply clear in his writings and didactic panels of the 1920s, those theoretic demonstrations and invaluable tokens of his teaching at the time.[93] Of course, in order to plunge into such analyses, one must possess a minimally precise knowledge of modern art, a knowledge that the "culturalist" (to use a term much warped by the exponents of a recent fashion) exegetes of Suprematism appear to be cruelly short of.

Malewicz has always pointed his readers to precise, indisputable sources of his development: it suffices to read his texts of the 1910s and '20s, not to mention his teachings at the Leningrad Institute of Artistic Culture (an inestimable aid in approaching modern art), to understand this. The repeated references to Cubism he again made in Moscow in 1918 evolved into key elements of his emphatic teaching to young students at Vitebsk.

[92] See Spira, *The Avant-Garde Icon...*, *op. cit.*, 2008.

[93] Presented in part in December 1925 in Moscow (in the Survey by the Scientific Section of the People's Commissariat for Education show at the Historical Museum) and subsequently exhibited in Berlin during the summer of 1927, these didactic panels are usually treated cursorily in discussions of modern art history. The artist's teachings in the 1920s cover a broad range of topics. Apart from their luminous analyses, the panels are evidence of his wide-ranging knowledge of art history in general. Byzantine painting is present in them but is given no more importance than any other art, medieval, baroque or (still less) modern.

CHAPTER 9

"KNOWING WHAT SPEAKING MEANS"[94]

One of the most common distortions of the way Suprematist paintings are viewed involves the way they are named. Alexander Benois initiated this practice when he violently downgraded the original *Quadrilateral* to a banal *Black Square*, a shocking diminishment and flagrant impoverishment of the essence of Suprematism, much the same kind of denigration that has been made in Paris as early as 1911 by critics of Cubism. Benois was bent on belittling a work that provoked his repulsion, for he had understood that with it Malewicz was ruthlessly upending the order of established values. As he put it explicitly, Malewicz was destroying what he held "sacred". In the eyes of the passionately anti-modernist critic, what was at stake was the very meaning of an image he recoiled from, since it destroyed his scale of values, the *raison d'être* of his world. It was thus that the most audacious work Malewicz had painted up until then was reduced to a vulgar "geometrical" hoax.[95] Denied the status of art by the critic, *Quadrilateral* was emptied of his aesthetic content, discarded on the rubbish heap of superficial platitudes.

In his first comments devoted to Suprematism, the painter explained unambiguously the nature of that form, i.e. its

[94] Concerning this French saying, see P. Bourdieu, *"Ce que parler veut dire". L'Economie des échanges linguistiques* (collection of essays), Paris: Fayard, 1982. English translation: *Language and Symbolic Power* (trans. G. Raymond and M. Adamson), Cambridge (Mass.): Harvard University Press, 1991.

[95] As early as 1913 similar geometrising reductions became standard in the satirical reception of Cubism in France and, much later, in Russia. See Nakov, *Tatlin*, 2020, chap. 3 and fig. p. 98.

63. *Pictorial Realism of a Peasant Woman in Two Dimensions*, otherwise known as *Red Square*, 1915 (Cat. S-126, first version), oil on canvas, 40.2 × 30.1 cm, private collection, on deposit at the Musée des Beaux Arts, Liège

63.

content. For the creators of the first abstraction a form could not exist without a content. As Kandinsky was to put it a few years later, a form without content was but a "hollow handle". In the "survey" of abstract art that the review *Cahiers d'art* undertook in 1931 (where Kandinsky's answer appeared), Piet Mondrian was of much the same opinion. In an important clarification made in Germany six years earlier, Kandinsky began his analysis of abstract art, which was much talked about at the time, with the statement that that what concerned him first was "the question of content and form" and went on to say that "the work is exclusively the product of *purely pictorial* means".[96] Other artists, for instance Jean Arp, answered

[96] W. Kandinsky, "Abstrakte Kunst", *Der Cicerone*, no. 13, Leipzig, 1925. English translation in *Kandinsky: Complete Writings on Art, op. cit.*, 1994, pp. 511–518.

64.

64. *Red Square 2*, 1916–1917 (Cat. S-127, second version), oil on canvas, 53.1 × 53 cm, State Museum of Russia, St Petersburg

negatively to the charge that abstract art – an art that seemed to have quietly reached a new level of recognition on the art scene of Paris – was "decorative" or "geometrical".

As for Malewicz, as early as 1916, he explained that *Quadrilateral* was a "being", an altogether extraordinary "being" in fact, since the artist presented him as a "royal infant". This condition of the painting's form (a Non-Objective one) is perceptible owing to its irregularity. To speak of it as a "square" is manifestly incorrect. Stemming from the Symbolist aesthetic, the existential, vital nature of the Non-Objective plane, which the painter described as one face of the quadrilateral, was manifested through the energy of the form – a form presented as existing in flight. The "being's" state was indicated by its energy level, as the artist said of each element in the Suprematist "construction".[97] As a matter of fact, when one examines the original *Quadrilateral* closely one sees that it is not a regular "square" in the strict sense of the word but a form resembling a square. One of its upper corners – the right one – points upwards. The form's vitality is more perceptible in *Red Square* (S-126) and to an even greater extent in that composition's second version (S-127), which the artist realised (in autumn 1916 or even later in 1917?).

While Benois' label shifted the painting from the province of the artwork, that is to say of "being", to that of common planes, the composition suffered another downgrading in the last few decades. We have seen it published under the apocryphal heading *Black Square on White Background*. The artist never called it this, nor did any of his students, and quite rightly so. Reduced to a simple planar reading, this title simply excludes the work from the field of Non-Objective art. From the standpoint of its aesthetic content *Black Square on White Background* is an erroneous, flatly impoverished description; it deprives the composition of its aesthetic identity and transforms it into a perfectly ordinary geometric figure. The same kind of positivist demotion, a purely descriptive and reductionist one, has turned *White Square* into *White Square on a White Background* or *White on White* in most recent publications, a non-artistic heading that should in no case be regarded as an indication of the work's true identity. Need we recall that this so-called title, which the artist never used, is totally alien to the composition. Its real title, used repeatedly

97 Malewicz used the term "construction" as of 1916.

by Malewicz in 1918 and later to assert its identity, remains quite simply *White Square*, a denomination one should read as personal statement: it is as though the painting were declaring *"I am (or my name is) White Square"*.

65.

CHAPTER 10

DIFFERENT WAYS OF HANGING A WORK ALTER ITS MESSAGE

65. *White Square*, 1918 (Cat. S-477), oil on canvas, 78.7 × 78.7 cm (rectified dimensions), MoMA, New York

[98] Barr's correspondence of the 1960s and 1970s, which has as yet been insufficiently studied, contains interesting information regarding this topic. This correspondence, part of which I was able to consult, is preserved in the archives of the New York MoMA.

[99] This exhibition had the merit of placing Suprematism on the map of modern art and of somewhat diminishing Kandinsky's – then dominant position relative to abstract art.

[100] I do not know exactly when this change occurred, but possibly it was on the occasion of a new hanging after the work had been returned from an exhibition elsewhere, or some similar occurrence. It would be presumptuous to suspect that it had been done on purpose; the change in orientation was most likely due to a banal decision by a minor museum staff member but later the difference went unnoticed by the museum direction.

Besides this lexical injury, *White Square* has been subjected to yet another distortion, a major one since it is of a visual nature. At some point during the 1970s (to tell the truth I do not know exactly when) its hanging was changed without warning and without a word of explanation. This probably happened after Alfred Barr retired. Since 1929, the date of the founding of the Museum of Modern Art in New York, Barr, one of the founders of MoMA (and mentor of Camilla Gray's work), had always been keenly interested in Russian Non-Objective art, particularly that of Alexander Rodchenko, Vladimir Tatlin and no less Kazimir Malewicz.[98] It was Barr who brought back several Malewicz paintings from Germany in 1935, including *White Square*, which featured in his Cubism and Abstract Art exhibition the following year.[99] In Germany he had been in touch with Hans von Riesen, Hugo Häring and Alexander Dorner, to whom the painter had entrusted the paintings he had left in Berlin in 1927. His relationship with Malewicz's work was thus fairly direct, if not exactly first-hand.

Barr's successors decided to change *White Square*'s hanging one day, "correcting" it by tipping it ninety degrees to one side.[100] (This change of orientation may well have been

66.

unintended but was nonetheless momentous.) The vertical orientation of the central form – the square – was modified: instead of soaring towards the top left the square was now suspended in mid fall. This change took place at the time the Neo-formalist fashion sweeping New York's art scene was gaining momentum, and at a time when the Neo-formalist

66. *White Square* (Cat. S-477), infrared reflectograph

67. *White Square* (Cat. S-477), X-ray

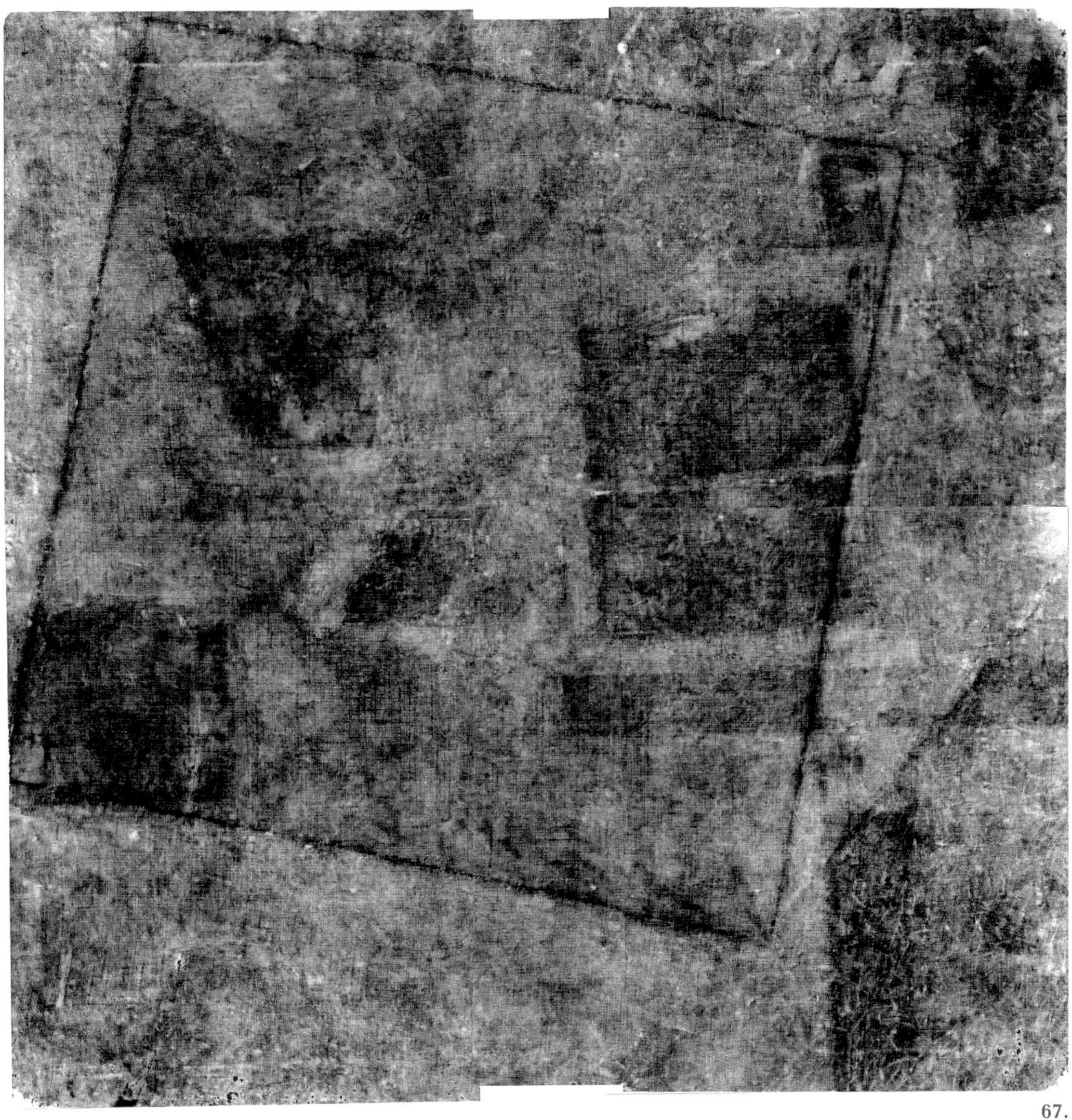

67.

[101] As evidence of this consider the opinions of the Neo-structuralists and other "geometricists", such as Sol LeWitt. (I refer to a personal conversation I had with that artist in Paris.) As for the new "Post-structuralist" vogue, it was represented at the time by the critics gravitating around the New York journal *October*, Annette Michelson, Benjamin Buchloh and others. I will not linger either

appropriation of Malewicz's aesthetic, which could be described as a kind of post-modern neutralisation, was in the ascendancy.[101]

Thanks to a study of *White Square*'s early stages by infrared reflectography[102] I was able to establish a good deal about the progression of the idea behind the composition.

As a result we now know about the successive levels of refinement that led to the final version and about the artist's affirmation of the square that, freed from the presence of secondary forms, expressed by itself the whole idea of "colourlessness" (White Suprematism). Thanks to this reading we are able to follow the affirmation of the composition's content (its sole form) as a single, powerful energetic source. Considering the subtlety of the white form's message, the alteration of its hanging under Barr, the new orientation is not just an error, it is a mistake. The original positioning of *White Square*, respected by both Barr and Camilla Gray in her pioneering survey of the Russian avant-garde,[103] is particularly instructive when the movement of its form is compared to that of the square in the original *Quadrilateral*. One observes an almost symmetrical opposition of the energetic forces in the two compositions: the motion of the black square is towards the upper right corner (as is obvious to the naked eye from its irregular form), while that of the white square emphatically faces the top left corner.

Used for teaching purposes, the eminently pictorial contrast between the "content" of the two forms confirms the explanation given by the artist for the "white" (or, in the artist's eyes, "colourless") phase of Suprematist painting.[104] More than just a culmination of the first period of Suprematism, that of the "black" compositions of 1915–1916, white Suprematism ended in 1918 by constituting a transformation, an ultimate metamorphosis of Suprematist painting involving a real qualitative transcendence of the very notion of the painterly practice (including that of Non-Objective painting). This evolution prompted the artist to write several sensational statements proclaiming the "end of painterly practice" and its transformation into the sphere of "pure action", i.e. the fact of going beyond the visual demarcation of planes. In this way the artwork had the capacity to leap over the conceptual barrier of philosophy, a veritable existential shift that deeply dismayed Malewicz's former avant-garde comrades in Moscow.

With the "white" phase we are consequently faced with more than just a stylistic change, but with a profound mutation of the essential nature of the practicing painter, who was now seen to rise above the bold practice of painting "like everyone". Henceforth the artist regarded himself as

on the altogether erroneous reproductions of this work, such as the one in Turowski's 2004 book where *White Square* is reproduced upside-down (*op. cit.*, p. 323).

[102] I was able to carry out this study in New York in September 2001 (see Nakov, *Malewicz*, 2007/2010, vol. 4, chap. 32).

[103] C. Gray, *The Great Experiment in Russian Art: 1863–1922*, London: Thames & Hudson, 1962, where *White Square* is reproduced in its correct orientation, as indeed it was exhibited at the time at the New York MoMA. It figures on p. 242 of the second edition of her work, *The Russian Experiment in Art: 1863–1922*, revised and enlarged by M. Burleigh-Motley, London–New York, 1986, but this time with the title *Suprematist Composition: White on White*.

[104] As set forth in Malewicz's written statements of 1918–1920.

a philosopher-painter. "There can be no question of painting in Suprematism. Painting became obsolete a long time ago, and the artist himself a prejudice of the past", Malewicz wrote in a dramatic, properly revolutionary statement dated 1920.[105]

* * *

We broke with Suprematism in a scandalous manner.
Malewicz suddenly went crazy and we got angry.

Nadezhda Udaltsova, journal entry,
22 November 1916

Understandably, the artist's comrades were at first deeply shocked at this statement, which destabilised the foundations and very essence of their artistic practice, it fundamentally (i.e. existentially) destabilised their inner aesthetic beliefs. The reaction came almost at once. As early as the autumn of 1918 Malewicz's "fellow travellers" (Alexander Rodchenko, Ivan Kliun and other "Constructivists" like Liubov Popova and Varvara Stepanova) rejected white Suprematism. *The Non-Objective Creation and Suprematism* exhibition, which was scheduled to open that fall in response to the artist "white" evolution, brought to light the breach between the painters who henceforth called themselves "Constructivists" and the partisans of Malewicz's "colourless" Suprematism.[106] His former companions lost no time in launching a "Non-Objective" movement in open opposition to Suprematism. From summer 1919 Malewicz was no longer welcome in Moscow. His few subsequent wanderings are only too familiar: Vitebsk, Petrograd, Germany...

During the 1920s the nucleus of "apostles" of the new religion dwindled rapidly. Apart from a few exceptional works by some of Malewicz's young students at Vitebsk who managed with difficulty to follow the Master to Petrograd, we know only of white reliefs by Kliun and a few white compositions by Nikolai Suetin and Ivan Kudriashov. The reaction that met, in 1923, the last public presentation of works of this type by Malewicz and his students was particularly significant

[105] K. Malewicz, preface to *Suprematizm 34 risunka* (Suprematism 34 Drawings, i.e. compositions), Vitebsk, December 1920 (English trans. in *K. S. Malevich, Essays, op. cit.*, 1971, vol. 1, pp. 123–128).

[106] Delayed for material reasons, the *Non-Objective Creation and Suprematism* exhibition opened late in Moscow on 27 April 1919. The catalogue, which included numerous position statements, marks the end of the period of the unbridled or rather idealistic evolution of abstract art in Russia.

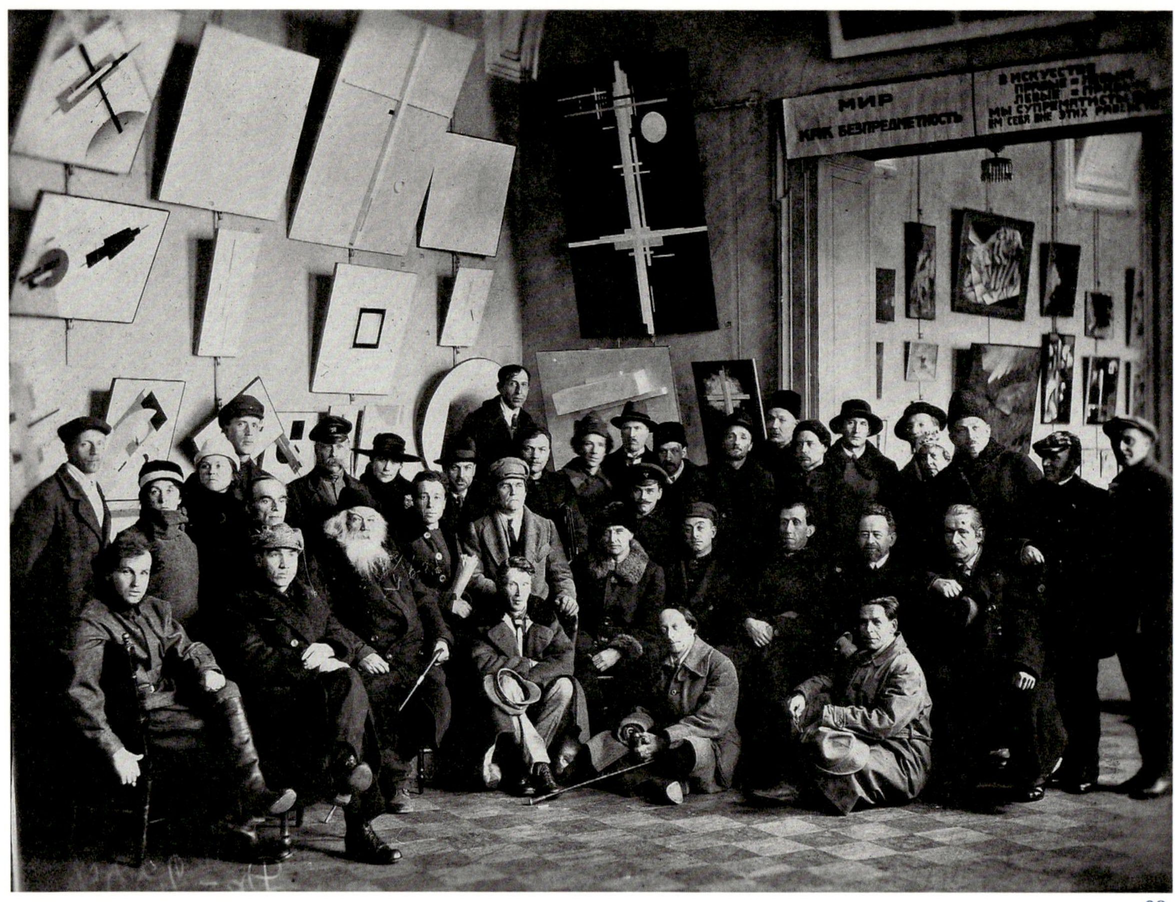

68.

inasmuch as the rejection of Suprematism had reached a new level. The all but silent but no less definitive rejection of painterly Suprematism left long-lasting traces on the very image of the aesthetic thought behind it. A new generation of avant-garde artists had by then rejected the philosophical transformation of Suprematism in its "white" phase. This time critics attacked the artist, not from the anti-modernist position previously defended by the manifestly reactionary Alexander Benois, but from a new "Productivist" vantage, the "activist", aggressively "avant-gardist", definitely materialistic practice that had emerged in Moscow during the autumn of 1921.[107] By then the notion of the avant-garde had already left the domain of artistic creation and had slipped into the arms of social ideology, taking a "technicist" and "productivist" materialist

68. *All Trends* exhibition, Academy of Fine Arts, Petrograd, spring 1923. Malewicz surrounded by "white" paintings and reliefs by the UNOVIS group. Seated next to him is Pavel Mansurov. Several works can be discerned on the right wall, among them an architectona by Ilya Chashnik

[107] See my comments on this subject in A. Nakov, *2 Stenberg 2*, Paris–London–Toronto, 1975.

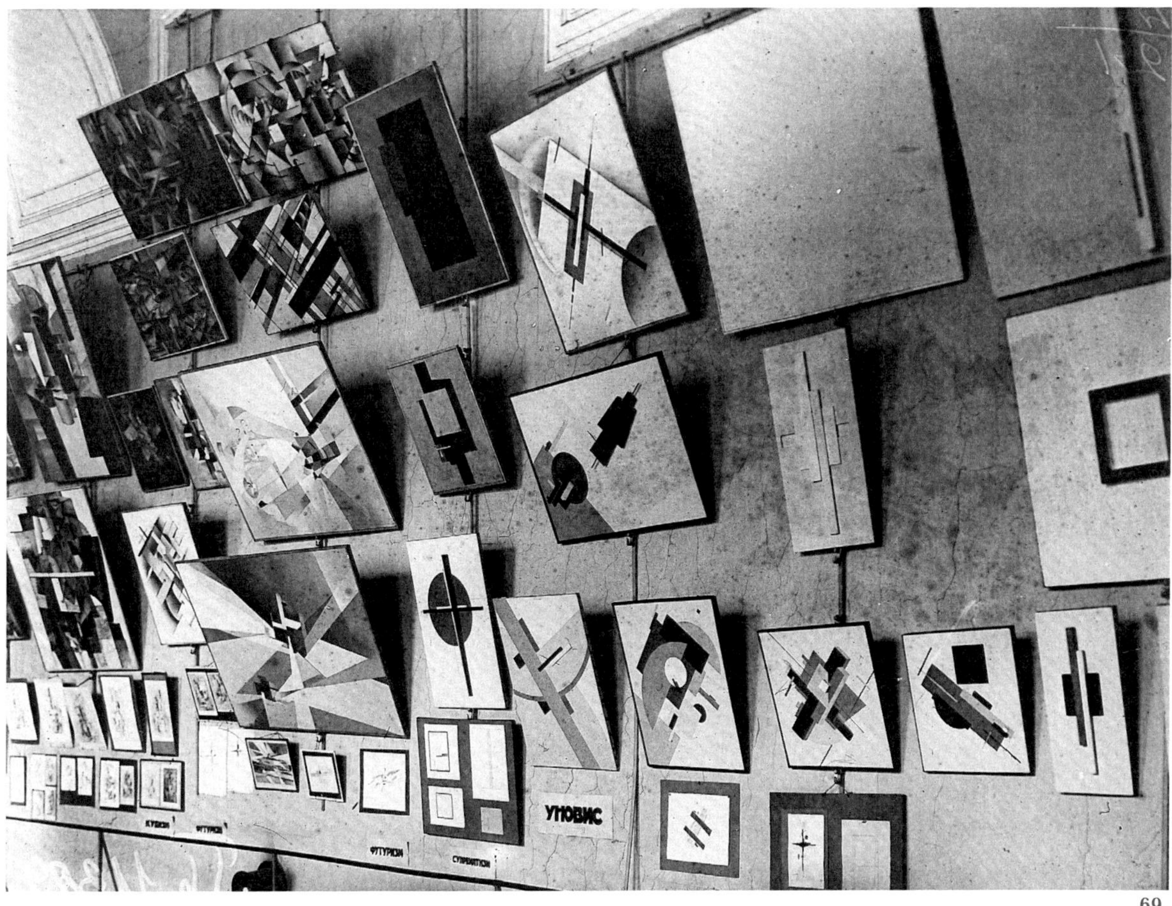

69.

69. Wall with Malewicz's "white" canvases at the *All Trends* exhibition. On the far left we discern the *Portrait of Matiushin* (Cat. F-401) above a Cubist canvas by Lev Yudin (now at the Tretyakov State Gallery in Moscow)

turn that was at the opposite end of the spectrum from the greatly and then finally metaphysical Suprematist aesthetic.

In one of the first issues of the then newly founded review *Lef* (Left Front of the Arts), the organ of the would-be "Constructivist" movement (a rather "Productivist" term denoting a "utilitarian", hence "materialist", approach at the time), there appeared a particularly acid review of the Petersburg *All Trends* exhibition, which included for the first time in that city a large UNOVIS section. Held for three months (15 May – 15 August 1923) in the rooms of the former Imperial Academy of Fine Arts (a symbol in itself), the exhibition included several of Malewicz's "white" compositions and a number of white reliefs, models of architectonas by students of the artist such as Ilya Chashnik, Nikolai Suetin, Lazar Khidekel and/or possibly others. Malewicz published on this occasion a new, and this time, ultimate, Suprematist manifesto.

Titled "Suprematist Mirror", this succinct text possesses a rare lyric intensity that is closer to a poetic incantation than to a painter's declaration. Its vibrant summons to a metaphysical absolute proved as shocking to contemporary tastes as the "white" works it accompanied. It can rightly be viewed, both in terms of its content and in terms of form, as a continuation and even a conclusion of the "White Manifesto" of the summer of 1918. Quite simply headed "Statement" (of colourlessness) and symbolically dated 15 June 1918,[108] it remained unread until the spring of 1920, when Malewicz included it in the *Unovis No. 1* miscellany, a virtually confidential publication since only five copies of it were produced. In 1923 the incantatory cadences of "Suprematist Mirror", which returns to and expands the 1918 themes, met with as much attention, not to say indifference, as the earlier manifesto had encountered. Nikolai Punin alone ventured to comment on it, but in rather unflattering, if not outright backward-looking, terms. To this day it remains a brief lyrical flash, a poetic fireworks in the metaphysical void of a period stifled by the torpidity of the "functionalist" (materialist) reaction. Malewicz's call for an absolute at once poetic and philosophic was rapidly thrust aside by the dramatic events that succeeded Russia's Civil War and the collapse of the idealist values of the Symbolist and Futurist avant-garde.

Most of the Symbolist themes that had marked Malewicz's rise to Non-Objectivity are summarised in the manifesto's vividly poetic style. Evoking his humanist convictions one last time, the artist gave a dazzling summation to the idealist origins of his aesthetic. The Symbolist element of that aesthetic was thus asserted in the philosophical absolute of an essential Non-Objectivity that was founded on both Odilon Redon's mystical silence (think of *Closed Eyes* of 1890, echoed in 1908 in the inspired introspection of Malewicz's first self-portrait) and on the philosophical transcendence of an Andréi Belyi, who had launched the concept of non-objectivity in 1910, both having paved the way for the infiniteness of the Suprematist aesthetic.

In short, in the spring of 1923, thanks to the coruscation of "Suprematist Mirror", Malewicz's Non-Objectivity was

[108] Malewicz's manifestoes are dated the 15th of the month in which they appeared. "Suprematist Mirror" was undoubtedly dated 15 June 1915, the symbolic date of *Quadrilateral* (or *Black Square*). The reader is reminded that all of Marinetti's manifestoes are dated the 11th for equally symbolic reasons, a detail that was probably known at the time.

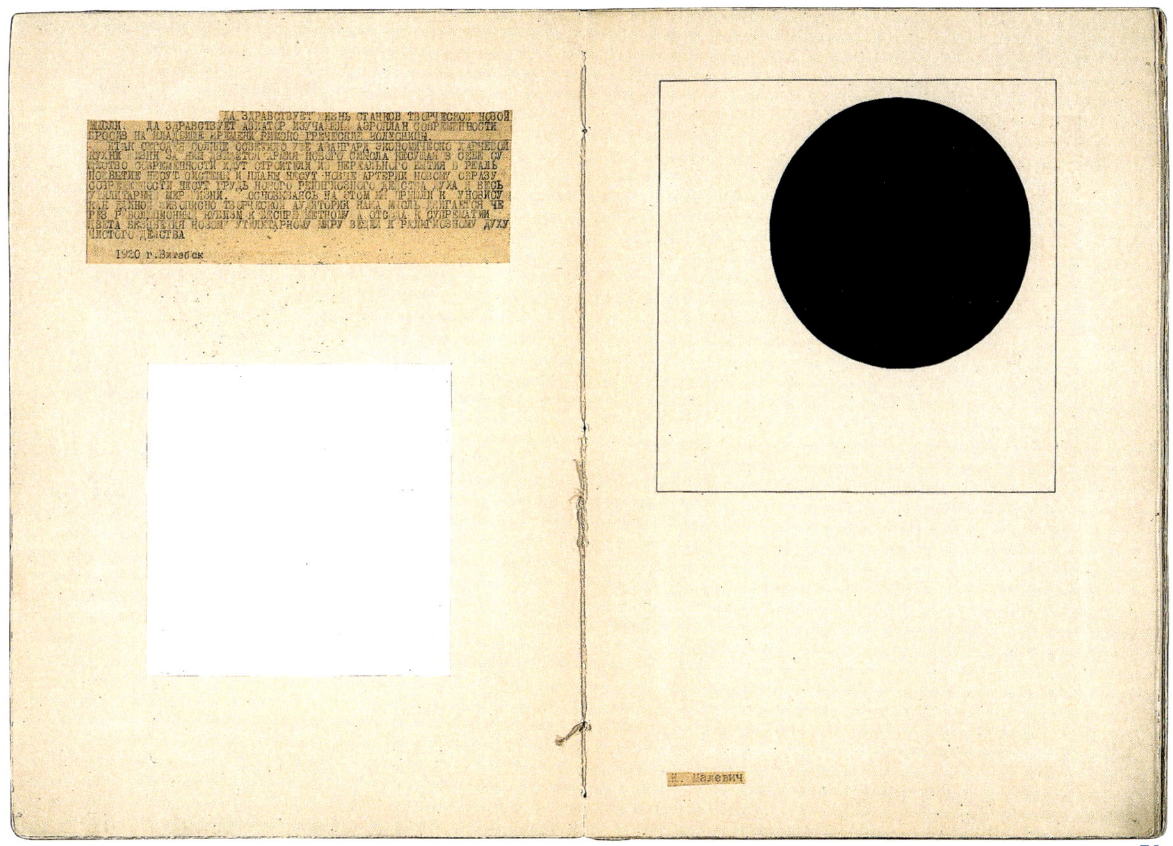

70.

70. *White Square*, version of May 1920 (Cat. S-478), gouache and sawdust (?), 35.7 × 22.5 cm (page), 13.5 × 13.5 cm (composition). Work included in the *Unovis No. 1* miscellany, Vitebsk, private collection

109 S. Yutkevich, "Sukharnaya stolica", *Lef*, no. 3, 1923. The young author and future film director was also attacking at the same moment the staging of Tatlin's spectacle *Zangezi*. Referring to the latter's 1915 reliefs, he described them as "it-sy-bitsy boards".

propelled into a new expressive dimension. In a period full of menace, it could only have met with the stupefaction and rejection of the "Productivist" generation in whose eyes the artist's cherished idealist values were merely hollow words, an alien manner of speaking. Given the context, Malewicz's evocation of a mirror, that thoroughly emblematic image of the Symbolist system, must indeed have struck a very strange note. His appeal for poetic introspectiveness was misunderstood: it belonged to a world that was already a thing of the past.

Denying any artistic content to Malewicz's "white" compositions, *Lef*'s writer Sergei Yutkevich dismissed them scornfully as "empty canvases".[109] And the fact is that in the spring of 1923 when "texturist" and other visually "materialist" works were being celebrated in Moscow, a "white" composition must have called on a completely different aesthetic sensitivity, a completely Dionysian Nietzchean vibrancy that was, *ipso facto*, intolerable to the "Productivist" point of view. Had not Osip Brik, the official ideologue of this neo-materialist current who was described at the time as a "Constructivist", declared in 1919 that any "pure" work, i.e. any work that was purely artistic, was "suspect"?[110] Malewicz, on the other hand, upheld his own "pure action", in other words ideal, metaphysical creation. The contrast between these two positions could not have been greater. Not unexpectedly, the image of *White Square* is missing from the only copy of the *Unovis No. 1* miscellany preserved in Russia (in the archives of the Tretyakov Gallery in Moscow). Yet it was there in 1920.[111] The page containing it was simply removed (when and by whom?). The traces of a history having been expunged, history is read differently; the history of the 20th century has taught us this sorry truth.

The anti-Suprematist reaction might have remained a passing moment in the history of modern Russian art had it not been for its lasting consequences. But such was not the case. White Suprematism was engulfed by the anti-modernist flood that initially presented itself under the banner of "Productivist" utilitarian materialism, but was actually a social, class, anti-elitist reaction. It lasted practically until the end of the Soviet regime. White Suprematism having indisputably been declared "beyond the pale" (of the new "sociological" standards), the painter's very existence was forgotten. As late as the early 1950s Malewicz had the image in Russia of being "American", for his Suprematist canvases, including the scandalous *White Square*, hung on the walls of a modern art museum in America, the New York MoMA.[112] Such is the censorship of white Suprematism in Russia that not a single "white" composition by Malewicz is to be found in his native country. Art historians, considered in Russia as established experts on the artist, know so little about the white Suprematist creation that until this day they have accepted uncritically the fashionable myth of the "empty canvases". Hence the path conducting to the understanding of Malewicz's white paintings of 1918, particularly the ones produced by him after 1920, still seems a very bumpy road indeed.

Transformed into a strictly manual, i.e. textural monochromy (take the example of Rodchenko), Malewicz's metaphysical

[110] See O. Brik, "Khudozhnik i Kommuna" (The Artist and the Commune), *Izobrazitelnoe Iskusstvo* (Visual Arts), Moscow, 1919. As this anthology was ready to print by summer 1918, the date of Brik's text ought to be given as one year earlier. Brik was involved in creating the review *Lef*. In the autumn of 1921, it was also at Brik's behest that a declaration advocating "abandoning pure creation" and calling for artists to take up "production" was voted at the Moscow INKhUK (Institute of Artistic Culture).

[111] Only five copies of this important anthology were made by hand; at present we know of just two of them, but only one, the copy presented to David Shterenberg (now in a private collection), includes the *White Square*'s image. The Tretyakov Gallery copy, which apparently belonged to El Lissitzky and later passed into the hands of Nikolai Khardzhiev who donated it to the Moscow museum, lacks the page with the *White Square*.

[112] I. Gavrilov, "Ched-evr XX veka" (A 20th-Century Masterpiece), *Vechernaya Moskva*, 28 March 1953, in which Malewicz is described as an "American painter [...] who 'in his time' benefited from a great success among New York snobs".

questioning had become a *style*, a simple *painterly practice*, and, in this artisanal guise, has survived a plethora of mutations in Europe and the United States during the second half of the 20th century.

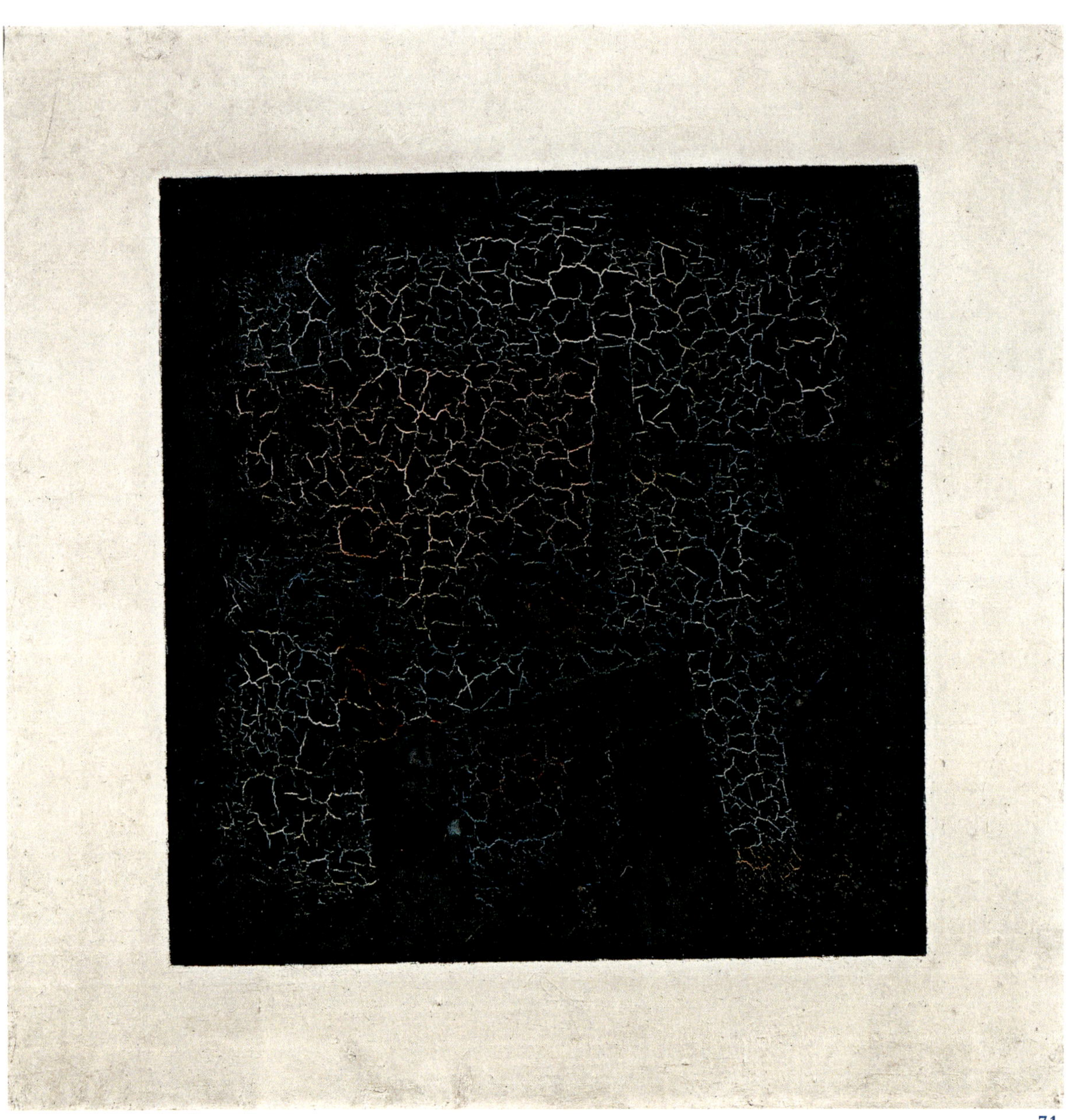

USELESS SCIENCE

71. *Quadrilateral*, commonly called *Black Square*, summer 1915 (Cat. S-116), oil on canvas, 79.5 × 79.5 cm, Tretyakov State Gallery, Moscow

Art history having its share in the vogue for "new alternatives", otherwise known as "fake news", an anecdotal event recently brought confusion to the way Malewicz's work is regarded. After initially (2015) considering it a minor epiphenomenon, I realized this winter that it had a startling if not negative impact. Hence the present *Postscript*.

A bizarre news item concerning *Black Square* appeared in Moscow in 2015 and, though a sort of ricochet effect, recently re-emerged in Paris. It concerns the so-called Parisian origin of the leading work of Suprematism. There was but a short step from the Muscovite myth to the "scholarly" French interpretation, and it has now been taken. As a result, we now find ourselves in the midst of an imbroglio worthy of a frothy operetta. The pretext came pre-packaged thanks to the discovery (perfectly genuine in this case) of an astonishing group of French late-19th-century works.[113] This quickly led to all kinds of elucubrations, and a number of artfully insipid publications donned academic robes for the occasion. Let us see what actually happened.

Early in the spring of 2015 a startling "discovery" was made in Moscow. It concerned Malewicz's *Black Square*

[113] See the article in the daily newspaper *Le Monde*, 4 February 2021, p. 21: "La résurrection des art incohérents. Dix-sept œuvres parodiques du mouvement légendaire du XIXe siècle ont été retrouvées dans une malle" (Resurrection of the Arts Incohérents. Seventeen satirical works of the legendary 19th-century movement found in a trunk).

(1915), a picture held since the end of the 1910s at the Tretyakov State Gallery, on which the "remains" (?) of an apocryphal much "damaged" (sic!) inscription that had supposedly not been spotted before – indeed, it could not have been spotted, since, as we shall see, it had not existed previously – was suddenly revealed. Very craftily inserted in the bottom white field of the canvas, this inscription (made with a pencil or perhaps even a ballpoint pen?) was added to the coat of paint that had dried decades earlier. It pretended to be a reference to the famous "April Fool's" prank of the French writer and humorist Alphonse Allais (1854–1905), a well-known joke presented at one of the *Salon des Arts Incohérents* in Paris in the 1880s and subsequently published by its author in a pamphlet containing several monochrome parodies of the same type.[114] Regarded since at least the last three decades as an "honorary" predecessor of the modern monochrome, Allais' provocative gesture is at present thoroughly familiar.[115] Camouflaged as the forerunner of the single-colour compositions of the second half of the 20th century (Yves Klein referred specifically to the humorist and laid new claim to the tone of his "incoherent" actions), Allais' approach possessed a certain satirical panache. It was a strictly formal parody, in the original sense of the term, of the abstract art of the future and, as such, was part of the repertoire of the jocular spoofing of modern art among the "bohemian, Hydropathic" (and other) milieu. Owing to its multiple layers of meaning, Allais' playfully provocative gesture has still not elicited the scholarly attention it deserves (like Émile Cohl's early films).[116]

Forgotten for decades (1920–1980), the proto-Dada exhibitions of the Incohérents (Paris 1882–1897, Nantes 1887), which as late as 1919 inspired the "rectified Mona Lisa", Marcel Duchamp's celebrated readymade provocatively titled *L.H.O.O.Q.* (an obvious reference to the Incohérents), awakened a renewed interest on the occasion of the large *Dada* show at the Centre Pompidou in Paris in the summer of 2005.[117] In the vein of the anti-modernist tradition of the Cubist spoofs (which saw its apogee in 1910–1912, first in Paris and then in Moscow, in caricatures of Cubism), Allais' falsely sacrilegious gesture had a lasting influence on modern publications devoted to monochromes (Yves Klein, Ad Reinhardt and others).

[114] See A. Allais, *Album Primo-Avrilesque*, Paris: Ollendorf, 1897. Often reprinted since then. Coined by Allais, the term "primo-avrilesque" refers of course to the tradition of April Fools practical jokes. The idea that inspired Allais is thought to have come initially from the painter Paul Bilhaud (1854–1933) who participated in the *Incohérent* salons; but I won't pursue this archaeological investigation any further.

[115] At present the bibliography concerning the topic is vast. One of the best-known studies in French is Denys Riout's *La peinture monochrome*, Nîmes: Éditions Jacqueline Chambon, 1996.

[116] The best work on the Incohérents, published in the wake of the modest show devoted to their movement at the Musée d'Orsay in Paris, is Catherine Charpin's book *Les Arts Incohérents 1882–1893*, Paris: Éditions Syros, 1990.

[117] After opening at the Centre Pompidou the exhibition travelled to the New York MoMA. I contributed to the material organisation of this event and published two essays in the catalogue to the Paris show. At the time I was working on a book about the Incohérents, scheduled to be published by Editions Fayard in Paris. My work on this movement, still to be finished, was interrupted by the task of completing my four-volume monograph on Malewicz.

Cleverly scribbled, for it presented itself as a half-erased annotation (a good job of faking!), the inscription that was suddenly "discovered" on the surface of *Black Square* excited the interest of Russian art historians who flocked to the existence of Alphonse Allais and the impish sources of the Montmartre avant-garde (Alfred Jarry, *Le Chat Noir* and so forth). Yet all these themes had been present on the Russian art scene before 1914[118] – a vast modernist breeding ground on which Symbolism and abstract art arose and then extended and transcended (Kandinsky, Apollinaire and, quite magisterially, Malewicz). Lacking historical knowledge of late 19th-century French art scholars in Moscow jostled each other to study the sources of inspiration of *Black Square* and its supposed origin in French art (though, as we shall see, they lie elsewhere). Taking the inscription to be genuine, they commissioned large-scale technical examinations of the composition (X-rays and other analyses). Almost immediately the Moscow museum trumpeted the news *urbi et orbi*, and in the autumn of 2015 it was reported widely in the international press (*The New York Times, The Art Newspaper*, etc.). The senior research scientist responsible for this "discovery" gave a conference in New York. Published in Russian by the Tretyakov Gallery the booklet on the topic was rapidly translated in Germany and issued in English by a reputable publishing firm in Cologne.[119] Other leading figures in the museum world in the West jumped on the bandwagon. But as I suggested in Moscow to my friend Irina Vakar, this fuss could have been avoided had a careful study been undertaken of the X-ray of the painting, a document I had commissioned from the Tretykov Gallery with some difficulty in 1992 in connection with my preliminary work on the Malewicz *Catalogue raisonné*.[120] In my view the comparison could have been of a Biblical simplicity: the inscription "found" in 2015 does not appear in the 1992 radiograph. Thus there is no point in rehashing the fanciful commentaries on *Black Square* that have been repeated *ad nauseam* since 2015.

Still more extravagant was the response to this item of fake news in the literature devoted to Malewicz in the West. In 2018, for example, the review of the Musée National d'Art Moderne in Paris ran a long text on *Black Square* manifestly reflecting the Tretyakov Gallery's "discovery".[121] In this pedantic piece,

[118] The Russian press of the period kept abreast of the then latest French fashions, as I have already pointed out, notably in my last book, Nakov, *Talin*, 2020.

[119] I. Vakar, *Kazimir Malevich, Chernyi kvadrat* (Kazimir Malewicz, the Black Square), "History of a Masterpiece" series, Moscow, 2015. The English-language version was issued by the eminent publisher Walther König. Solicited by Irina Vakar to lend a photograph of Malewicz I responded favourably. However, at the time I was unaware of the content of the publication in question.

[120] The document was produced in several stages that had to be adjusted into a coherent whole, a rather acrobatic task though it was finally accomplished. The English-language version of my text appeared under the title "Devices, Style and Realisation: Professionalism in Malewicz's Painting Technique", *Artibus et Historiae*, no. 57 (vol. XXIX), 2008, pp. 183–239, and as chapter 31 (vol. 4) of my *Malevich*, 2010, pp. 133–190.

[121] J.-Cl. Lebensztejn, "Sous-couches du Quadrangle de Malévitch", *Cahiers du Musée national d'Art Moderne*, vol. 144, Paris, summer 2018. The same journal had distinguished itself a few years earlier by publishing a group of fake Malewicz drawings of such poor quality that it should have aroused the suspicions of the editors. See my own comments in the second part of this book.

the author, a French academic, put forward with the utmost seriousness a number of extraordinary claims in this regard. From the outset he was not embarrassed to admit that not only had he never set eyes on the original, he did not even speak Russian (as was the case with others who had preceded him down that path of ignorance[122]). Apart from the fact that it took the assertions of the Moscow museum seriously, the 2018 article contained numerous clichés concerning the painting's "ruined state" which the author, whose knowledge of the original was limited to a few reproductions he moreover described as "mediocre", unhesitatingly portrayed as "the worse for wear".[123]

At this point let us recall the physical history of the work. In fact, the artist himself damaged its surface in 1928. With a view to including it in his exhibition at the Tretyakov Gallery the following year he undertook to restore in person its black surface, which had dried too quickly (the rapidly superposed layers had resulted in numerous fissures and cracks). Unsatisfied with the outcome of his work, the artist had rapidly given it up and, at the suggestion of the museum's director (Mikhail Christi), had almost immediately made a copy of it. Yet the material condition of the 1915 original is to this day stable, even entirely satisfactory – as I was able to judge for myself when in 1987 I held it in my own hands – though it is true that the rough look of the surface as left by Malewicz in 1928 is rather unpleasant. As a matter of fact the museum administration invokes the latter as a reason for refusing to lend it. (The curators of other museums in the world give similar arguments, which is fair enough.)

There is but a short step between announcing the painting's "disastrous condition"[124] and elaborating an original theory about the artist's utilisation of "cracks", which the author of the 2018 text unhesitatingly took. Thus the act of cleaning the composition that Malewicz himself engaged in and, by his own admission, failed at, for he was no picture restorer (even though he now and then did not recoil from retouching the surface of certain Suprematist compositions), was transformed by the 2018 commentator into a deliberate utilisation of cracks in the paint. Thus an enterprise as specious as it was sophisticated suddenly acquired a hitherto unsuspected originality. Of course the cracked pane of Marcel Duchamp's *Large Glass* of 1926 provided a convenient justification.

[122] See Martineau, *op. cit.*, 1977. I have already commented briefly on this text in these pages.

[123] Among these reproductions was a photograph taken by Karel Neubert and published in the Prague review *Výtvarne Uměni* in 1967. The quality of this image was far from "mediocre", for Neubert was one of the great photographers of his time.

[124] This type of comment crops up in most publications. The example of Denys Riout is one of the most egregious (*op. cit.*, 1996).

The acme of the *primo-avrilesque* interpretation of *Black Square* concocted in Moscow in 2015 took place in Paris in February 2021. It is this event that finally prompted the present Postscript. On the occasion of an original presentation of seventeen works by Incohérent artists, the rediscovery of which I mention at the beginning of this essay, a Paris gallery, with the goal of adding lustre to its exhibition, referred explicitly to the authority of the French 2018 article cited here. Accompanying the written explanation of Malewicz's work and referring to the Moscow "discovery", a reproduction of *Black Square* was enthroned in the middle of the gallery's selection of Incohérent works. The latter are perfectly authentic and interesting in themselves but their value was instantly enhanced by the presence of *Black Square*. Thus an acrobatic reversion of invented themes and influences has turned Malewicz into a pope (by succession) of the Incohérent movement and a semi-real semi-false cultural ping-pong of fantasy influences has crossed borders it had never previously crossed (at least not in this manner).

Naturally there remains the question of possible connection between Malewicz and the thematic matter of the Incohérents, that is to say Allais' famous "monochromes" which one cannot help now interpreting in the light of Yves Klein's so to speak backward-looking telescope. As it happens, at the time of the artist's ascension towards the Parnassus of modernism these themes were discussed in the Moscow press. As early as 17 December 1911 an item headed "An Artistic Parody" appeared in the daily *Russkoe slovo* (The Russian Word)[125] informing the newspaper's readers of a jocular event staged by the students of the Moscow Art School in response to Alphonse Allais's example. The note referred briefly to an "artistic parody" (of the Incohérents).

Does this mean that Malewicz was aware of their art? It is highly likely that he was, for a few days later, precisely on 24 December of the same year, he contributed to the same newspaper a declaration concerning his own aesthetic stance.[126] Brief as it is, this text was the painter's first artistic credo and needs to be read in the light of Russian Post-Symbolism (compare with the theories of Andréi Belyi). Malewicz speaks of "the essence of knowable form", light years away from the jocular tone of the Incohérent stunts. Armed with his

[125] "Khudozhestvennaya parodiya", *Russkoe slovo*, no. 290, 17 December 1911, p. 7.

[126] See *Russkoe slovo*, 24 December 1911, p. 6. This was the artist's first public statement. I comment on it in vol. 1 of my monograph (pp. 112–113 of the 2007 French edition; p. 118 of the 2010 English-language edition). The artist sent this text as an "open letter" to the editors of the paper from Malewicz as "secretary" of the future Donkey's Tail group.

spiritual convictions, he situated his action in an aesthetic perspective far removed from the playful satires of the Paris group. The evolution of his art, which was to lead three years later in a perfectly coherent manner to the philosophy of Non-Objectivity, had by 1915 not only left the critical stance of the Incohérents far behind; it was also a complete transcendence of their position. Such was the birth of Suprematism.

2

CATALOGUE RAISONNÉ:
SUPPLEMENTARY COMMENTARIES

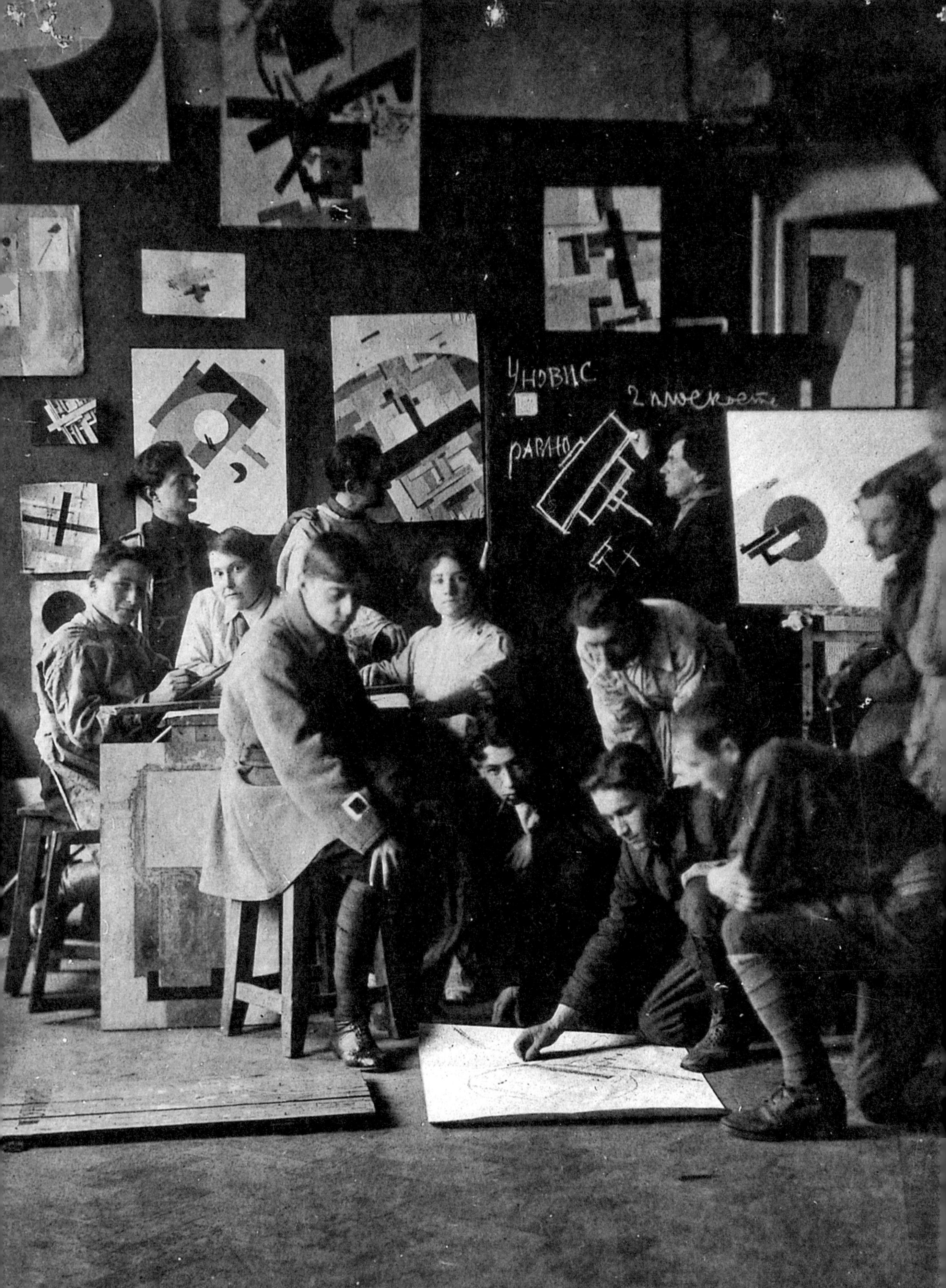
УНОВИС
2 плоек
равно

[1] See "Addendum au catalogue raisonné de
2002", in Nakov, *Malewicz*, 2007, vol. 4, chap. 32,
pp. 188–191. (Being already published this section was not included in the English-language
edition, *Malevich*, 2010.)

Compiled during the 1980s, revised at the end of the 1990s and published in bi-lingual English-French version in 2002 the Kazimir Malewicz *Catalogue raisonné* (Paris: Adam Biro, May 2002) has now been in existence for nineteen years. In this interval new commentaries resulting from fresh information have proved necessary.

Without putting into question either the overall structure of that inventory or the essential information it contains, I nevertheless feel obliged to inform readers of certain changes of detail, supplementary information or corrections that in most cases stem from recent (and not so recent) documentary discoveries. Since errors and involuntary omissions are always possible, I take this opportunity to revise or to complete some of the original entries, as well as to reply to certain questions that recur regularly due to a less than attentive reading of the catalogue. In 2007 I published a first correction of various printing errors and, more exceptionally, added additional information.[1]

As indicated clearly in the introduction to the 2002 catalogue, far more than dates of creation, not always easy and sometimes impossible to establish, the order in which the Suprematist works, which comprise the most substantial and important part of the book, are listed was dictated by the stylistic logic of the series I proposed to establish. The highly intuitive brilliance of Malewicz's art suggested infinite different classifications, for it opens on a multitude of directions. Endeavouring to impose a linear logic of any kind on such a constantly shifting mass of materials would not only have been foolhardy; it would above all have been unproductive.

On several occasions during the second half of his creative life (1920–1935), the artist sought to re-examine the evolution of his Suprematist work. Quite naturally pursuing its own path, his art was thus the locus of a permanent reconstruction, an essentially evolutive growth. This perpetual reinvention of Suprematism is easily comprehensible, as the latter remained a living adventure for Malewicz, who was forever renewing it in novel formal constellations. Like a source of life, the gushing fountain of Suprematism was for him a completely natural creative exploration, an infinite ever-shifting universe. This is patent right up to his final architectonas of the 1932–1933 period and especially his astonishingly diverse Post-Suprematist œuvre, accomplished in spite of the grave existential obstacles he faced in the last dramatic years of his life. The latter especially bear witness to his extraordinary stylistic diversity, his multidirectional creative openness in every way equal to the multiple stylistic possibilities of Suprematism itself. Surely it would be unreasonable to expect an artist of such creative vitality to become an archivist of his own production.

In its 2002 version the catalogue thus calls for new interpretations, especially in the section devoted to the artist's extremely varied Suprematist drawings. Apart from the sequences awaiting reconstruction in the light of the drawings and the manner in which the compositions were completed (some of them highly accomplished, the artist having used them after 1919 in his teaching, others in contrast remaining in an extremely fragmentary state), various sketches that have been forgotten or have survived the disasters of aesthetic and or social censorship (even certain almost accidental thumbnail sketches) require cataloguing.

In the mid-1920s Malewicz undertook to classify his work in series indicated by letters and numbers which his assistant Anna Leporskaya inscribed (but not systematically) in green ink on the back of his drawings.[2] But even in the case of this fragmentary project, already begun in Vitebsk in the early 1920s with Latin characters and numbers, we find ourselves in the presence of a sketchy idea rather than a definitive, clearly structured, solidly announced and explained system of classification. The task of reconstructing sequences on the basis of the size and type of paper in subsequently dismembered sketchbooks is far from easy at present. Moreover, nothing guarantees that the sketches from these sketchbooks were made in chronological order and are thus a sure indication of the artist's stylistic evolution. For the time being, then, this remains a task for the future.

[2] See my remarks in the introduction to the *Catalogue raisonné* (Nakov, *Catalogue raisonné*, 2002).

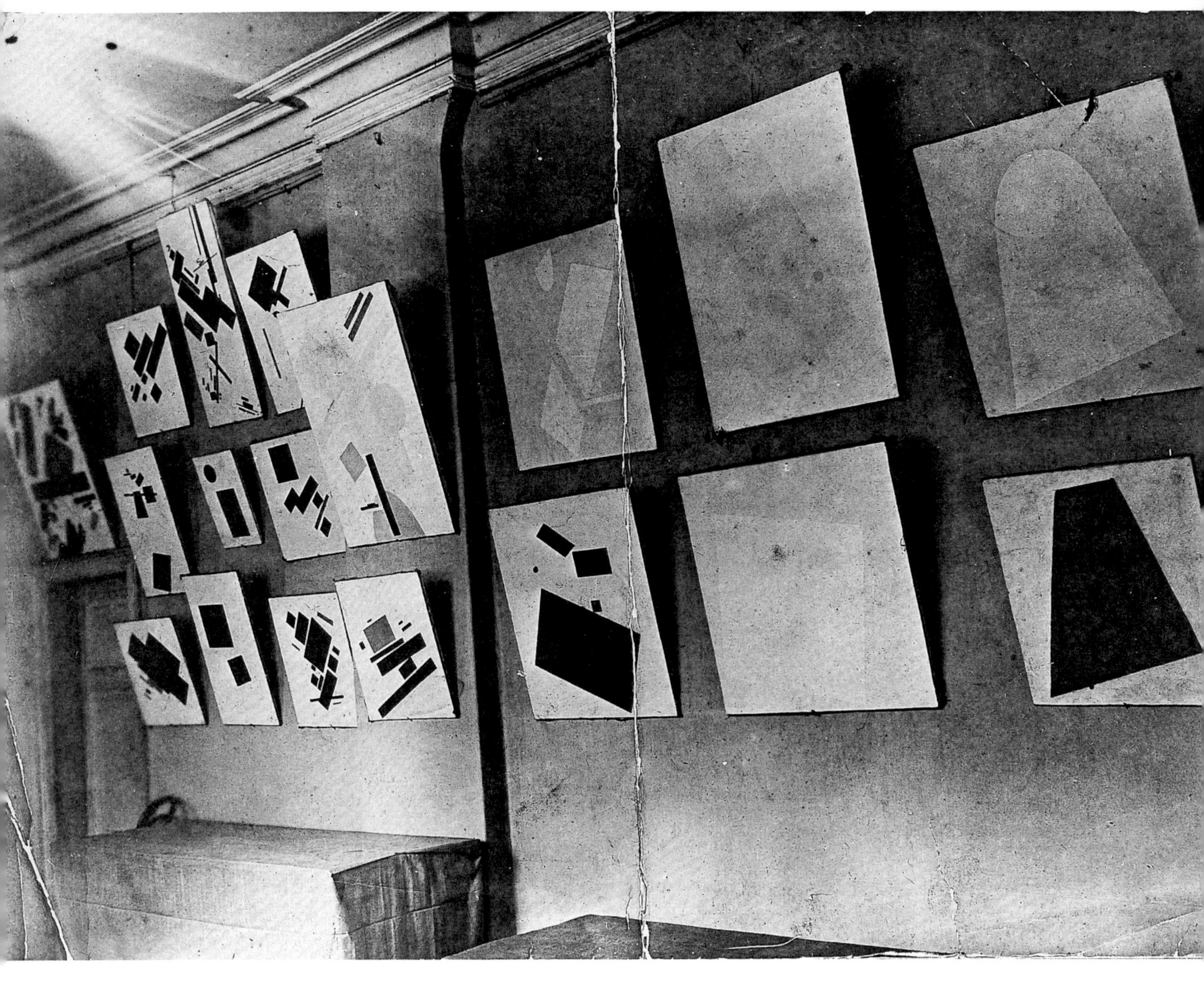

THE QUESTION OF HANGING: HOW TO MAKE HEADWAY IN INTERPRETING THE ŒUVRE?

73. Kazimir Malewicz, solo show, Moscow 1920. This was the second and last time that the artist showed his "white" (colourless) paintings in Moscow. *White Square* is among the paintings in the lower tier but is presented upside down as in the absence of the artist the hanging was realised by Aleksei Gan

^{3} The history of these "restitutions" remains to be written. Note that they could not be made before the death of the artist's daughter in 1989, as Una Uriman was resolutely opposed to them.

Since the late 1980s there have been numerous exhibitions of Malewicz's Suprematist works. Brought out from the reserve collections of Russian and Western museums, a number of paintings (some of which have been returned to the artist's more or less distantly related heirs[3]) have found their way into commercial circles, which means that they have circulated widely. Their hanging has now and then varied according to stylistic interpretations arising from feelings of incredulity produced at their first public presentation in December 1915 – and still provoked today. These changes in orientation reflect not just the vitality of the Suprematist aesthetic but chiefly interpretative difficulties invariably stemming from a lack of assimilation with this type of abstraction, an altogether revolutionary innovation at the time.

Ever since the beginning of the Suprematist adventure (summer – autumn, 1915) the logic of Malewicz's Non-Objective work was distinguished by a fundamental principle, an innovative approach in terms of the logic behind the "realist" (actually illusionist) system practised previously in Western painting, including the then most recent periods

(Cubist, Expressionism). The Non-Objective (abstract) forms in the Suprematist repertory have a different nature to the object-related (erroneously called "realist") forms surrounding us. Suprematist compositions are Non-Objective "constructions", as the artist himself called them.[4] The forms that could be perceived in them were ruled by different laws than those that govern our world, the world of normal experience. One of the basic principles of Suprematism is weightlessness, the property arising from the Non-Objective (or extra-material) nature of these forms, which the artist defined as the state of the "free flight of forms". As he specified in his first texts of the 1915/1916 winter, these forms are radically different from those of our "terrestrial" world. Faithful to the vitalism of the Symbolist tradition, he looked on these forms as "beings", each endowed with its own energy, its own identity. Thus the principle characteristic of the Suprematist "constructions" is, relative to our "reading" of Non-Objective forms, the "free flight" of the compositional components. The notion of material weight having vanished, the *sui generis* invention of Suprematist compositions assert their identity solely through their dynamic thrust, their essential property as "beings". This means that, in contrast to our "mimetic" manner of looking at the world, forms that seem heavy to us must in fact not be perceived as such. Dematerialized by the artist, they should be seen to rise, to soar freely. Their autonomy, the main attribute of their existence, is a function of their inherent energy. However, the normal spectator (whether he is an ordinary onlooker or a specialist, an art historian, critic or other) is still atavistically drawn to stable, static constructions, to objects firmly anchored in a sort of "still life". Owing to this ancestral survival of "old-fashioned" habits of perception a number of Suprematist works have been presented upside down (according to the static logic of objects subject to gravity), with the visually heaviest element at the bottom, as if they were solidly anchored in a kind of physical reality. Their composition thus appears lifeless, in keeping with the ancient rules governing inanimate materials. But these do not apply to Malewicz's Suprematist creations.

The example of Ivan Puni (or Pougny) is particularly instructive in this regard. A chance follower of Suprematism, the Petersburg artist adhered as rapidly, if not accidentally,

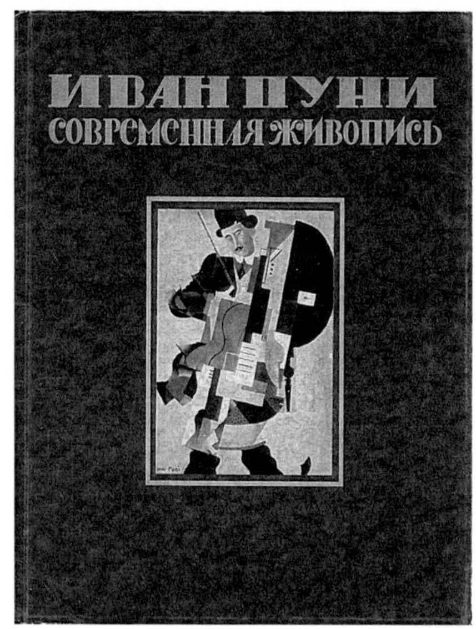

74.

74. Cover of Ivan Puni's book *Sovremennaya zhivopis* (Contemporary Painting), Berlin, 1923

[4] By "constructions" Malewicz meant what we might call an *ex nihilo* inventions produced solely by his own volition. A "construction" did not refer therefore to an actual object.

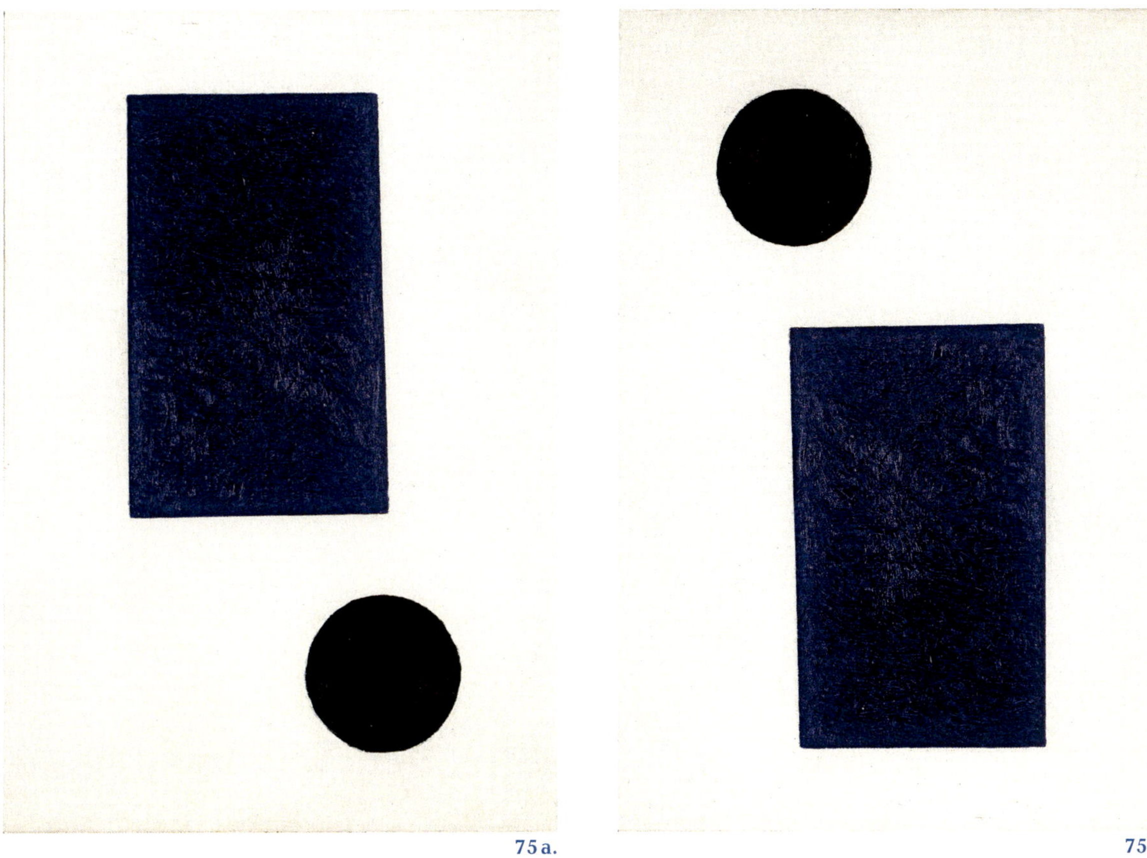

75 a.   75 b.

75 a and b. (Suprematist composition), 1915 (Cat. S-216), oil on canvas, 43.2 × 30.8 cm, private collection (formerly Busch Reisinger Museum, Cambridge, Mass., USA). Two different (inverted) positions

[5] See my remarks on this subject in Nakov, *Tatlin*, 2020, in particular *Appendix 1*, p. 329.

[6] See the London Tate Gallery 2014 catalogue. In the 2017 Moscow exhibition (VDNH; *Kazimir Malewicz. More than the "Black Square"*, ed. by A. Shatskikh) it was given the same incorrect orientation.

to the logic of Non-Objective art, as he then abandoned it. As early as 1923 he published reproductions of a number of Malewicz's Suprematist compositions, as well as several Tatlin Non-Objective works, wrong side up, freezing them in a material ponderousness that contradicted the very logic of Non-Objectivity (which was also the logic underlying Tatlin's initial reliefs).[5] This misunderstanding of the Non-Objective nature of Suprematist art has left traces that persist today. Thus, for instance, *construction* (as Malewicz used the term in 1916) S-216, a work that left a museum to enter the circuit of private collections in the last decade or so and has consequently travelled frequently. It continues to be shown in a way that suggests a static reading, with the rectangular shape at the bottom.[6] Presented in this way, the rectangular form rests heavily at the foot of the composition and has the effect of

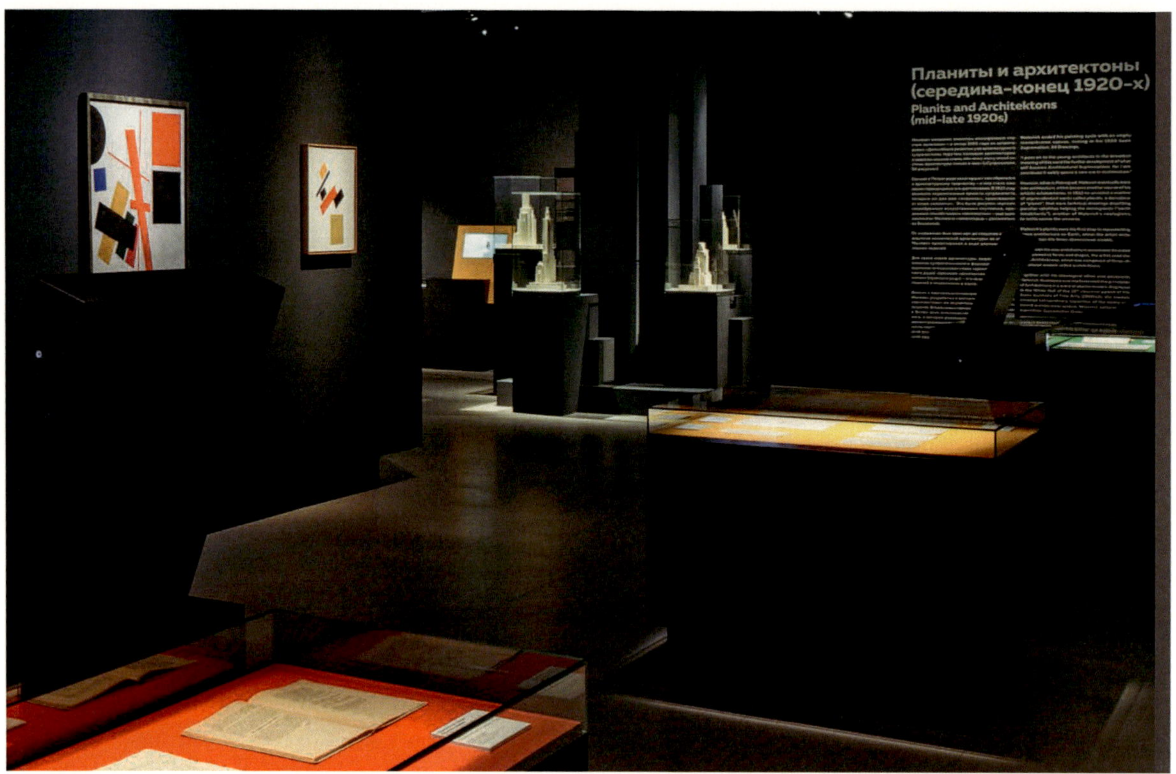

76.

eliminating the composition's soaring dynamic. (It is one of the artist's earliest Non-Objective compositions featuring a small round form projecting upwards – in visual terms – from a heavier rectangular form). The same remark applies to composition S-31, a Suprematist painting at the Ivanovo Museum (Russia), which recently was still displayed with the "heavy" form (the rectangle) at the composition's base,[7] though according to the principles of Suprematist dynamics it should be at the top of the composition (as demonstrated clearly by drawing S-30, a preparatory version of painting S-31, which includes annotations in the artist's hand, concrete indications that obviate the need for any comments).[8]

Certain "magnetic" compositions of 1916 (S-295 to S-300, S-341, S-420) present other difficulties of interpretation. In their case the artist manifestly experimented with positioning forms and "circular" evolutionary arrangements of formal combinations. There is obviously no question of a "correct"

[7] Reproduced, again incorrectly, in the catalogue *Avangard spisok No. 1, k 100-letiju muzeia zhivopisnoi kul'tury* (Art of the Avant-Garde: List No. 1 of the 100th Anniversary of the Museum of Painterly Culture), Moscow: Tretyakov State Gallery, 2019, cat. 127, fig. p. 157.

[8] It sometimes happens that, with the "best of intentions", similar mistakes are made by copyeditors who venture to correct visual material. This happened to me with S-420, which was incorrectly positioned in the 2002 catalogue, an error I corrected in the monograph, *Malewicz*, 2007, vol. 2, fig. p. 147.

76. Photograph of a room in the exhibition *Kazimir Malevich. More than the "Black Square"*, VDNH exhibition space, Moscow, winter 2017. On the left wall notice the inverted hanging of paintings S-31 and S-420

77. Suprematist composition, 1915 (Cat. S-31), oil on canvas, 54.3 × 53.5 cm, Ivanovo Museum of Art

78. (Composition 21c), 1915 (Cat. S-30), pencil on squared paper, 10 × 9.7 cm, preliminary study for S-31 (the inscriptions next to the forms confirm the orientation proposed here), private collection

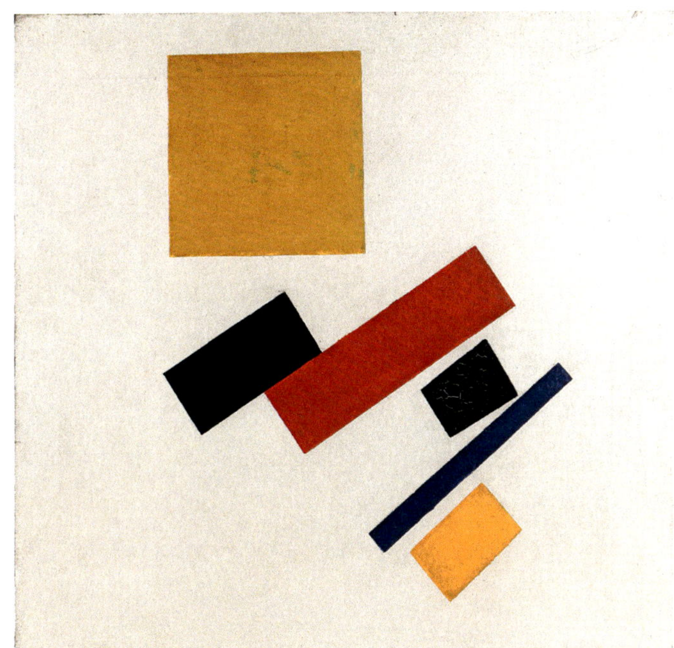

77.

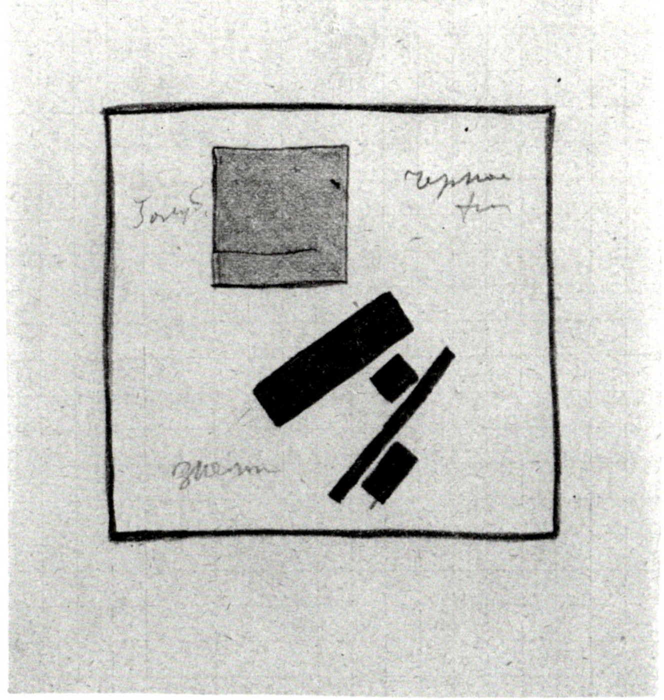

78.

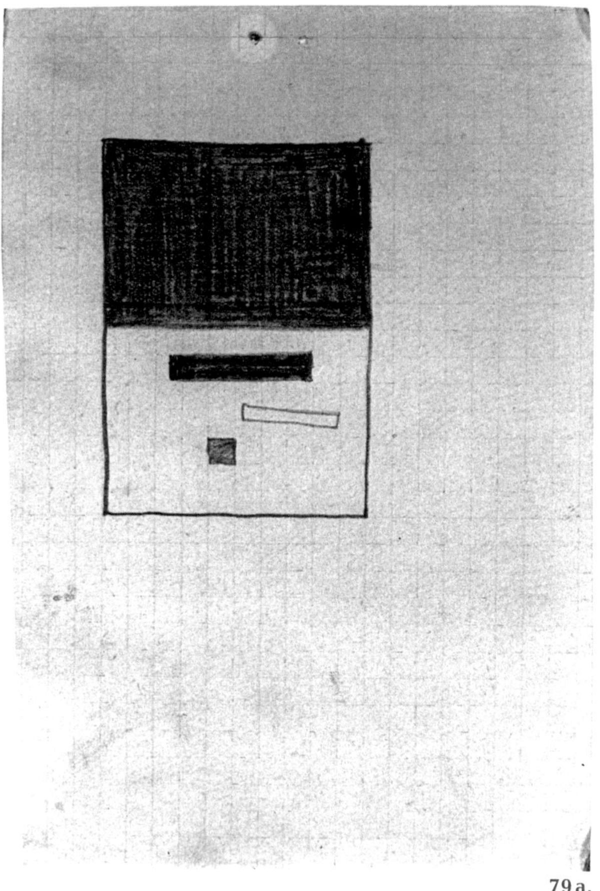

79 a.

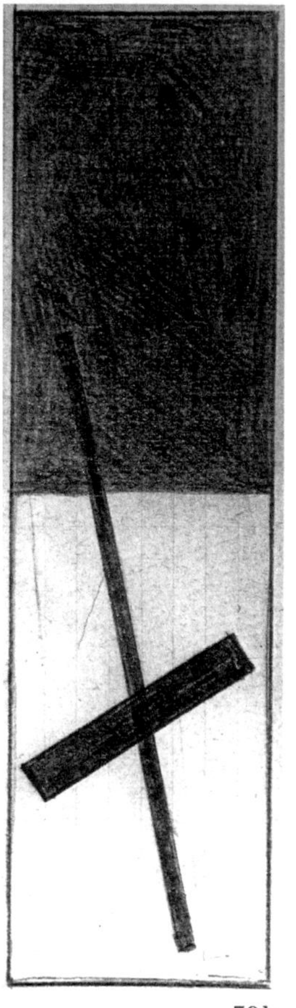

79 b.

orientation of these works. At this point Suprematism had attained a new level of independence, a new freedom, from "terrestrial" laws. That is why the 1916–1917 period is particularly problematic for determining the orientation of some Suprematist compositions, for it was at this point that the artist immersed himself in a new phase of spatial experimentation. In short order this euphoria, an extra-terrestrial (or, as Malewicz himself put it, "planetary") vision of Suprematism, was to lead to a new "leap into the infinite" – that of the "white" compositions of the winter of 1917/1918 and the ultimate break with material references to what he called the world of "flesh and bones".

We know that after 1918 each presentation of Suprematist works provided the artist with another opportunity to try out

79 a and b.
a. (Suprematist composition),
1915 (Cat. S-103), pencil on paper,
16.2 × 11.2 cm, private collection
b. (Suprematist composition), summer
1915 (Cat. S-105), pencil on paper,
16.6 × 10.8 cm, Museum Ludwig, Cologne

80 a.

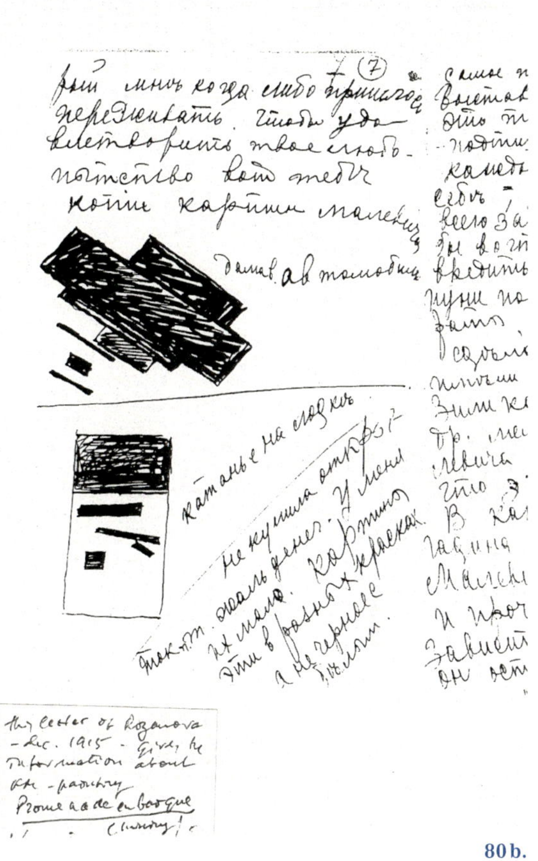

80 b.

80 a and b.

a new formal (stylistic) arrangement. An exhibition wall was, in Malewicz's eyes, an opportunity to create a Suprematist constellation possessing a character of its own, that is to say as a grouping of canvases in a single composition that thus became a new Suprematist work, i.e. a fully-fledged composition. This explains why certain paintings changed orientation in different presentations, since on each occasion they contributed to another grouping, another total composition. Consisting originally of diverse Non-Objective forms, the individual assemblage of non-objective entities on the museum wall became in turn elements in a grouping, as the wall itself became a composition in its own right. One could cite the arrangement of Suprematist paintings at the Warsaw exhibition of March 1927 barely a few weeks before the Berlin show of

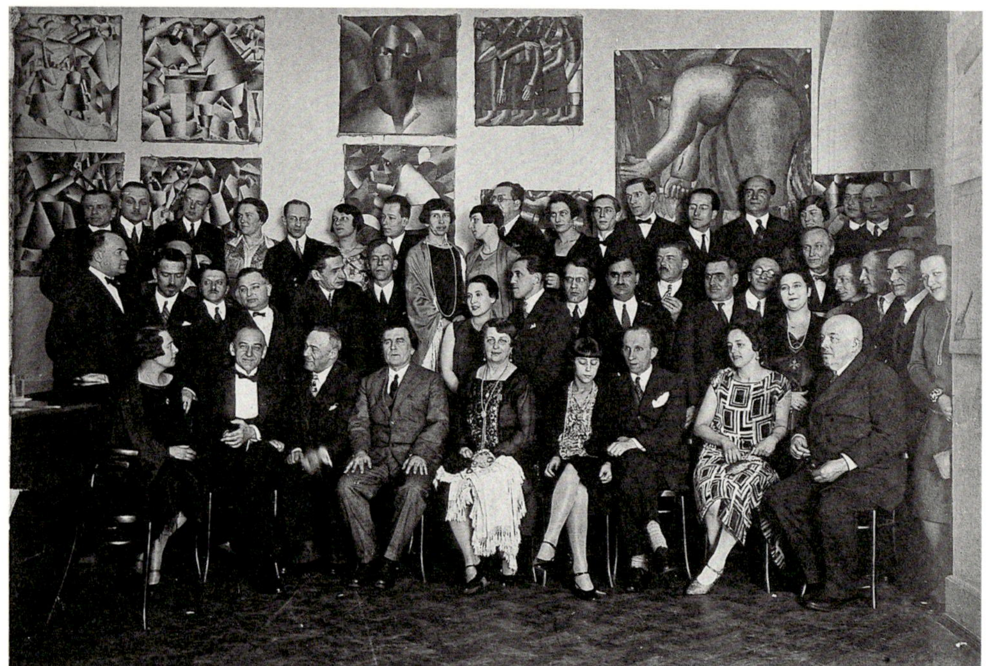

81 a.

the summer of 1927, both hangings orchestrated by the artist himself. The Warsaw hanging is particularly instructive in this regard for it was organised with a lyrical élan in what looks like a highly restricted space, revealing a new spatial treatment of previously familiar works.[9]

With the exception of the *0,10* exhibition, where the hanging of only half of the 39 paintings on show is known to us through a contemporary photograph (December 1915), the grouping of Malewicz's Suprematist canvases does not generally appear to have been determined by the artist. The hanging arrangement in the photographically well-documented 1920 Moscow retrospective, in particular, was determined by the "Constructivist" critic Aleksei Gan, a recent enthusiast of Malewicz's Suprematism. The photos taken on this occasion were sent to Malewicz who was in Vitebsk at the time; they can hardly be viewed as a trustworthy source, since Gan himself was responsible for the presentation.

81 a and b. Banquet in honour of Malewicz in conjunction with his exhibition of March 1927, Hotel Polonia, Warsaw. The difference with the orientation of the Suprematist canvases at the Berlin exhibition is clearly visible

[9] The mechanical or rather digital "reconstruction" of this hanging arrangement by A. Turowski (see his *Malewicz w Warszawie, op. cit.*) strikes me as incompatible with the logic itself of Suprematism (see his *op. cit.*, 2004).

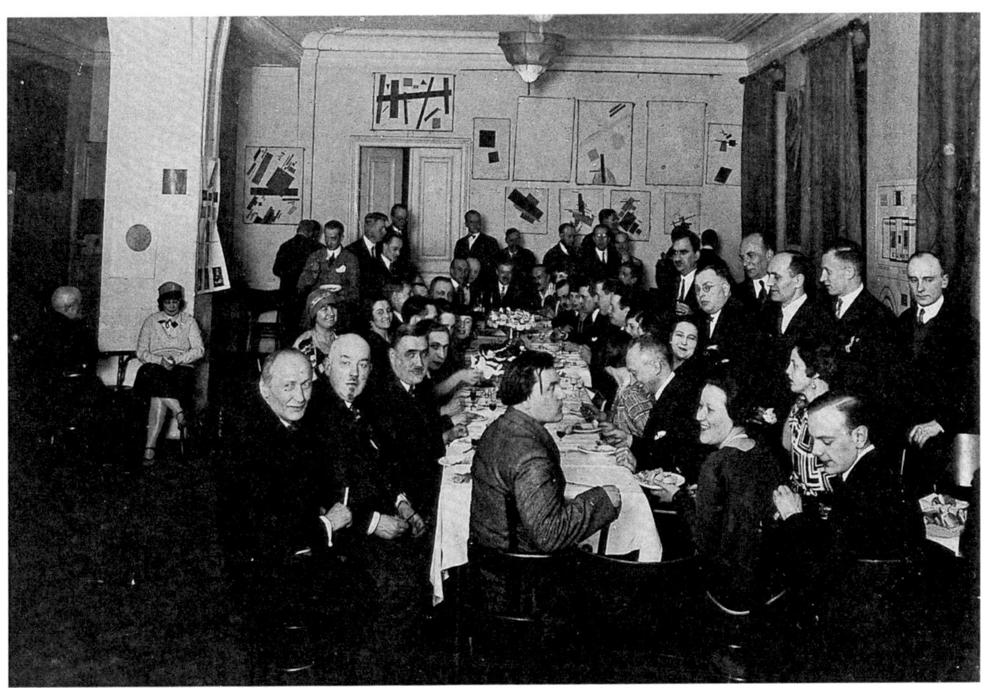

81 b.

* * *

¹⁰ Khardzhiev gives this opinion in writing in a document preserved in his Amsterdam–Moscow papers, N. Khardzhiev, "Zametki... o knige" (his critical comments on a book by D. Sarabianov and A. Shatskikh, *Kazimir Malevich. Zhivopis. Teoria*, Moscow: Iskusstvo, 1993), archive reference 1994–22.

¹¹ I refer to the artist's statement of 19 February 1914 in which he publicly "renounced Reason" ("Knave of Diamonds" evening debate in Moscow).

Two "transrational" works of 1914 – *Vanity Case* (F-420) and *Through Station Kuntsevo* (F-421), both painted on wood panels – in the collection of Moscow's Tretyakov Gallery, pose yet another problem of orientation. Traditionally reproduced in a vertical format, these small Cubo-Futurist compositions, both heavily overlaid with a particularly elaborate fragmentation of geometric forms, should in fact be presented horizontally, according to Nikolai Khardzhiev, who got the appropriate instructions directly from the artist (or persons close to him). (It was not in the latter's habit to specify the sources of his information.) These indications, which I obtained at first hand from Khardzhiev, who passed them on with his usual lively insistence, ought to be understood, it seems to me, as a sign of conceptual revolt on the part of the artist.[10] As the reader may see for himself, Malewicz's vigorous Alogist declaration of February 1914[11] shows that he was capable of "reversing

133

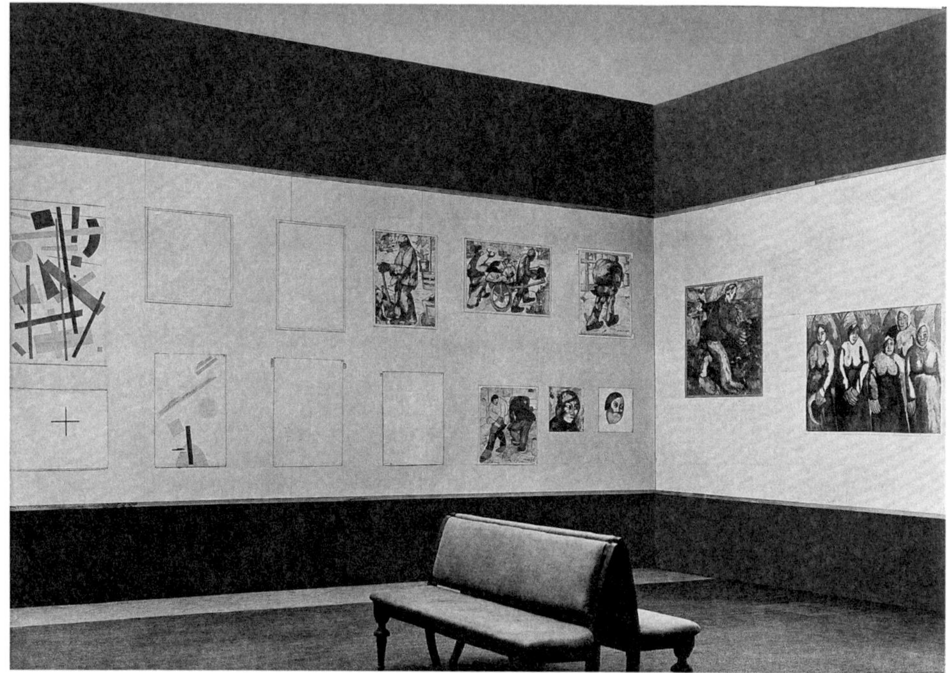

82 a.

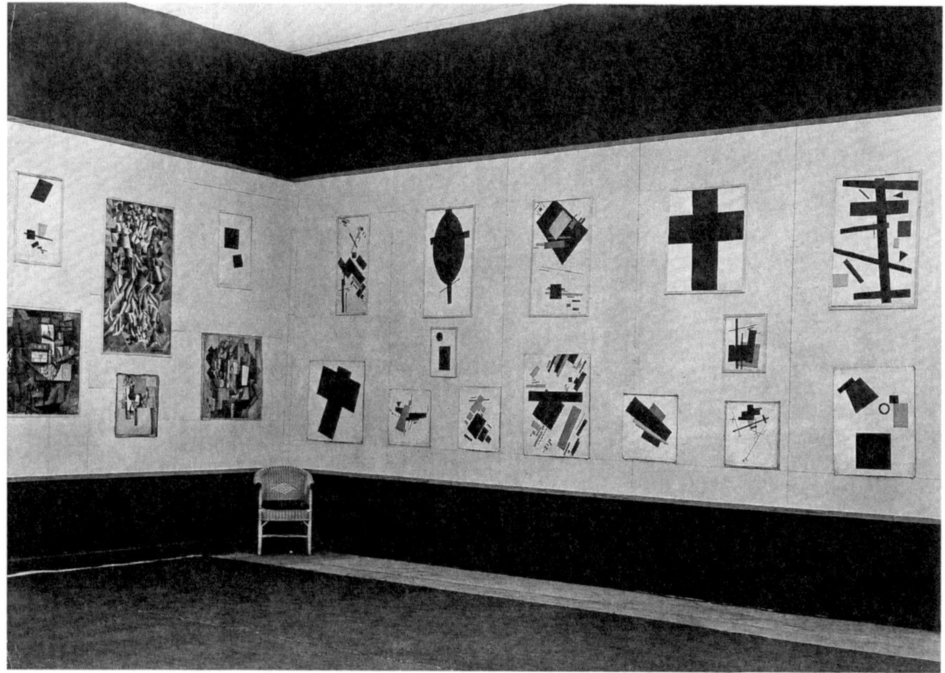

82 b.

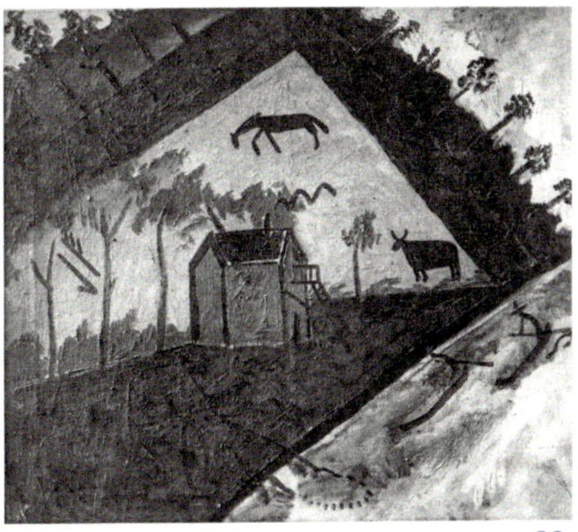

83.

82 a and b. Malewicz's solo show (*Sonderausstellung Malewitsch*) at the Grosse Berliner Kunstausstellung, Lehrter Bahnhof, Berlin, 1927

83. David Burljuk, *Landscape Seen from Several Viewpoints*, 1913, oil on canvas, lost/destroyed? Nakov Archives, Paris

the perspective" of a Cubist or Post-Cubist composition to signify the "insurrection" – an Alogist subversion – of the figures or objects within the work. One may conclude from this that the orientation of the two works shifted between the moment when they were actually painted and the time when the artist gave them an Alogist interpretation. This type of spatial disruption belong to the conceptual (spatial and/or thematic) ambit of the spectacle *Victory over the Sun* in the immediate continuation of which the two compositions, F-420 and F-421, are to be placed. One encounters a comparable approach in the same period in the meta-Cubist work of David Burljuk, but on a more modest, even rather naïve scale, as in the latter's *Landscape Seen from Several Viewpoints*, a painting that subsequently became a kind of manifesto of Burljuk's Cubo-Futurist practice.[12]

An inscription on the back of the Cubo-Futurist painting *Lady at Piano* (F-437) appears to confirm this hypothesis. In the artist's hand, it is a peculiar inscription in that it is written "in reverse" (i.e. upside down) relative to the "logical" or "normal" reading of the forms in that Cubo-Futurist work. It would thus seem to indicate a shift, a "back-to-front" reading of the composition subsequent to its realisation, therefore surely an Alogist *interpretation* of the work substituted for the "normal" understanding of the composition as it was initially painted. That an artist could be mistaken about the orientation of his work seems highly improbable.[13]

---

[12] The composition itself has been lost but Burljuk referred to it repeatedly. A reflection of it can be found among the artist's drawings in the Futurist miscellany *Moloko kobylits* (Milk of Mares), 1914. Burljuk was to use this compositional device frequently in the years 1915–1916.

[13] I wish to thank the Krasnoyarsk Art Museum, and in particular its curator Ilya Zhigaev, for kindly communicating to me the details of this inscription on the verso of the canvas.

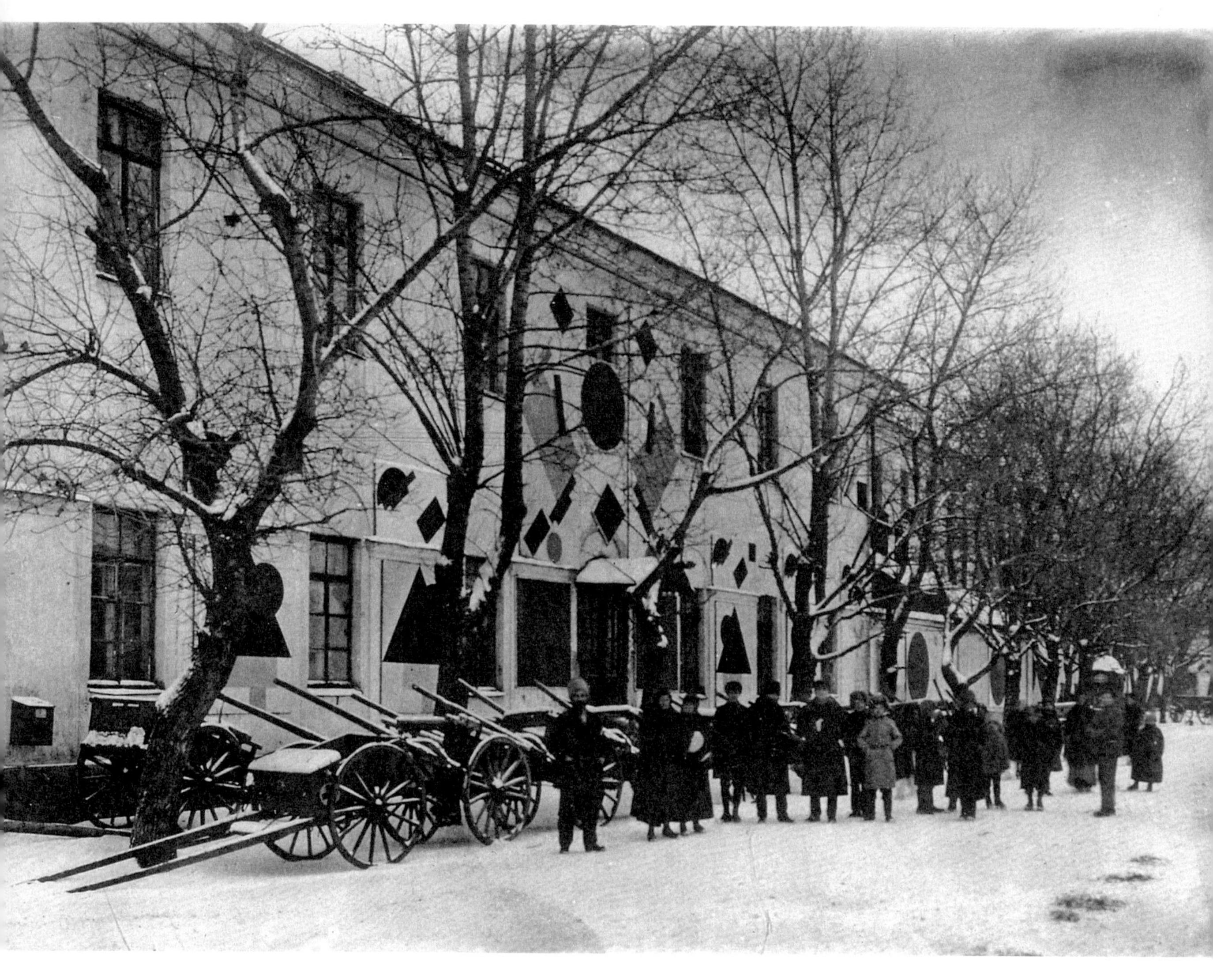

CHAPTER 12

REVISIONS AND CORRECTIONS, ADDITIONAL DOCUMENTS

S-670

The research I undertook in 2016 for *The Advent of Abstraction* exhibition,[14] of which the key feature was Lissitzky's 1923 *Proun 8 Stellungen* (Proun 8 Positions), led me recently to examine that artist's abstract production more closely. In the process, I reached the conclusion that Malewicz's drawing S-670 was in actual fact a work by Lissitzky.[15] This change in attribution derived from a careful study of the style and execution (the texture and luminosity) of the different Non-Objective forms in the graphic composition. It was thus the result of a strictly stylistic reflection. As a matter of fact, while writing the entry in the 2002 catalogue, I had already indicated implicitly the stylistic closeness between the two artists, without however drawing the ultimate conclusion from this observation, since at the time I was faithfully following the indications provided by the owner (somebody I respected dearly). The visual experience I acquired in the course of my work for the Canadian catalogue allowed me to gain a greater familiarity with Lissitzky's graphic work and his pencil strokes.

84. Vitebsk, January 1920. Buildings with suprematist decorations, made by the UNOVIS on the occasion of the "Fight against unemployment", photography, *Unovis No. 1*, 1920. Nakov Archives, Paris

[14] National Gallery of Canada, Ottawa.

[15] At this time, I made the attribution on the basis of the owner's belief. The latter was, in my opinion, plainly in good faith.

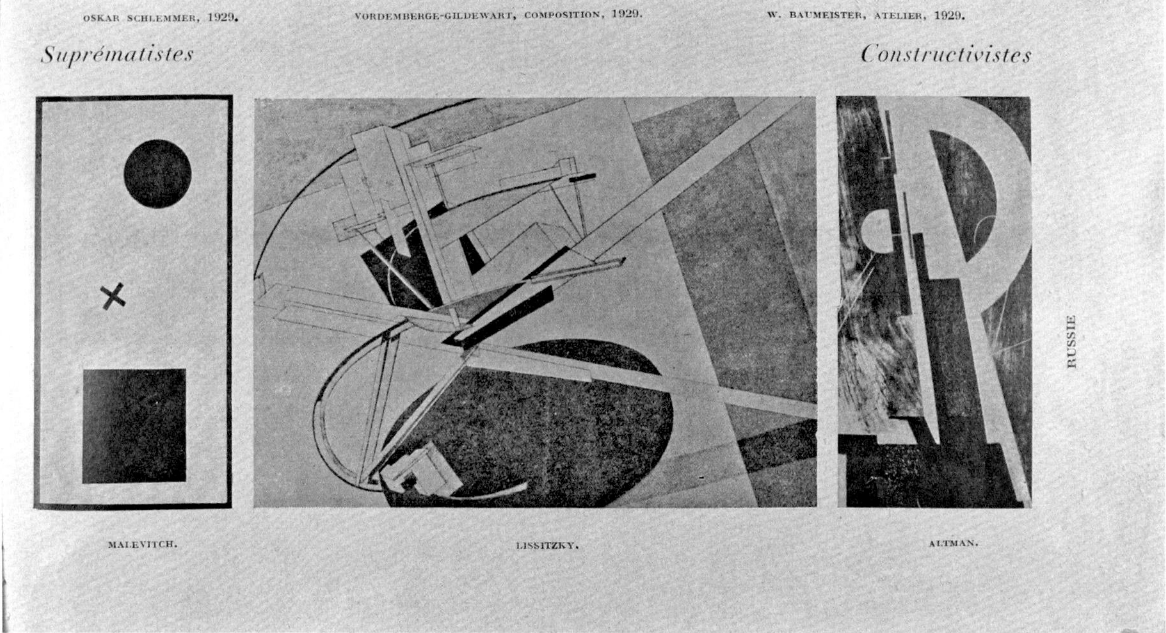

85 a.

S-220 Supplementary Comments

Page 22 of issue number 1, 1930, of the Parisian review *Cahiers d'art* features a three-part illustration reproducing abstract works by, from left to right, Malewicz, Lissitzky and Nathan Altman. Malewicz's work is a Suprematist composition whose "motif" appears in two versions in the *Catalogue raisonné*: S-220 and S-221.[16] Two variations on this arrangement – S-222 and S-223 – are also known to exist. The reproduction in the Parisian periodical allows us to identify one of these compositions, which, judging from the frame visible in the illustration, seems to have been an oil on canvas. The association of the three works would suggest that Lissitzky was the direct or indirect source for the triple image. The reproduction allows us to identify the initial image of the motif in S-221, the original composition having disappeared.

The periodical's date of publication was marked by a series of contacts between Christian Zervos, the publisher and chief editor, and the German circles at the Bauhaus, Berlin and Frankfurt, with a renewed interest in abstract art, a "survey" of

[16] Once again I am obliged to insist on the difference between the date when these compositions were executed and the date of the "motif". Readers of the catalogue frequently do not make this distinction.

85 a and b.
a. *Cahiers d'art*, no. 1, Paris, 1930,
p. 27, illustration of Malewicz's now
lost composition Cat. S-220. In addition
to S-220, from left to right works by
El Lissitzky and Nathan Altman.
b. Suprematist composition with three
basic elements (Cat. S-220, detail),
motif of the early 1920s, pencil on paper,
10.5 × 16.8 cm, present whereabouts
unknown

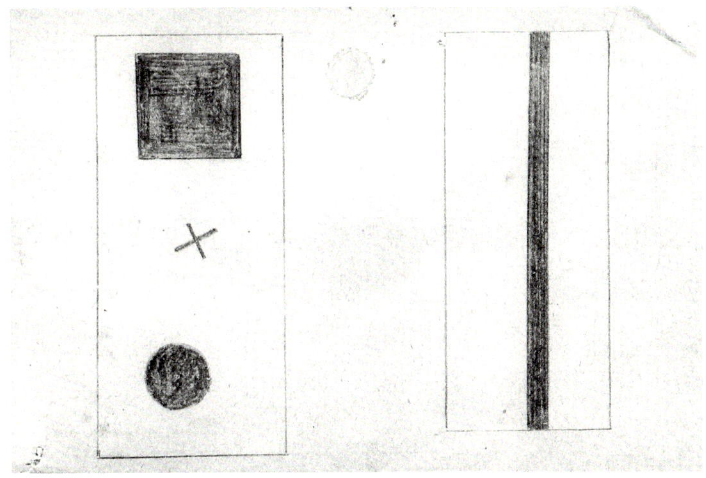

85 b.

which Zervos was to publish in the ensuing months. However, rather intriguingly, Russian abstract art was as yet covered rather scantily in *Cahiers d'art*, unlike recent developments in Russian architecture, a recurrent topic in several issues of the journal.[17]

S-119 Supplementary Comments

Subtitled by the artist "Vtoraia stadiia kvadrata" (Second state of a square), this drawing includes a substantial marginal note written in Russian in pencil:

2 я стадия квадрат[а]
с белыми полями

изображение квадрата было началом его культивирования в другие формы живописные в супрематизме живописном направлении новых форм подсознательности выявлен[ие] квадрата как живописной формы
*   [КМалевич – вписано]*
как само стоятельную единицу найдет[нную?] в сознательном порядке, а так же его дальнейшая культура формы (его виды) момента, когда инстинктивное изчезает и перех.[одит?] в ясное. Белое есть тело на котором [яснее и сильнее?] развивается форма,

17 Christian Zervos was later to publish some comments on Russian abstract art. See Ch. Zervos, *Histoire de l'art contemporain*, Paris, 1938, pp. 363ff.

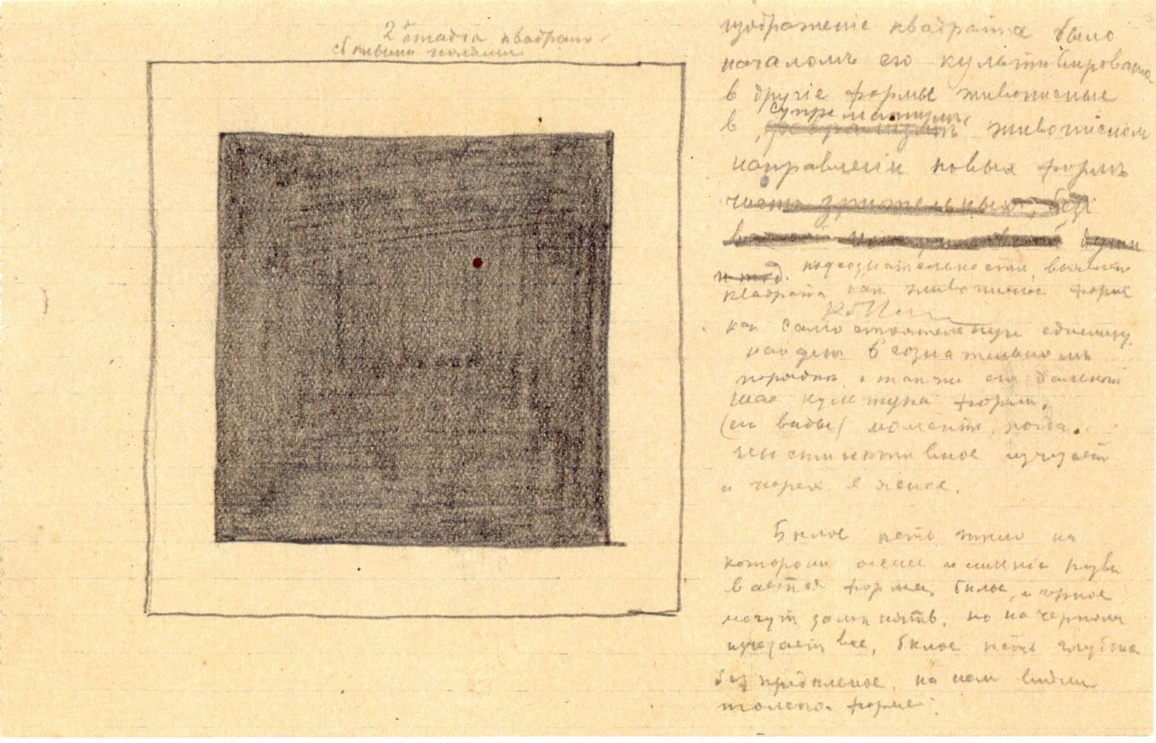

86.

белое, и черное могут заменять, но на черном исчезает все, белое [есть] глубок[ое] без предельное, на нем вид[ны только формы]

Translation:

The representation of the square was the beginning of its culture (development) in new pictorial forms in the direction of the pictorial movement of Suprematism, unconscious manifestation of the square as a pictorial form

KMal [authentic signature later inserted in the body of the text]

as an independent unit [the square?] will find in the order of consciousness, as well as in the subsequent development of its formal evolution, forms where (that are) instinct vanishes and passes into clearness [consciousness].

White is the body in which form evolves most powerfully [more clearly?], white and black can be interchanged, but while everything disappears in black, white is deeper, infinite, in white one only sees the forms [themselves].[18]

86. *Second State of a Square*, motif of 1915, drawn in 1920/1921 (Cat. S-119), pencil on paper, sheet 12 × 16.4 cm, composition 9.9 × 16.1 cm, Art Institute, Chicago, prov. Irving Stern•

• Acquired by the Art Institute of Chicago in 2014, this composition from the 1920s constitutes a reflection on the topic of "whiteness" and was probably written in connection with the lithographic versions produced at Vitebsk in 1920.

[18] Translated from the French translation by Andréi Nakov (translator's note).

Here the artist opens an important chapter of his Suprematist thinking, echoes of which are to be found in his "white" compositions. Seldom studied, not to say largely ignored, this part of his reflections on "whiteness" has left traces in the notes of his students at the Vitebsk UNOVIS, Lev Yudin and Nikolai Suetin.[19] At first glance rather disjointed, fragmentary though extremely intuitive, Malewicz's comments pave the way to a major phase in his art of the early 1920s.

* * *

Thanks to group of three photographs discovered at Kursk and displayed at the A Ya Gallery in that city in March 2011 an exhibition can now be added to the list of public events organised there in late April 1913.[20] On the eve of Easter this exhibition was held on the rooms of the Second High School for Girls (*Vtoraya zhenskaya gimnaziya*) in the context of the activities of the Society of Kursk Artists (TKH: *Toverishchestvo Kurskikh Khudozhnikov*), of which Malewicz had been an early member as of 1898. This event, the association's fourteenth exhibition, confirmed the importance of the artist's beginnings in Kursk, a point he had always insisted on but concerning which there was little concrete evidence.

The 1913 exhibition was arranged by Malewicz's close friends in the city, in particular the painter Lev Kvachevsky.[21] It ran for a few days only. The photographs of the rooms enable one to identify several of Malewicz's works known thanks to the catalogue of the Donkey's Tail exhibition in Moscow (11 March – 8 April 1912), among them *Argentine Polka* (F-194), *Head* (F-280) and *Female Harvester* (F-248). Apart from the well-documented paintings in the Moscow show (some of them known from preparatory drawings), one can distinguish a number of works on the walls of the High School for Girls which have so far only been known through sketches, such as the large gouache of *Seated Man* (F-224).

In a review published on 23 April 1913 in the local paper *Iuzhnii krai* one reads: "Up to now the Cubists and Futurists have exhibited exclusively in the large cities Moscow and St Petersburg. They are unknown in the provinces. Kursk is the first provincial city… (etc.). The local painters Loboda and Kvachevsky have offered us this pleasure. Most of the works

---

[19] In particular, Yudin's notes in *Lev Judin, Skazat'– svoe Dnevniki, Dokumenty, Pis'ma* (Lev Yudin, Speaking One's Mind: Journals, Documents, Letters), ed. by I. Karasik, Moscow: RA, 2017, as well as some of Suetin's pencil drawings of the same period, several of which contain marginal notes.

[20] Anastasia Sokolova in Kursk kindly shared most of the following information with me. I wish to thank her as well as Elena Kholodkova, a curator at the city's Deineka Picture Gallery. The photographs were displayed at the A Ya Gallery on 6 April 2011 in conjunction with a social action for preserving the house on 17 Pochtovaya Street, which was slated for destruction, where the artist and his family lived in the early 20th century. (The demolition work was suspended in 2011.)

[21] See Malewicz's letter of 1913 to Kvachevsky, cited in I. Vakar and T. Mikhienko (eds.), *Malevich o sebe. Sovremenniki o Maleviche. Pisma, dokumenty, vospominaniya, kritika* (Malevich about himself. Contemporaries about Malewicz. Letters, Documents, Memories, Criticism), Moscow, 2004, p. 26.

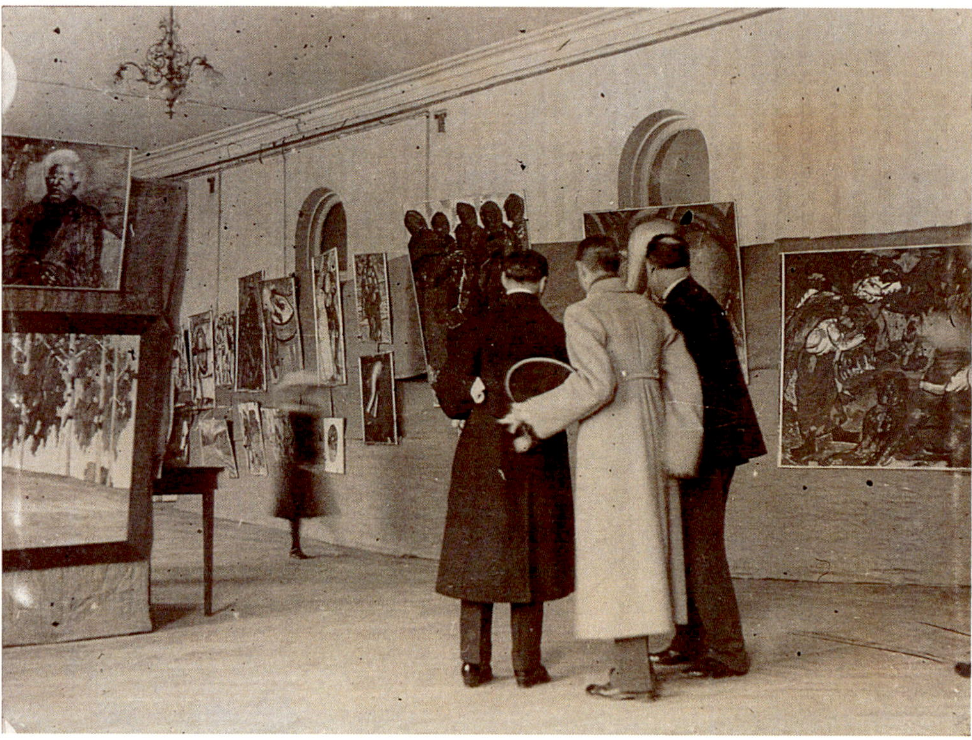

87 a.

on show were produced by Mr Malewicz, who is personally present at the exhibition. He thus offers us a rare example of a living Cubist. Malewicz is not only a Cubist; he paints according to the principles of Cubism and of the Russian folk image (*lubok*), as well as those of Byzantine frescoes, shop signs, Roundism, Futurism and 'anything-goes-ism', in the jocular words of his fellow artists at the exhibition".[22]

In contrast, another article reviewing the same exhibition is frankly negative. It describes the innovative artists in the show as "mental cases or swindlers". The author writes that "there are incomprehensible works. [...] To speak seriously of productions of this kind should not be permitted".[23] Such articles, typical examples of the usual journalistic treatment of modern art outside of Moscow and St Petersburg, nevertheless contain information concerning the works on display, including *Portrait of Kliunkov*, *Carpenter* (several versions), *Young Peasant Girls*, *Female Harvester* and other paintings, which can all be identified in the photographs.

87 a, b and c.
Exhibition in the Second High School for Girls (*Vtoraya zhenskaya gimnaziya*), Kursk, April 1913. Presentation of paintings by Malewicz in the framework of the annual Exhibition of the Kursk Society of Painters, of which he was one of the founders

[22] *Iuzhnii krai*, no. 11369, Kharkov, 23 April 1913, p. 6.

[23] "Cubists, Futurists and Co.", in *Kurskaya byl'*, no. 91, 1913, p. 4.

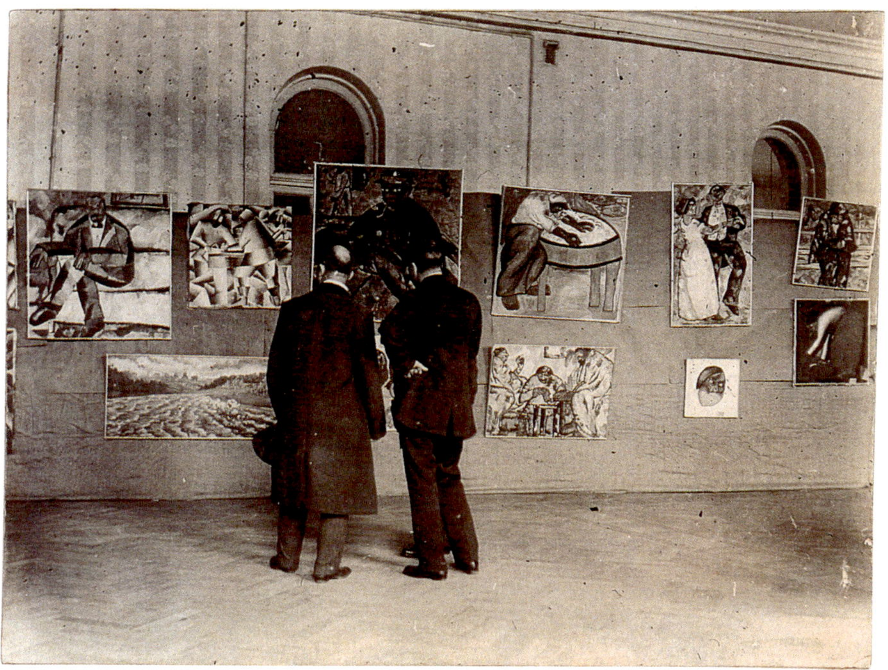

87 b.

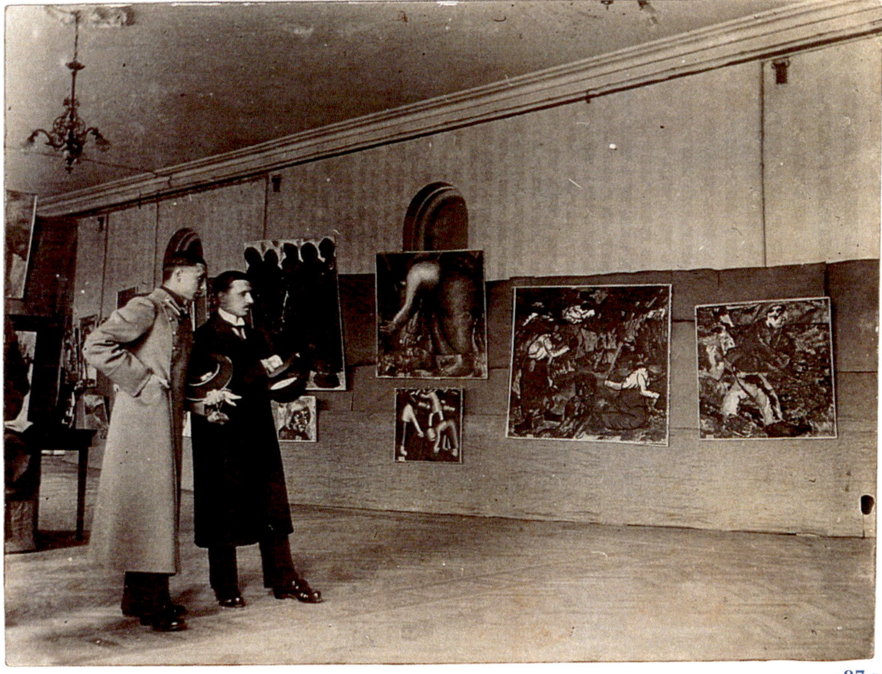

87 c.

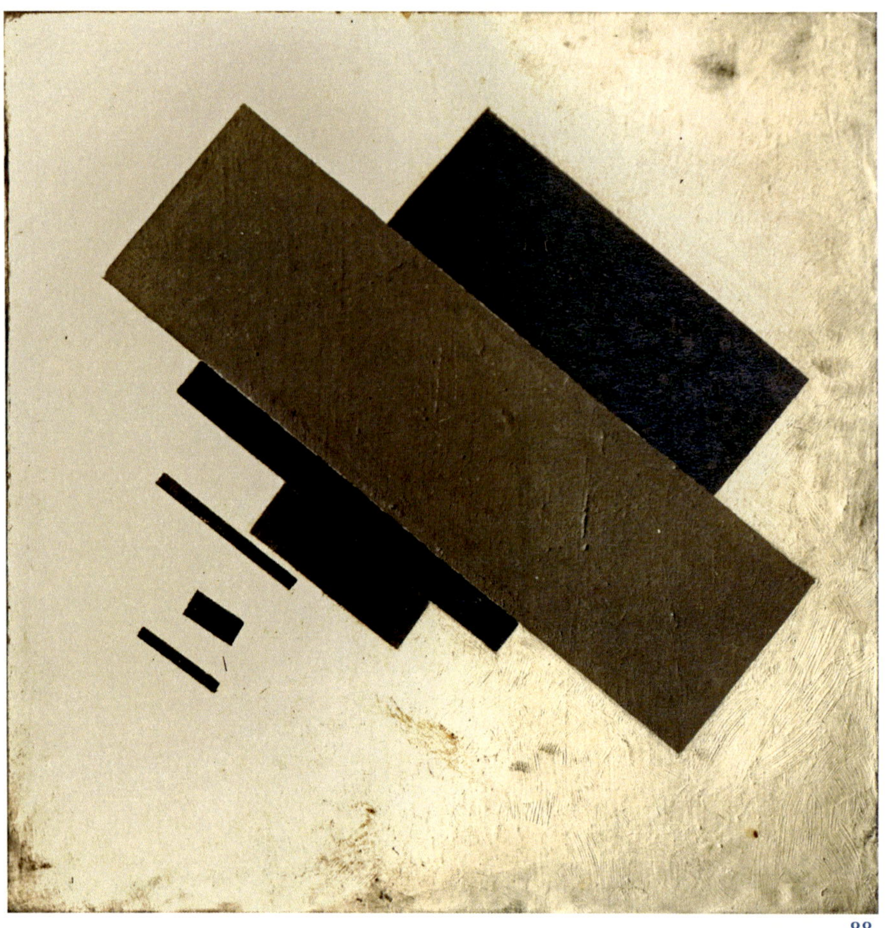

88.

The exhibition has the merit of allowing us to document the artist's autobiographical statements. On several occasions Malewicz stressed the importance of his beginnings at Kursk and his contacts with the small modernist milieu with whose activities he was initially closely associated. This aspect of the artist's life was practically unknown before the early 1990s.[24]

88. Suprematist painting, 1915–1916 (Cat. S-52), lost gelatin silver print, reproduced in *From Cubism and Futurism to Suprematism*, Moscow, 1916. Former Costakis Archives, State Museum of Modern and Contemporary Art, Thessaloniki

S-52

In 2016 in the course of my work in the Costakis archives at the Museum of Modern and Contemporary Art in Thessaloniki, Greece, I discovered an unpublished photograph of the

[24] Considered a "strategic" city up until then, Kursk was off limits to foreigners. In 1991 I was probably the first art historian to visit the city in order to study this hitherto blank page of Malewicz's life. I was warmly welcomed by descendants of the Shuklin family and obtained access to certain facts and documents concerning the dramatic history of the Polish Catholic community in Kursk during the 1930s.

144

89. Suprematist composition, 1916, pencil on paper, unidentified work, whereabouts unknown. Former Miroslav Lamač Archives, Prague

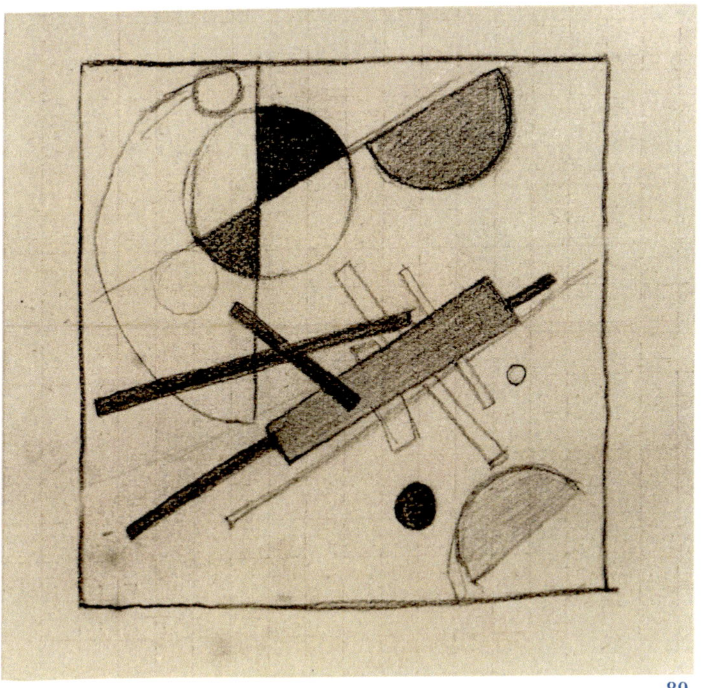

89.

Suprematist composition S-52. This document (gelatin silver print, 10.5×10.5 cm) is sufficiently rare to merit being mentioned, for the Suprematist works to have been the objects of a single photograph during the artist's lifetime are very scarce. Given that the composition was reproduced in autumn 1916 in the booklet *From Cubism and Futurism to Suprematism* it seems likely that the photograph was taken for that specific purpose. The copy in the Costakis archives is of excellent quality. It shows the surface of the painting clearly, including the artist's brushwork. The inscription on the back (in pencil) indicating that the painting is the composition *Supremus 52* seems to date later than the work itself (summer – autumn 1915). Since the existence of the painting is not documented after 1920, the date of the artist's Moscow retrospective, the composition can be considered "lost", probably destroyed.

Regarding such documentary "complements" one might also mention the existence of a few rare works known only through images unaccompanied by physical information, for instance an extremely interesting drawing of the Suprematist type from the winter of 1915/1916. Unfortunately, this

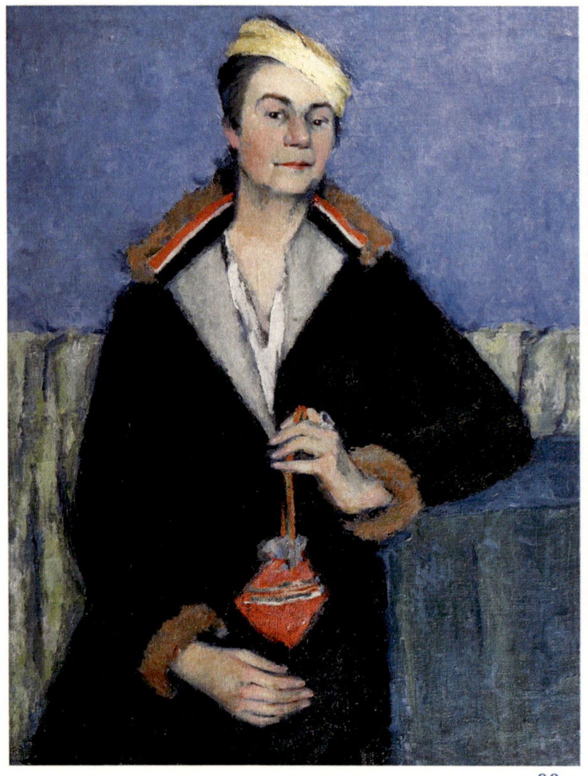

90 a.

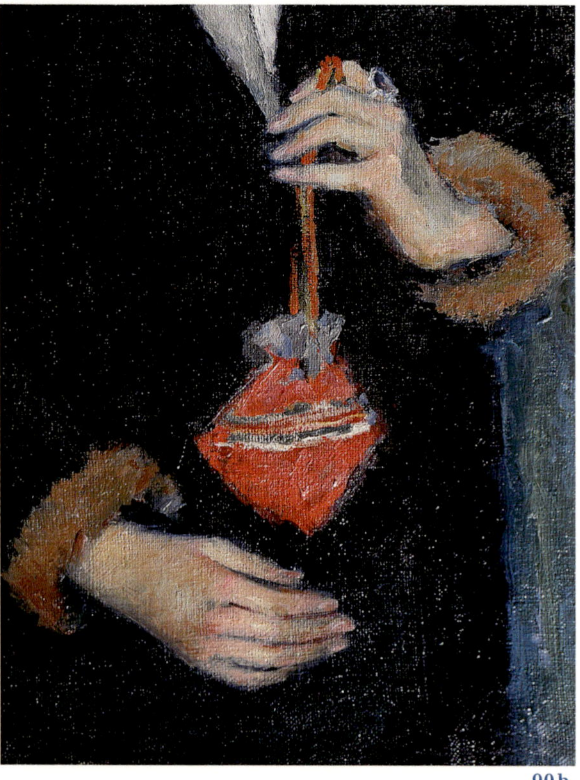

90 b.

document from the former archives of Miroslav Lamač does not include any details about the work's dimensions, location, etc.

90 a and b.
a. Maria Dzhagupova (?), *Portrait of E. Yakovleva*, formerly attributed to Malewicz (Cat. PS-253)
b. *Portrait of E. Yakovleva* (detail)

The Master said:
"Yu, shall I tell you what it is to know.
To say you know when you know,
and to say you do not when you do not,
that is knowledge."

Confucius[25]

The recent publication of documents connected with Malewicz's Cubist teaching at Vitebsk in 1920 has led me to revise the attribution of a painting that figured in the 1923 *All Trends*

[25] D. C. Lau, *Confucius: The Analects*, Harmondsworth: Penguin Books, 1979, Book 2, no. 17.

91. (Emblematic composition),
c. 1928–1930 (Cat. PS-174), pencil on
paper, 10.8 × 10.9 cm, Khardzhiev-
Chaga Cultural Foundation, Amsterdam
(on deposit at the Stedelijk Museum,
Amsterdam)

92. Hands and cross, *c.* 1930–1931
(Cat. PS-22), pencil on paper, 22.5 × 35 cm
(composition 11.5 × 9.8 cm), private
collection

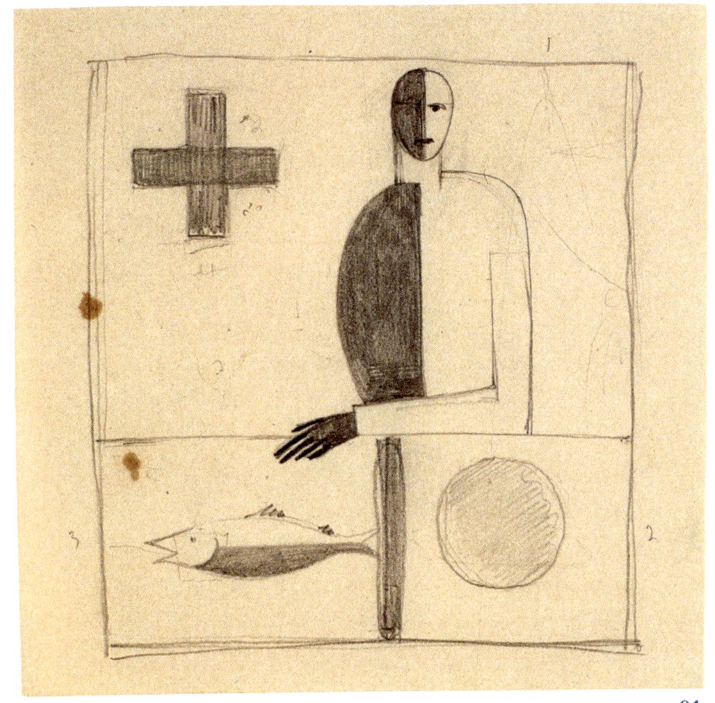

91.

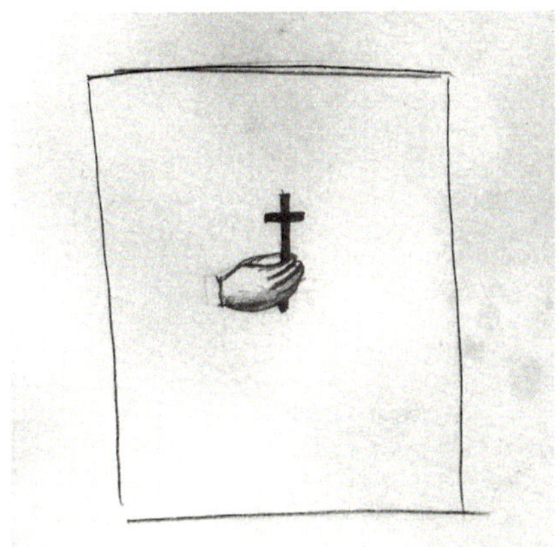

92.

exhibition in Petrograd. The fact that all of the works displayed in this show were listed in its catalogue under the collective UNOVIS heading does not preclude them being identified separately. But at the time I was revising the *Catalogue raisonné* in 2000 I had only a single photograph to go by, admittedly of a rather poor quality, of the UNOVIS wall. In the absence of other information it was difficult to identify Cubist works in particular. At the time I also manifestly placed too much trust in the statements of Maria Gorokhova, the widow of the painter Lev Yudin, a member of the UNOVIS at Vitebsk and, later, in St Petersburg.[26] I was also able to interview Evgenia Magaril (1902–1987), another former student at the Vitebsk UNOVIS. I was privileged to be acquainted with her in Leningrad in the 1970s; in certain respects she was an important source of information concerning the Vitebsk UNOVIS. As recently revealed in connection with Malewicz's Cubist teaching, the composition is in fact probably a work painted in Vitebsk by Lev Yudin (1903–1941), another young student in the UNOVIS

[26] In the mid-1970s I made several visits to Maria Gorokhova (1903–1991) and was able to collect her recollections and consult a number of documents relative to the teaching at Vitebsk. Most of the documents are now preserved in the public library of St Petersburg. They were published in 2017, see *Lev Judin, op. cit.*

classes, who followed Malewicz to Petrograd.[27] For decades it was concealed by a figurative work – *Dawn* – painted on the back of the same canvas by another of Malewicz's students (but this time at Leningrad), Konstantin Rozhdestvensky, from around 1930. Under the aesthetic criteria of the USSR, this "bucolic" painting was considered "acceptable" at the time, and exhibited publicly instead of the composition from the UNOVIS Vitebsk period. This was in effect an instance of censorship in the name of so-called "Social realism". It seems all the odder in that Rozhdestvensky did not become a member of the UNOVIS group until the mid-1920s Leningrad.

PS-253

This portrait was rediscovered in St Petersburg in the 1980s. On first encountering the original I was immediately impressed by the power and geometric impact of the composition, which, in my opinion, unquestionably indicated that it was painted after a compositional model that Malewicz had originated. I still have this impression.

Yet certain details call for caution. In the *Catalogue raisonné* entry I pointed out that the inscriptions on the back were not in the artist's hand. A close look at the radiograph of the painting (to which I subsequently did not have access) seemed to indicate that there were two distinct types of brushstroke at the centre and along the edges of the composition. As a result of recently published research the attribution has been switched to Maria Dzhagupova (1897–1975), an artist who was in touch with Malewicz in Leningrad and especially with the informal circle of students connected with him from the late 1920s on.[28] However, as Malewicz did not actually teach painting in this period, it seems difficult to assert that Dzhagupova was actually a "student of Malewicz's", as has recently been advanced.

The documents relating to this painting do indeed suggest that it is not solely the work of Malewicz, however this does not resolve the question of the model it is based on, i.e. the composition properly speaking. The little we know about the production of Maria Dzhagupova, an artist who worked mainly in the applied arts, in particular in the field of decorating

[27] Yudin's compositon, an untitled oil on canvas (125 × 85 cm) now in the Tretyakov State Gallery in Moscow, was exhibited in 2018 as "Cubism". It is very likely the same work as no. 1254 in the *All Trends* exhibition catalogue, as part of a group of not individually identified works under the collective UNOVIS heading. By itself the photograph of the UNOVIS display does not provide a sufficient identification of the composition. It was not shown publicly until 2018 (see the exhibition catalogue *Chagall, Lissitzky, Malévitch. L'avant-garde russe à Vitebsk 1918–1922*, Paris: Centre Pompidou, 2018, fig. p. 159). The painting is not reproduced either in the voluminous edition of the artist's "Journals", based on the papers his widow bequeathed to the St Petersburg Public Library (see *Lev Judin, op. cit.*, Moscow, 2017).

[28] See K. Akinsha and V. Thorpe, "Rediscovered Masterpiece Work of Malevich's Pupil", *The Guardian*, London, 7 April 2019, and A. Vassiliev, "Vystavliaia kartinu kak Malevicha..." (Exhibiting a Painting under Malewicz's Name...), *The Art Newspaper Russia*, 20 April 2019.

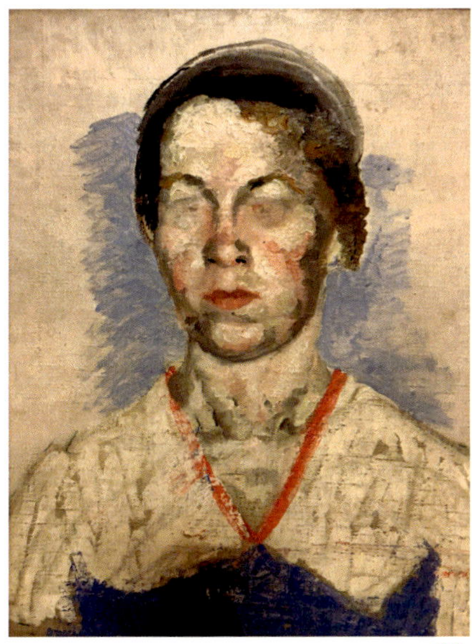

93. Unknown artist (attributed to Malewicz), *Portrait of Anna Leporskaya, c.* 1928–1935, oil on canvas, 98.3 × 77.5 cm, ABA Gallery, New York, former Anna Leporskaya Collection, Leningrad

fabrics, does not allow one to attribute to her the full originality of a composition as rigorous and ambitious as this, one whose apodictic structure points to the authority of a prior model, if not a direct work. The question of a Malewiczian model remains open to scrutiny and analysis, all the more so that the final period of the artist's output has still not been structured in terms of a stylistic interpretation. We are now far from the era when the works that Malewicz produced between 1927 and 1934 were lumped together under the misleading label "second peasant period" (sic!).[29] Quite the contrary, the stylistic diversity of the works executed towards the end of the painter's life is extremely impressive. At the time I was compiling the *Catalogue raisonné* I was already referring to the artist's "Post-Suprematist" period, but within this category several very different stylistic groups should be recognised. They range from highly realistic compositions (primarily the portraits PS-263 to 273) to relatively abstract works (apart from reprises of certain thematic concerns of the 1910–1912 years, PS-2, PS-6, PS-55, PS-157, PS-175, PS-180, PS-197 to PS-201).

The concepts of planar (post-abstract) symbolisation that orientated the artist's production of different stylistic sequences from 1926 on have as yet to be identified and only then can they be interpreted. No painter of Malewicz's Russian milieu equals his stylistic richness and compositional sharpness in the late 1920s and early '30s. The possibility of his involvement in the inception of the portrait's composition is still open, but this by no means precludes the name of the artist who painted it *in fine*.

Sketch for a Female Portrait

The same type of question is raised by a vaguely defined oil sketch of a portrait thought to be by Anna Leporskaya but reattributed to Malewicz at the latter's exhibition in St Petersburg's Russian Museum in autumn 2018. Until 1996 this composition had been exhibited as a work by Anna Leporskaya (the date was corrected in 2004[30]). Technical (material) examinations of this work would probably provide little information, for even if we knew them the materials used at the time in the

[29] This strange stylistic categorisation was launched in Russia towards the end of the 1980s when the artist's last period was particularly misunderstood.

[30] This re-attribution was made by Elena Basner, who revised her own opinion of 1996 (see the brief note of the "Blow Up" section of the journal *Pinakoteka*, nos. 18–19, Moscow, 2004.

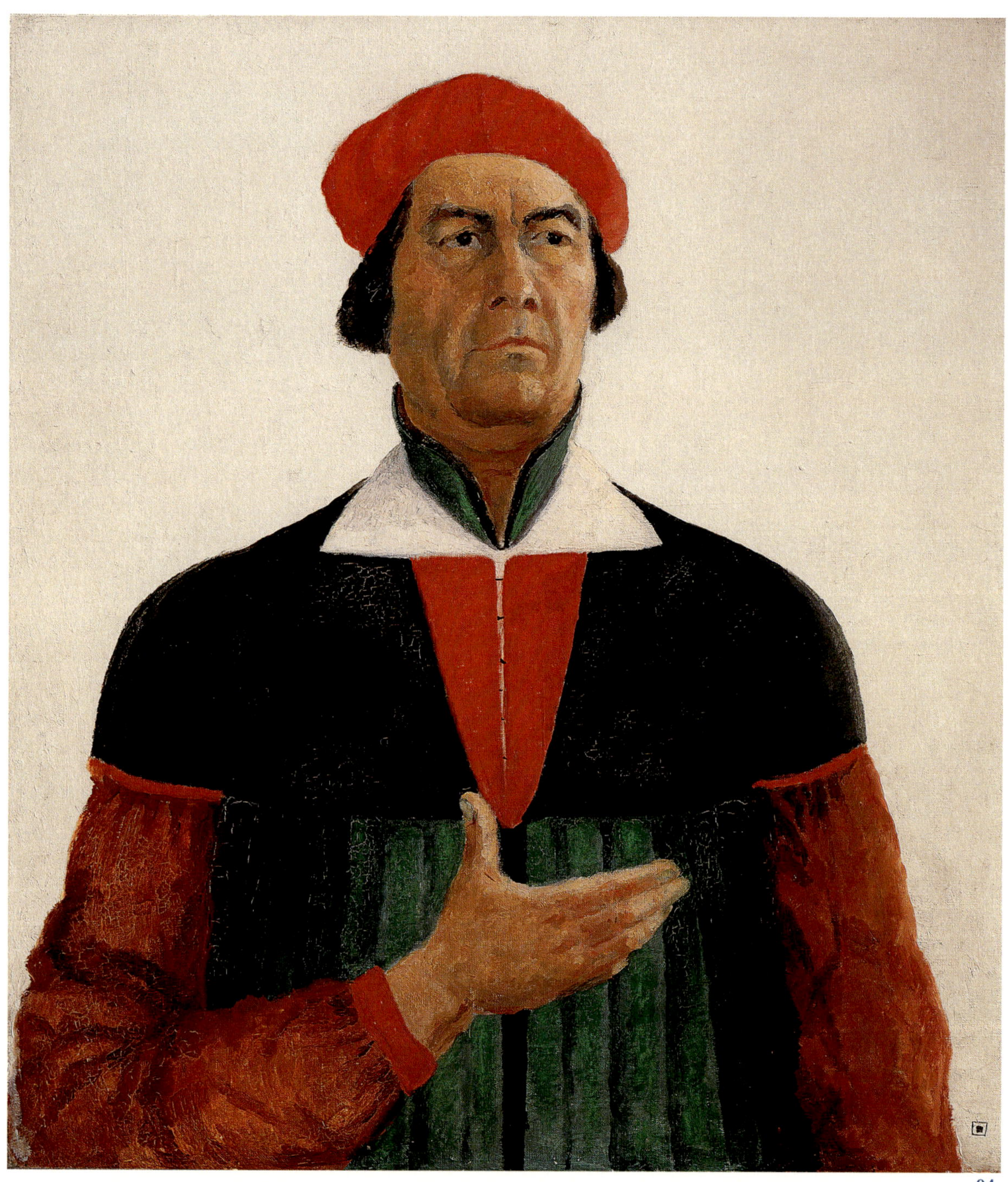

94.

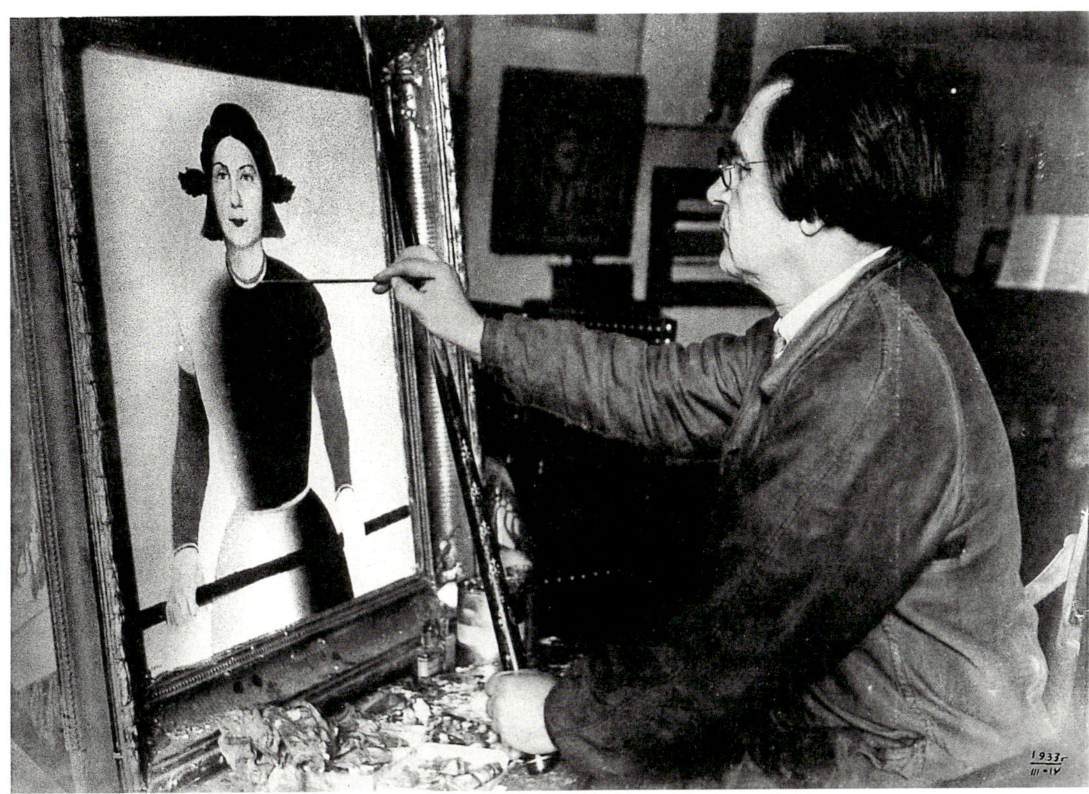

95.

94. *The Painter* (self-portrait of the artist),
1933 (Cat. PS-251), oil on canvas,
73 × 66 cm, State Russian Museum,
St Petersburg

95. Nikolai Suetin, Malewicz in the pose
of an academic professor, Leningrad,
c. 1928–1932, gelatin silver print.
Nakov Archives, Paris

96. Nikolai Suetin, "academic"
presentation of a Malewicz painting
(*Portrait of Nikolai Punin*, Cat. PS-250)
on the artist's easel, Leningrad,
late 1920s, gelatin silver print.
Nakov Archives, Paris

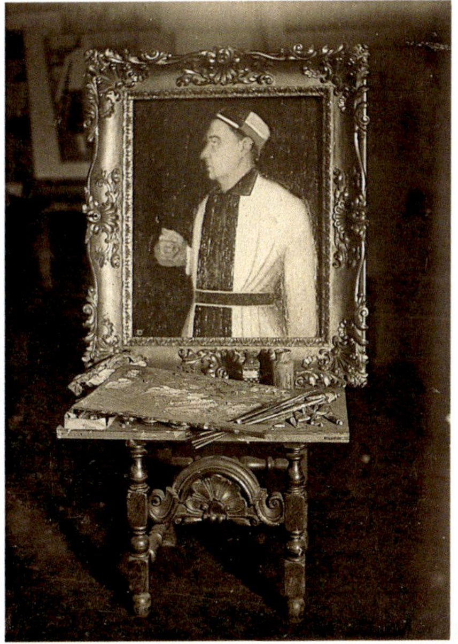

96.

same circles would not permit attributing it specifically to this or that hand. Thus the question of style is once again a prime stylistical factor in our discussions relating to this attribution. A scholar of art owes it to himself to consider first and foremost the manner in which forms are arrived at, the style of the work. That is why the Italian term *critica d'arte*, somewhat forgotten if not actually scorned today, still seems operative.

Concerning the Attributions

Published in 2002, the *Catalogue raisonné*, as I said, suffered from the delay in the publication of the monograph, scheduled to come out that same year but which only appeared in 2007 with another publisher. As initially planned, it was to be part of a single project comprising the monograph as well. This did not happen and as a result the original edition was issued without of the complete list of bibliographic references mentioned in its entries. The additional bibliography was only included in the fourth volume of the monograph, which was issued five years later in French (2007) and eight years later (2010) in English. However, the list of exhibitions that figured in the *Catalogue* was not reprinted in the French edition of the monograph although it is given in full in Chapter 33 of the English-language edition.

As indicated in the *Catalogue raisonné*, a reference to a text or to an exhibition catalogue in one of the above publications means that I have taken into consideration the Malewicz work or attribution contained therein. Thus if a work mentioned in an article or essay I have listed does not appear in here this means that I have discarded its attribution to Malewicz.

I published a first supplement and list of corrections to the *Catalogue raisonné* in the French edition of the monograph (2007), vol. 4, chap. 32. Two oil paintings of the artist's Impressionist period, which featured in the Moscow 2017 exhibition, concern Malewicz attributions since 2007: *Zimniy peyzazh* (Winter Landscape), 1929, 36.8 × 35.5 cm, reproduced on p. 174 of the exhibition catalogue, and *Dom s verandoi* (House with Veranda), 1906, oil on cardboard, 19.2 × 30 cm, fig. p. 25 of the exh. cat. These attributions seem plausible but need to be examined in depth.

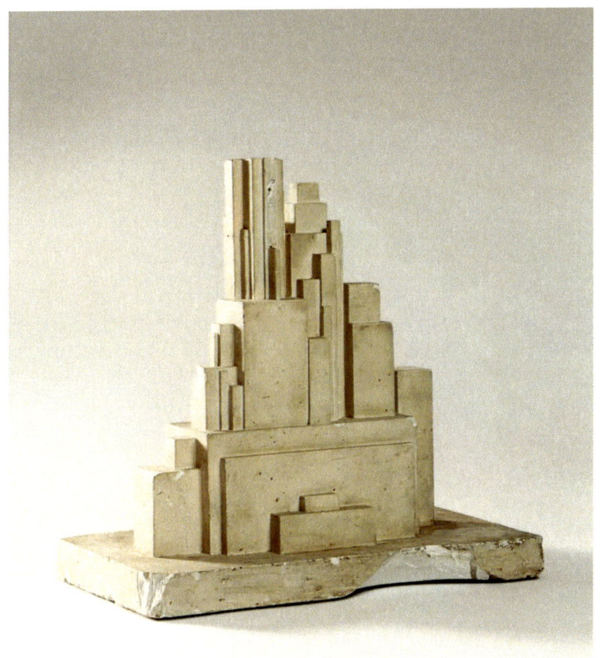

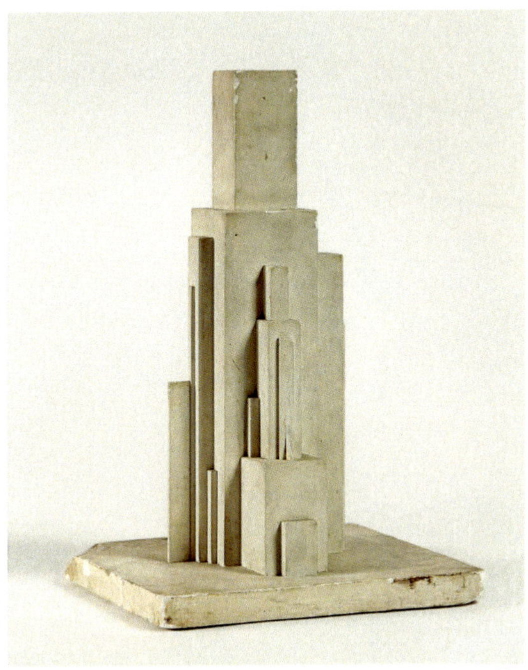

97 a.   97 b.

Architectonas and Details of Architectonas

Three *architektona* in plaster figured in the 2017 Malewicz exhibition in Moscow:

Portal (Portal), 34 × 21.5 × 21 cm (fig. p. 162);

Gorod (Town), 36 × 23 × 37 cm (fig. p. 164);

and *Bashnia* (Tower), 66 × 23 × 23 cm (fig. p. 165).[31]

These pieces seem to be part of a fairly large group of works that seem directly or indirectly connected with the artist's architectonic work: details of architectonas and a large number of humanoid figures exhibited in Vaduz, Liechtenstein, in 2013 and, later, in Baden-Baden, Germany (one does not know exactly how many pieces there are in this series; their number does not seem to have been specified). In 2017 a selection – perhaps most? – of these objects was shown in the exhibition *Chagall, Lissitzky, Malevich – The Russian Avant-Garde in Vitebsk 1918–1922* (the English-language catalogue, translated from the French edition edited by Angela Lampe, was published in 2018 by Prestel Publishing in Munich).

[31] A. Shatskikh (ed.), *Kazimir Malevich, Ne tol'ko chërnyi kvadrat* (Kazimir Malevich: Not Only Black Square), Moscow: VDNH exhibition space, 2017.

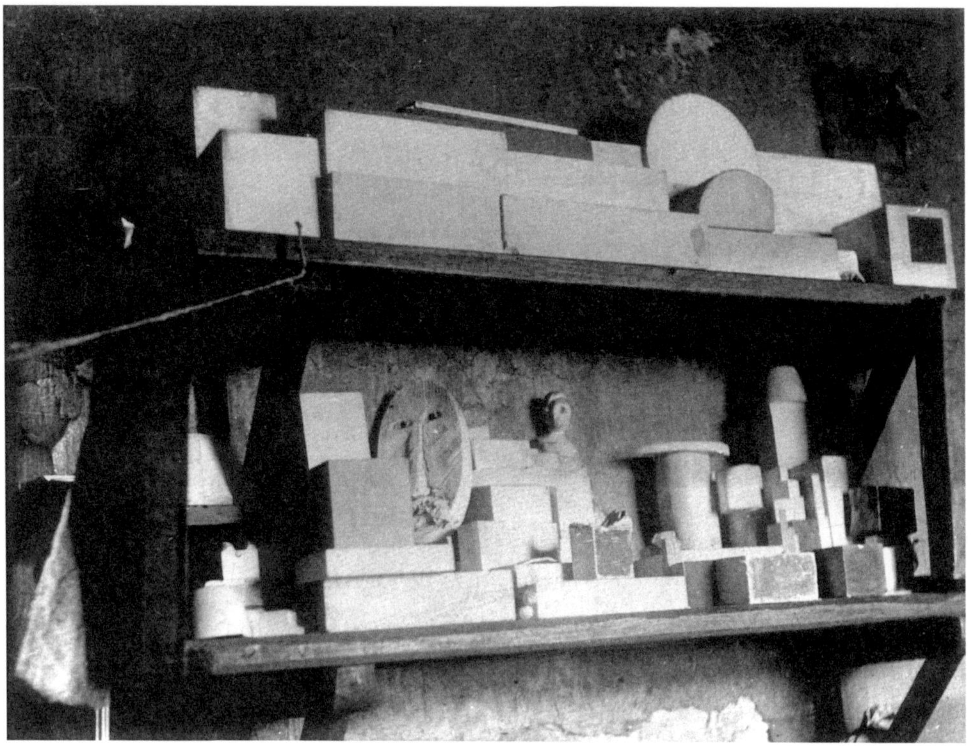

98.

However, some of the pieces shown in Vaduz and again, in 2017, in Moscow (in the VDNH space) bear little resemblance, in my opinion, to the architectonic output of Malewicz and his closest collaborators (Nikolai Suetin and Ilya Chashnik). I would first cite reasons of a stylistic order, even though they could be dismissed as subjective. In the absence of documentary evidence it is criteria of this type that guide one's judgement concerning attributions in the visual arts. The proportions of the elements the artist uses in his compositions and especially their texture and his manner of positioning them, that is to say the relationship between forms, determine the "internal" image of the artwork, or in Platonic terms, its – ideal – "model".

To begin with, the items discussed here do not exhibit the ideal proportions of Malewicz's *architektona*. On the contrary, they present themselves as arrangements of volumes marked by a certain "heaviness" (for example the work displayed under the title *Gorod* [City]). The lyric aspect and the precision of

98. Architectural elements in plaster, 1930s, kept in the Suetin–Leporskaya studio, Belinski 11 street, Leningrad. Photograph of the late 1960s taken by Prague photographer Karel Kuklik. Nakov Archives, Paris

the proportions that characterise both the horizontal (S-684 or S-690) and vertical (S-697 or S-702) architectonas is missing in them. In short, the poetic dimension of Malewicz's architectonas does not seem to belong to the vocabulary of this series. Secondly, apart from the above considerations relative to the proportions of the volumes and their positioning, compared to what we know about the artist's architectonic manner, the materials used here differ from those employed in well-known, documented architectonas (S-690, S-688 and S-700). The material of these pieces is lustreless, cream coloured. The patina and strangely compact consistency differ from the white plaster of the known, unquestionably authentic pieces, such as S-699, which Nikolai Suetin preserved after the artist's death and which later passed into the safekeeping of his companion Anna Leporskaya. They were placed on the top shelves at the entrance of her studio at number 11 Belinski Street, where I saw them frequently and was able to hold some of them in my hands.

The pieces exhibited from early 2010 on include a quantity of small humanoid figures. Besides considerations of style and execution, miniature figures of this type are not associated with any of the artist's architectonas. Indeed, judging from the documents we know of (drawings and photographs), Malewicz very seldom if ever included such figures in his architectonic projects, limited to Non-Objective volumes, which were arranged in a Suprematist, i.e. an ideal, manner. His architectonic production was rather abundantly photographed at the time and is in particular documented in numerous sketches and drawings by the artist and by his close students Chashnik and Suetin, none of which includes figures.[32]

In 1932, at the end of his architectonic production, the artist designed a large figure of Lenin to set atop the *Column of Soviets* (S-703). With different proportions and stylistically far removed from the miniatures shown in 2017, the figure of the "Guide" is unlike anything in the artist's architectonic work and is limited solely to Malewicz's last columnar architectona. Attesting to a painful socio-political compromise, this figure, quite unique in his production, has a figurative look that differs fundamentally from the recently exhibited figurines discussed here.

[32] See in particular the diagrams of S-675 to S-687, which the artist published in the 1920s, as well as his free sketches like those of the composite families S-675 to S-677. One of the first Western publications to appear after the catalogue of the 1988–1989 retrospective is the one compiled by Jean-Claude Marcadé (*Malévitch*, Paris: Nouvelles Éditions françaises).

"Doctor Mabuzo"

Among the Suprematist-type works recently attributed to Malewicz is a canvas containing the inscription "Doctor Mabuzo" (Doctor Mabuse). Belonging for decades to the collections of the Tretyakov Gallery, this painting appeared since the late 1990s in publications on Malewicz based on Russian sources. Moreover, to my great surprise, it figured in the artist's retrospective at Amsterdam's Stedelijk Museum in 2013 (*Kazimir Malevich and the Russian Avant-Garde*). It was also included in 2013 in the exhibition at the Bundeskunsthalle in Bonn and in the modified version of the same show at the Tate Gallery in London in 2014. It was subsequently displayed permanently at the Tretyakov Gallery, where it could still be viewed in 2019.[33] Its stylistic closeness to the compositional stereotypes of Constructivism notwithstanding its strictly Suprematist spirit, which is far removed from the latter (and should make interpreters reflect), meant that it was warmly received in Western Europe, especially in Germany, the country where Constructivism has indisputable roots.[34]

Earlier, in September 1987 I had an opportunity to examine this canvas closely in the course of a study visit to the reserves of the Moscow museum. My scrutiny of its surface, its original colours (which were greyish and therefore unlike Malewicz's register of hues) and above all of the somewhat mechanical touch of the execution (flatness of the brushstroke) rapidly convinced me that the attribution to Malewicz was erroneous. I was already familiar with it through a good black-and-white photograph taken in Moscow by the Prague photographer Karel Neubert in the second half of the 1960s.

On pursuing my investigations in the late 1980s I was able to establish that a work similar in all respects to the Tretyakov Gallery canvas (probably the same picture) featured in the mid-1920s in an exhibition of works by students at the Decorative Institute in Leningrad.[35] In those years Ilya Chashnik taught occasionally at the Institute, hence the presence of a Suprematist composition rerouted to the field of the applied arts (film posters or other designs of the same order) and thus suitable for a student's assignment, as indicated in the periodical referred to here. (Chashnik's production contains numerous examples of this type of work, however, the composition's brushwork does not support an attribution to that artist.)

[33] See the catalogue of the Stedelijk Museum's exhibition, *Malevich and the Russian Avant-Garde* (Amsterdam, October 2013 to February 2014), ed. by S. Tates, K. J. Kelly and L. S. Boersma, fig. p. 150. This illustration is faithfully reproduced in Jean-Claude Marcadé's *Malévitch. Écrits*, Paris: Editions Allia, 2015, p. 375. The painting was included in the permanent display of the Tretyakov's collection in 2015, as shown by the photograph in *Kazimir Malevich. Chernyi kvadrat* (Kazimir Malewicz. The Black Square), ed. by I. Vakar, Moscow: Tretyakov State Gallery, fig. p. 55 (in German translation: *Kazimir Malewitsch. Das schwarze Quadrat*, Vaduz: Kustmuseum, 2018, p. 55). The date that seems most appropriate for this painting would seem to be around the release of Fritz Lang's film in Russia, i.e. 1924. Declared "decadent", the film was soon forbidden by the authorities, but aroused such interest among certain avant-garde filmmakers that Sergei Eisenstein and Esfir Shub did a special montage of it in 1924.

[34] See the leading reproduction in *Süddeutsche Zeitung*, Munich, 4 April 2014, and the article by Catrin Lorch, "Helige im Quadrat", illustrated in an eye-catching encapsulation of the themes singled out in the large-circulation press: icons, "peasant" images and the poster for "Dr. Mabuso". The display of this work at the Bonn Kunsthalle was even more startling, as the composition was attributed the date "1916" (for what reason?). The possible date would be the launching of the German film on the Russian screens – 1924.

[35] See V. I. Denisov, "Vystavka plakata v Dome Pechati" (An Exhibition of Posters at the Press House), *Zhizn iskusstva* (The Life of the Arts), Leningrad, no. 51, 21 December 1926, pp. 12–13.

99. Commentary of the exhibition at Leningrad's Institute of Decorative Arts, 1926. Illustration in the review *Zhizn iskusstva* (The Life of the Arts)

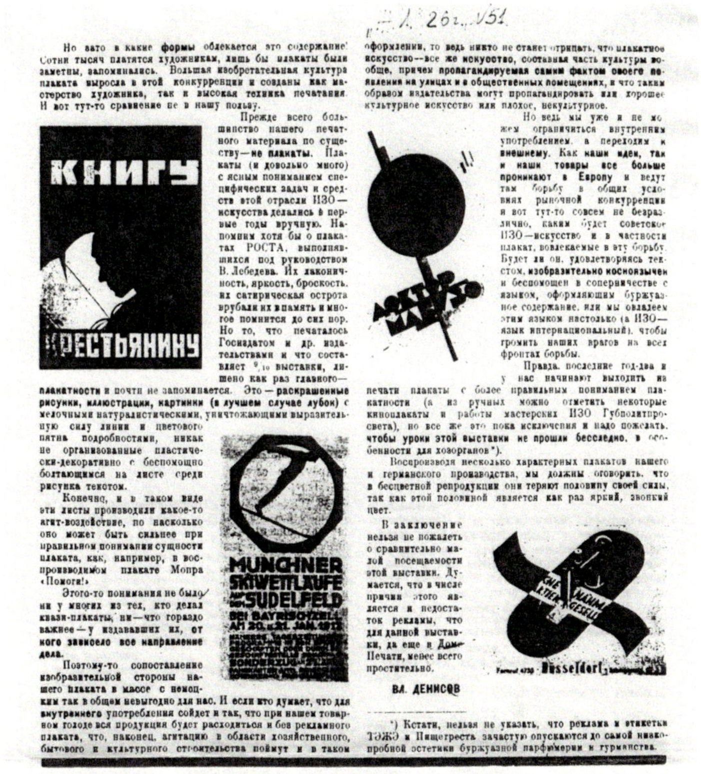

99.

To this could be added the fact that among the photographs that Neubert took in the Soviet Union towards the end of the 1960s, the same series at the Tretyakov included several highly unusual geometric compositions of a crystal variety which I would call "in the Vasarely manner", at the time associated with Malewicz's name. (They have since been disqualified.) They attest to the flagrant ignorance surrounding the Suprematist corpus in Soviet Russia in an era when abstract art of any kind was violently rejected.

* * *

As the precision of the bibliographic entries in the *Catalogue raisonné* was not immediately obvious I was questioned several times over these last few years concerning an attribution

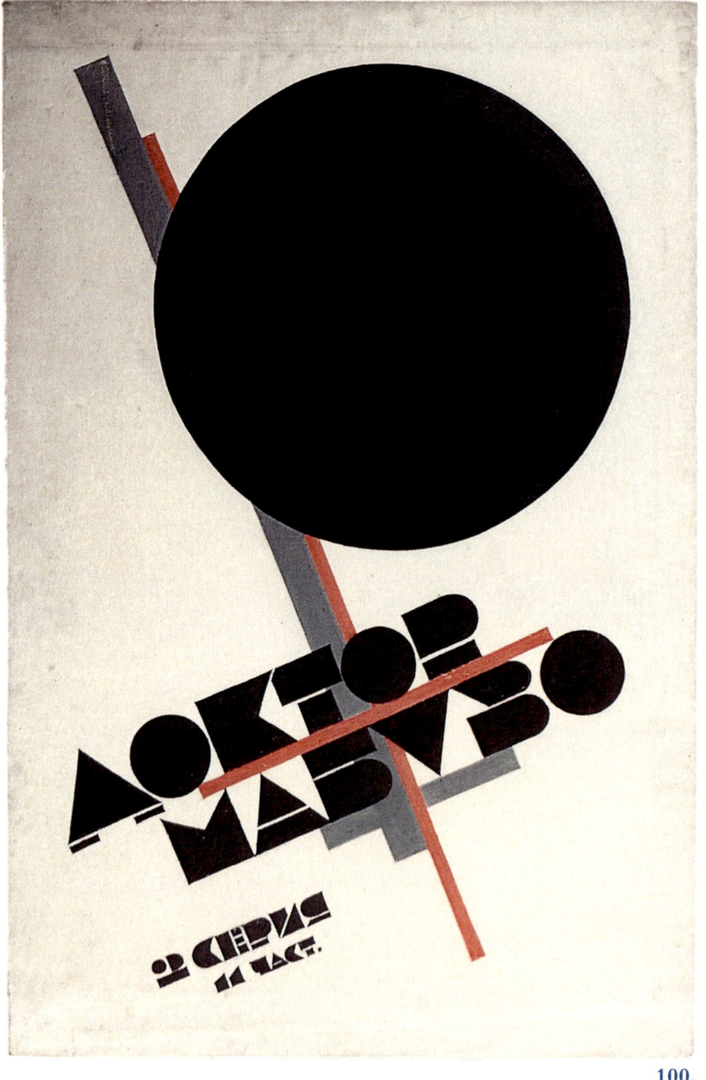

100.

100. Unknown artist, "Doctor Mabuzo",
c. 1924–1926, oil on canvas, 105 × 70.6 cm,
Tretyakov State Gallery, Moscow[*]

[*] Attributed to Malewicz. In conjunction with
the first Russian screening of Fritz Lang's film
Dr. Mabuse

to Malewicz of a Suprematist type composition – an oil on
canvas – that Pontus Hulten published in 1987. At present this
work (still?) belongs to the Menil collection at the eponymous
museum in Houston, Texas.[36] In the late 1980s Dominique
de Menil asked me for my opinion concerning this attribution, and I told her in person and quite categorically that I did
not accept it. I repeat this judgement here and point out that
it is based on precise considerations of style and execution,

[36] See *The Menil Collection*, New York: Harry
N. Abrams, 1987, fig. p. 191 (listed in the bibliography of my monograph, *Malewicz*, 2007/2010).

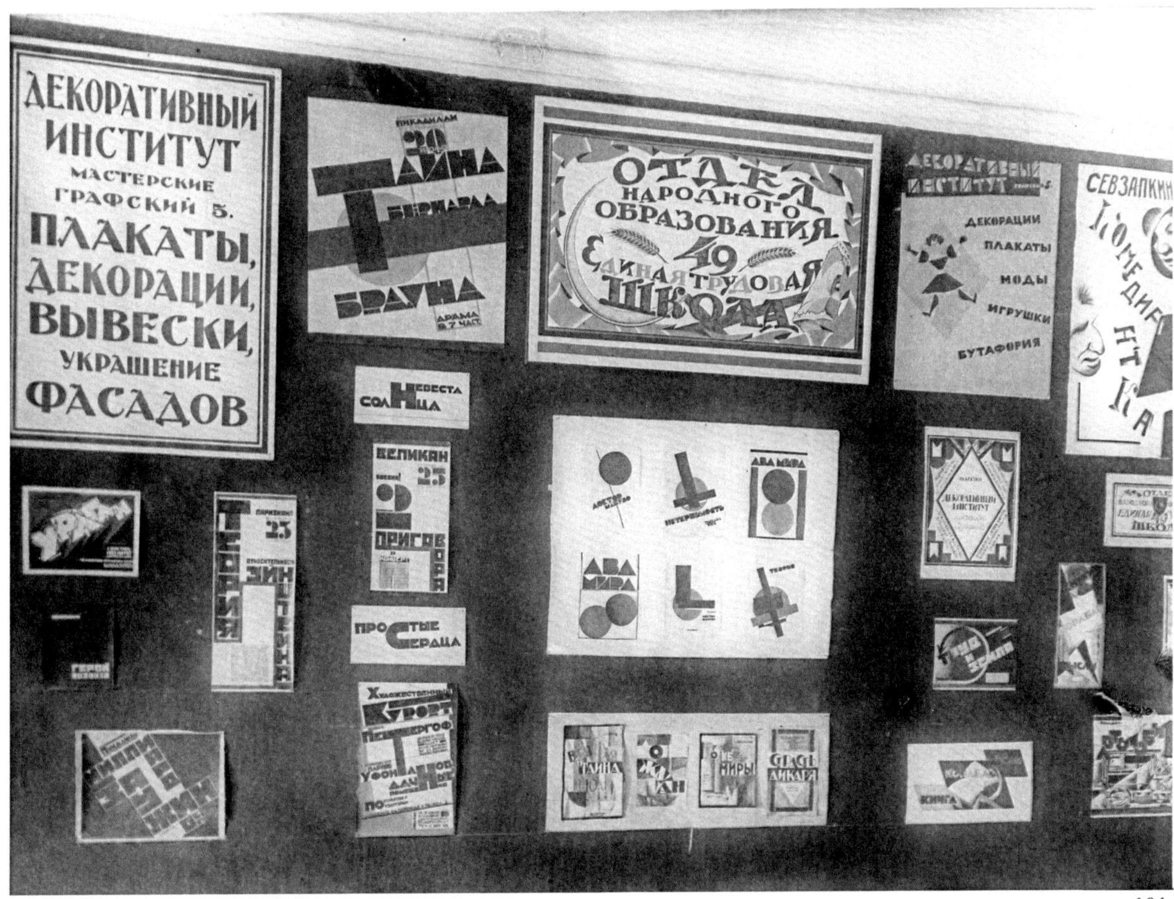

101.

101. Exhibition of works by students of the Decorative Arts Institute in Leningrad, 1926. In the centre a work (a painting?) inspired by *Dr. Mabuse*

37 See F. Miele, *L'avanguardia tradita: Arte russa dal XIX al XX sec.*, Rome: Carte Segrete, 1973.

38 A. Turowski, *Malewicz w Warszawie: rekonstrukcje i symulacje* (Malewicz in Warsaw: Reconstructions and Simulations), Kraków: Universitas, 2004 (also listed in the bibliography of my monograph, *Malewicz*, 2007/2010). This publication was issued in Poland in spring 2004, but is antedated 2002, a date that coincides fallaciously with the publication of the *Catalogue raisonné* in the spring of 2002. As usual, the author makes no mention of my publications on Malewicz.

as corroborated by the work's provenance (Franco Miele's preposterous Moscow-Rome "collection" of the late 1960s, today greatly disqualified.)[37]

In the mid-1970s a large group of pencil drawings of the Suprematist type surfaced in Germany. Consulted on two occasions by the owner of a German gallery, I concluded after examining the originals that their attribution to Malewicz was fallacious. I stated this opinion in no uncertain terms to the owner (or presumable owner) and repeat it here. In 1987 Andrzej Turowski published the drawings in *Les Cahiers du Musée National d'Art Moderne* in Paris (duly listed in the bibliography of my 2007/2010 monograph). The same author reproduced the same set of drawings in 2004 with the same attribution, this time in colour.[38] Since that date several of the drawings seem to have been acquired by a public collection in Poland.

In the years following the death of Chashnik's son Ilya (like his father) in 1977 and especially that of Anna Leporskaya (1982), copies (most of them enlarged) and "variants" of Malewicz drawings have appeared in various exhibitions (especially in Switzerland and the USA) and have then made their way into private as well as public collections. A certain number of authentic works preserved in the Belinski Street studio and photographed during Ilya Chashnik junior's lifetime, found their way, often enlarged, to the US[39] or to Russia.[40] Another group of drawings, made (traced directly?) from the originals, surfaced in Moscow in 2000.[41] The exact references at my disposal and my examination of the paper (a sheet of which, I have kept as a sample) enabled me to distinguish between the copies and the originals, at present an extremely difficult exercise.

This is why the inventory of the works left in the Suprematist studio in Leningrad is vitally important. Drawn up by Miroslav Lamač in 1966–1967,[42] this inventory, which the Czech art historian initially communicated to me in 1980, was on my demand quite recently (2013) confirmed by Karel Kuklik (1937–2019), a Prague photographer who on this occasion also worked as Lamač's informal assistant in 1966.[43] At the time the inventory was to be part of the monograph scheduled by the Cologne publisher DuMont Schauberg, in particular its director Karl Gutbrod.[44] The content of this inventory, as published by me in 2002, has recently been contested by Troels Andersen.[45] As always, refusing any debate, this author states his position peremptorily, without the least documentary proof. After verifying his assertion and again consulting Karel Kulik in person, I confirm the information given in my 2002 *Catalogue raisonné*.

* * *

In the last thirty years or so the production of imitations of Malewicz's work has increased exponentially and reached truly extravagant proportions. There is no longer any point in dwelling on this inflation. Yet one matter deserves to be

[39] Among many other publications see the catalogues *Of Absence and Presence*, New York: Kent Fine Art, 1986, and *Kazimir Severinovich Malevich*, New York: Leonard Hutton Galleries, 1995. Some of these drawings were exhibited again in Moscow in 2018 on the occasion of the commemoration of the Nikolai Khardzhiev archives. The catalogue accompanying the *Kazimir Severinovich Malevich. Drawings for a New World* exhibition at the Meadows School of the Arts, Southern Methodist University, Texas, USA, 1997, a selection of works that had featured in the Leonard Hutton show, presents an almost farcical version of this type of enlargement.

[40] See in particular the catalogue *Mutiuiushchaia utopiia / Les utopies mutantes*, Moscow, 2010, previously shown in Paris at the Passage de Retz, figs. pp. 28–33.

[41] See the above catalogue, which includes copies of F-433, F-457, F-476 and F-479.

[42] An acknowledged authority on modern art, especially Czech Cubism, Miroslav Lamač was the first historian of Western art to produce relevant interpretations of Malewicz's œuvre. After a grave illness he died prematurely in 1992. See the commemorative article by Tomáš Vlček, "K životnímu jubileu Miroslava Lamače" (On the anniversary of Miroslav Lamač), *Umění* (Arts), Prague, 1989, vol. XXXVII, pp. 79–81, followed by an exhaustive bibliography of his writings by Zuzana Všetečková, pp. 81–88.

[43] A highly esteemed photographer in his own country (see Jaromir Zemina, *Karel Kuklik*, Prague, 2004), Kuklik worked in the 1960s for the Prague review *Výtvarné Umění*, of which Miroslav Lamač was the editor-in-chief. At our last meeting in Prague in February 2013 Kuklik gave me a detailed account of the part he played in establishing the inventory of the Malewicz works in the possession of Anna Leporskaya in Leningrad in the second half of the 1960s. He shared his personal recollections with me and, from memory, supplied technical details and described the precise conditions under which he carried out this work on two separate occasions (besides his skill as a photographer, widely recognised in the Czech Republic, he also spoke Russian and was thus able to serve as an interpreter in the course of these missions). During our last meeting Kuklik formally recognized several drawings in the group of compositions he had photographed in the Leningrad studio, which Anna Leporskaya had handed to him (she also made him a gift of a couple of Malewicz drawings). Andersen has disputed the authenticity of these works. Kuklik later made a written statement on this subject (a document, dated 10 February 2013, which I keep in my files, like the complete photographic record he made in Leningrad).

looked at more closely, and not just for anecdotal reasons, for it attests to the mercantile debasement of Malewicz's work in general and, more specifically, to that of his post-Suprematist œuvre. In the context of an informal exhibition at the Fine-Arts Museum in Ghent, Belgium, in addition to blatant imitations of Lissitzky, Alexandra Exter, Kandinsky and other artists of the "Russian avant-garde", there appeared a number of "folk" items purporting to belong (not without a good deal of extravagance) to the post-Suprematist type, all attributed to Malewicz.

After a moment of shock at a display as comical as it was ridiculous, I began to wonder about the possible origin of these "giftware products" inspired by the folkloric dimension sometimes garbing Malewicz's last period (after 1927), which was referred in a certain period as his "second peasant period" (what was the first one?). Since 1998 we have witnessed the appearance of various "post-Suprematist" objects, mainly dolls of the "matryoshka" variety sold in gift shops in certain museums.[46] Such items undoubtedly inspired the odious manufacture of post-Suprematist style giftware. The example of this type of commercial venture rashly underwritten by a major European museum surely marks the low point (?) of the present mercantile popularisation of Malewicz's work.

[44] A widely cultivated person and a remarkable art publisher, Karl Gutbrod was the son-in-law of Willi Baumeister, the German artist who in 1927 was personally in touch with Malewicz in Berlin. In addition to his involvement with abstract art Baumeister participated in the Grosse Berliner Kunstausstellung in 1927 along with Malewicz, with whom he became friends. On this occasion they also exchanged works.

[45] See T. Andersen, *K. S. Malevich. The Leporskaya Archive*, Aarhus: Aarhus University, 2011. As for his objections to Lamač's work, he has draped himself in a silence befitting a greater cause. My offer to debate in person with him, an offer I made through the intermediary of Geurt Imanse, a curator at the Stedelijk Museum, has also gone unanswered.

[46] According to information kindly given to me by Alexandra Balash of St Petersburg, the production of these by-products began in 1998. Initially it took the form of ceramic products; dolls were manufactured later (see A. N. Balash, "Muzeinyi predmet i muzeinyi suvenir" [The museum object and the museum souvenir], UDK, U6901).

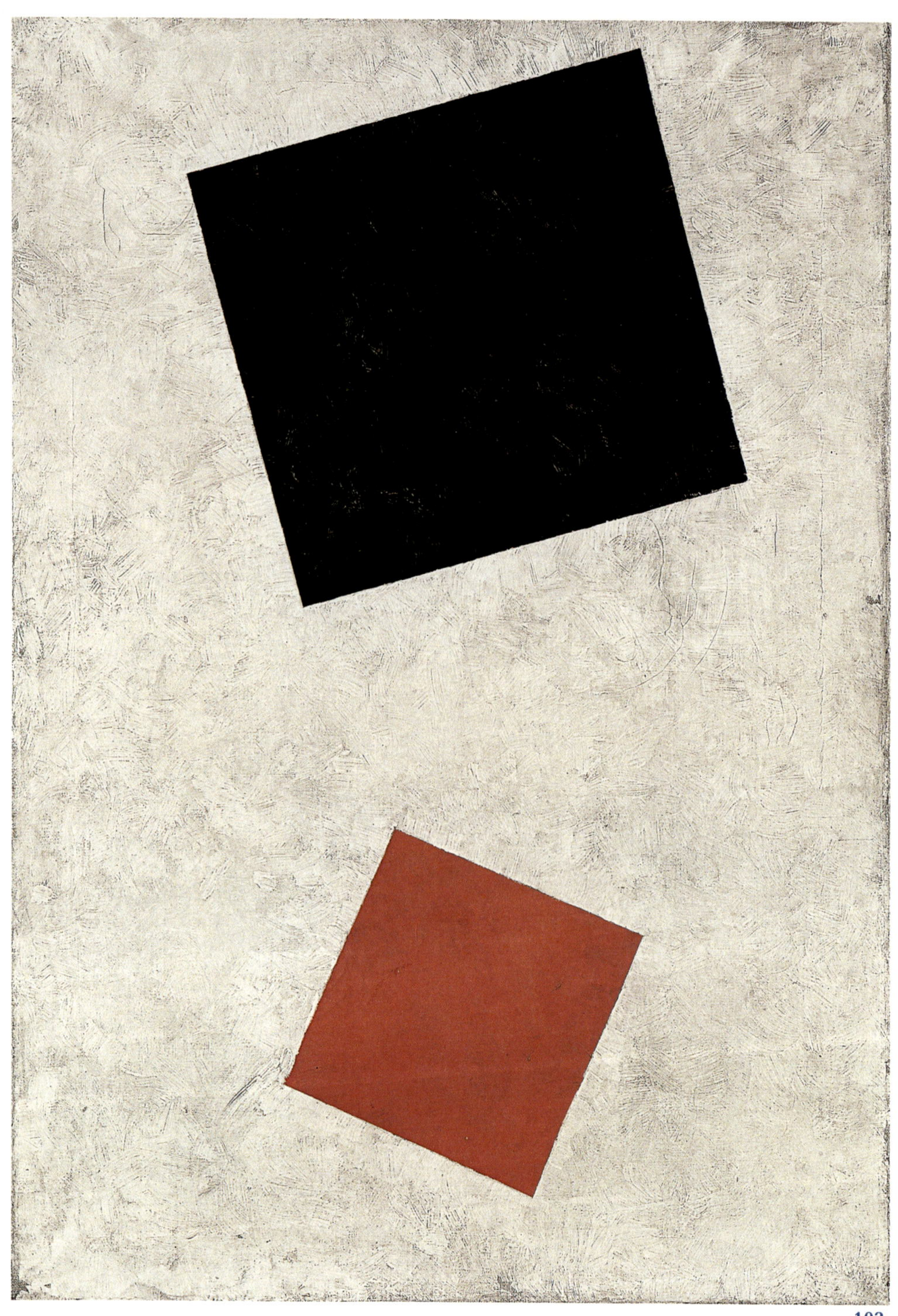

102.

A TEMPEST IN A TEAPOT

*He who wants to drown his dog
says it has rabies.*

French proverb

I n November 2017 an extravagant dispute erupted in the German press: it concerned the authenticity of the Suprematist painting *Red and Black Squares* (S-141).[47] Having belonged since 1973 to the very knowledgeable German collector Wilhelm Hack, this canvas was exhibited for years at the Wilhelm-Hack-Museum in Ludwigshafen, an institution founded that same year to house the important Hack Collection formerly in Cologne. In the late 1950s Hack had been the first European collector to acquire a Suprematist painting by Malewicz (S-240 in the *Catalogue raisonné*), a work now in the Hack Museum. (The donation of the greater part of his collection to Ludwigshafen in 1973 led to the construction of the museum that bears Wilhelm Hack's name, adorned with an impressive tile wall designed by Joan Miró.) Hack, a pillar of the Cologne Kunstverein and a colourful figure in German and even European art circles, was one of the very few collectors to be interested at the time (the late 1950s) in avant-garde Russian art and in particular the work of Malewicz.[48] S-240, the first Malewicz composition that Hack acquired, came from the German-Russian Riesen family, with whom the artist had lodged in Berlin in 1927.[49] One of its

102. *Red and Black Squares*, motif of 1915, later version, *c.* 1918–1920 (Cat. S-141), oil on canvas, 82.7 × 52.3 cm, former Wilhelm Hack Collection, Kunstsammlung Nordrhein-Westfalen, Düsseldorf

[47] See the articles by Helga Meister in *Die Westdeutsche Zeitung* of 9 November 2017, the *Handelsblatt* of 10 November and her "Offensichtlich nicht echt", in *Frankfurter Allgemeine Zeitung* of 11 November 2017.

[48] Wilhelm Hack (1899–1985) was a major collector of modern art in Germany. In addition to choice works by Delaunay, Mondrian, Macke, Schwitters, Pollock and others his collection included an important group of medieval and, especially, 16th-century German sculptures. Most of these works are now housed in the Wilhelm-Hack-Museum. Hack was able to persuade Joan Miró to design the tile mural for the museum's southern façade, realised by the ceramicist Artigas. He was an important figure in the German

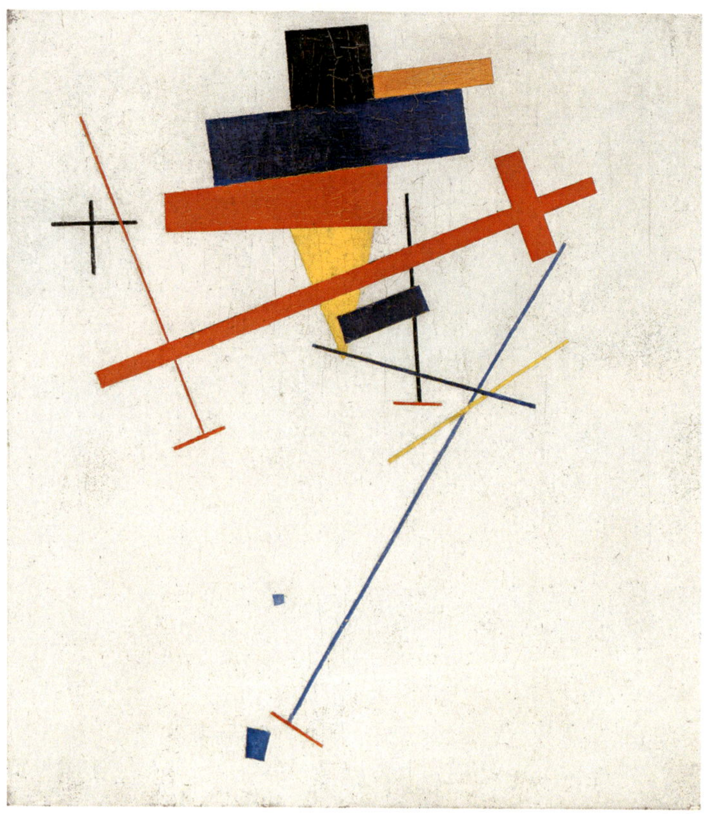

103.

members, Alexander von Riesen, was the German translator of his *Non-Objective World* published in December of that year by the Bauhaus press as *Die Gegenstandslose Welt*. In addition to works by major Western artists, the Hack Collection above all included a trove of Russian Non-Objective compositions by Exter, Lissitzky, Popova, Rodchenko, Kliun and others – and of course Kazimir Malewicz. Hack was a passionate Malewicz collector, probably more so than for any other artist, and in addition to the Suprematist composition just mentioned, his Malewicz collection, which he held "on deposit" in Ludwigshafen, also comprised a great number of Malewicz works plus *Red and Black Squares*, attesting to the high emotional status of this painting for the Cologne collector. At Hack's death in 1985 the works "on deposit" passed into the hands of his son, Harald Hack, and, on the latter's death in 2012, into those of his widow, Marlene Hack, who

art world, particularly that of Cologne. During the 1960s and 1970s he was active in that city's Kunstverein. Fascinated with Malewicz, he initiated a major publishing project with DuMont Schauberg.

See the remarks about him in an article signed by G. Heydenreich, I. Hajdas, D. Blumenroth and S. Dietz in the annual report of the Eidgenössische Technische Hochschule (ETH) in Zurich, Switzerland. The description of Hack as a "German businessman who invested his wealth in a collection of fine art, mostly modernist paintings" is not only extravagant but truly shocking (*"Malevich (?) Painting Analysed"*, Laboratory of Ion Beam Physics, Annual Report, 2017).

[49] A key work in the Hack Museum, this painting is among the few Suprematist works never to have been restored and is thus irreplaceable for the study of the artist's technique.

[50] In *Malevich IV: the Artist, Infinity, Suprematism. Unpublished Writings 1913–33*, Copenhagen: Borgen, 1978, p. 255, n. 26. It would be cruel to reveal the limits of the compiler's knowledge of Malewicz, but quoting Woody Allen "nobody is perfect"... The errors in his publications are typical of the 1960s: a poor knowledge of the artist's Symbolist and esoteric sources (Uspenski), references to works that have since been catalogued differently, a restricted understanding of the 1927 exhibition, and other failings. This by no means invalidates his role as a forerunner, but nonetheless points out the limits of his work. It would now be inelegant to mention the objections of Wilhelm Hack and others to the Danish scholar.

[51] With one notable exception of 1977 at the Kunstverein Hannover: *Malewitsch-Mondrian. Konstruktion als Konzept. Alexander Dorner gewidmet.*

[52] See my remarks on this subject in chap. 32 of *Malewicz*, 2007/2010.

[53] Yet in the early 1920s it had been interpreted in terms of its Expressionist profusion. See B. Arvatov, "Dve grupirovki" (Two Groups), in *Zrelishcha* (Shows), Moscow, 17–23 October, 1922 (cf. my French trans. "Deux groupements", *Change*, nos. 26–27, Paris, 1976, pp. 252–253). In 1974 the American artist and art critic Donald Judd reached the same conclusion. His article is exceptionally clear on this point and is a particularly illuminating discussion of Malewicz's painting technique (see D. Judd, "Malevich: Independent Form, Color, Surface", *Art in America*, vol. 62, no. 2, New York, 1974, pp. 52–58).

[54] The project was initially placed under the responsibility of Karl Gutbrod, a close friend of Hack's. After several authors bowed out, the project and especially the task of compiling the documents relating to it passed into my hands in 1979. These documents were supplemented with the photographic record of the Leningrad studio and later with the Lamač archives that his family transferred to me.

in 2014 gifted them most generously to the Modern Art Museum in the city of her residence, Düsseldorf (Kunstammlung Nordrhein-Westfalen). Together with a group of Suprematist drawings, *Red and Black Squares* was exhibited in that institution in 2014. Several years later rumours, always difficult to trace, cast suspicion on this group of compositions, notwithstanding the fact that some of them (several important 1915 drawings, such as F-465) as well as *Red and Black Squares* have an extraordinary expressive power. Troels Andersen had already voiced doubts regarding the latter,[50] though he had not had an opportunity to examine the canvas at first hand, since Hack kept it in his Cologne home until 1979.[51] It was only then that it was publicly displayed at the museum in Ludwigshafen. Hack was not in the habit of hiding in front of his guests, including myself, his negative opinion of the Danish scholar's artistic judgements, especially those reflecting his narrowly geometric vision of Suprematism (which the recent rejection of the drawings has in effect confirmed).[52] The notion of a flat, mournfully geometric Suprematism current in the 1960s and '70s (at the beginning of the 1960s Malewicz's so-called "geometric" production was still being ranged under a vaguely "Constructivist" heading) was at the opposite pole of the artist's Expressionist exuberance, and both Hack and I firmly believed in its plenitude.[53] Hack, highly respected at the time, was indisputably a connoisseur of modern art and his opinions invariably had the force of genuine assumptions. Malewicz was not just one of his passions, it was definitely his greatest one. He was moreover deeply involved in the project of a monograph of the artist that the Cologne publishers DuMont Schauberg had initially commissioned Hans von Riesen to write in the mid-1950s. Riesen having declined to pursue this task, the project was then entrusted to the Czech art historians Miroslav Lamač and Jiří Padrta.[54] In the course of a visit to Prague in the company of Karl Gutbrod, Hack encouraged both scholars warmly.

Aware of my own interest in the subject, Hack invited me to his residence in Cologne in spring 1973, and I had the privilege of being one of the few persons actually to hold *Red and Black Squares* in my hands. Hack pointed out several details of the picture, among others the highly worked fringes of the Non-Objective forms, the energy of the artist's touch, the fingerprints that Malewicz left on the edge of the canvas, which he must have picked up before the paint he had just laid down had time to dry. I stated that the composition's surface (which I then considered, and still consider, very dirty) needed cleaning, but Hack would not hear of it and outlined his principle of "respecting the life-memory" of the work. It took me years of apprenticeship and especially the experience of several cases of excessive cleaning to understand how valuable Hack's position was.[55] Similarly, it took me an extra fifteen years to persuade the directors of the Stedelijk Museum in Amsterdam to undertake a radical "restoration" of the "white" compositions in their collection.[56]

After the first moment of surprise at the "sensational revelations" of a large circulation press known to be avid for scandal, I sought to discover the "scientific proofs" upon which these allegations rested. But at this point I ran into a strange obstruction of information. After lengthy discussions the Düsseldorf museum merely agreed to let me look briefly at a report by a chemist at the Technische Hochschule (Technical School) of Cologne.[57] I was taken aback on discovering that the man, whose name I had never come across before, called himself an "expert on modern art" and on the work of Malewicz in particular. Yet his report did not cite or even mention the few bona fide studies on the subject, those of Ann Hoenigswald, to say nothing of my own work.[58] Even more surprising, early in January 2019, after my visit to the museum in December 2018, I received a threatening letter from the administrators "forbidding" me to refer to or cite even an extract from the report, which I had already been informed I was not to copy, even by hand (thus I had merely noted the passages that interested me in the course of reading it). My request to have a copy of the radiograph I had been able to consult during the same visit was also refused.[59] Only after the helpful action of a German lawyer did the Düsseldorf museum finally consent to let me have a copy of the report (but not the X-ray, with which I was fortunately acquainted through other sources).[60]

The laboratory report of the Cologne Technical School stated that the pigments identified in the work did not raise any problems of dating and indeed seemed consistent with those used in the early 20th century, by Malewicz in particular.[61]

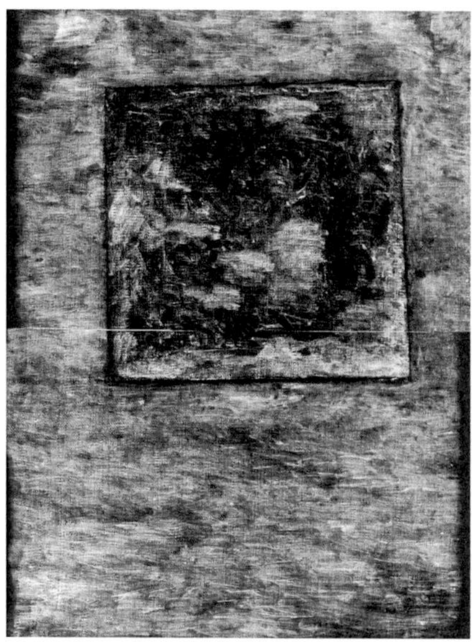

104.

104. *Red Square* (Cat. S-126), X-ray

[55] See my remarks in chap. 32 of the French edition of my monograph, *Malewicz*, 2007. The most surprising not to say distressing example of this is the "cleaning" of a Suprematist composition in the Peggy Guggenheim Collection (S-306), *vide* the photographic document from the 1950s published here.

[56] This work was initiated solely in connection with the 1988–1989 retrospective. At that time I was able to convince the museum director to change the hanging of certain Suprematist paintings such as *Self-Portrait in Two Dimensions* (S-21).

[57] Gunnar Heydenreich, Untersuchungsbericht 15-0151, Technische Hochschule Köln, dated 8 June 2016.

[58] A. Hoenigswald, "Kazimir Malevich's Paintings: Surface and Intended Appearance", *Conservation Research 1996/1997*, National Gallery of Art, Washington D.C. (*Studies in the History of Art*, vol. 57, 1997, pp. 109–125).

[59] The letter dated 8 January 2019 contains the sentences: "Wir können Ihnen keine Röntgenaufnahmen zur Verfügung stellen" (We cannot place X-rays at your disposal) and "Wir gestatten keine Zitate aus dem Gutachten" (We do not allow quotations from the expert report).

[60] I contacted the Berlin lawyer Peter Raue, who is well known in the German art world. Thanks to

105. (Suprematism), 1916 (Cat. S-306),
former Peggy Guggenheim Collection,
Venice. Photograph made during the
work's restoration in Italy in the mid-1950s

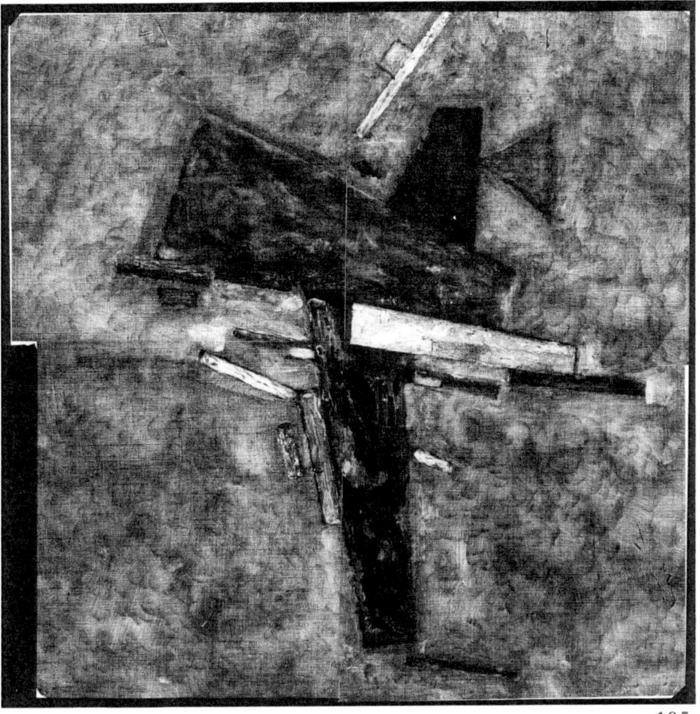

105.

On the other hand a comparison of the brushwork visible in the X-ray of *Red and Black Squares* with another composition by the same artist, *Painterly Realism of a Boy with a Knapsack* (S-139), in the New York MoMA, revealed significant differences in the execution of both forms and background, opening the way to question as to its attribution to Malewicz. This did not surprise me, as the two works were painted at widely different times. The MoMA canvas was one of the artist's very first, as yet hesitant, Suprematist compositions from the summer of 1915, expressing a Suprematism of "narrative memories" (as Paul Klee would have put it around the same time), whereas I placed *Red and Black Squares*, as specified in 2002 in my commentary of the *Catalogue raisonné*, towards the end of Malewicz's first Suprematist period, hence several years after his first Suprematist canvases, when his Suprematist painterly practice was fully mastered and what I would describe as the work of a "virtuoso of the brush".

At this juncture I noticed that the information and the dating I gave in the *Catalogue* had simply been ignored. In fact

his intervention I was able to obtain a copy of the 2016 expert reports.

[61] See Untersuchungsbericht 15-0151, 8 June 2016.

167

the very difference I established between the date of the *motif* and the actual *realisation* of the painting was simply not mentioned, thus allowing the authors of the report to draw a specious comparison further producing inevitably mistaken conclusions.[62] Another statement in the report drew my attention, namely the affirmation that the surface of the composition had been "patinated artificially", a gratuitous pronouncement in my view as it rested on no precise observation or proof and was contradicted by the SIK Institute's earlier analysis of S-284 (2016).[63] Naturally, the Cologne report did not contain any detailed commentary with regard to the execution of the forms. To speak in these terms about a painting whose execution is imbued with vitality and in which even the artist's fingerprints are visible struck me as not only specious but as altogether shocking.[64]

A single objective argument remained: the date of the work by the carbon-14 method. The study published by the Zurich ETH, i.e. by an "outside" (therefore independent) laboratory, concluded in a date for S-141 in the "mid-1970s". I was completely taken aback by this for it contradicted my own experience of having the painting in my hands in the spring of 1973.[65]

As the Cologne report was based on the ETH study, I wanted to know more about it and contacted the ETH laboratory. When I voiced doubts about the exactness of their findings, mentioning my own direct contact with S-141 in 1973 and after stating that I had traced its existence to at least the mid-1960s (a date I was able to establish in 1976 thanks to my conversations with Ilya Chashnik's son and to the fact that he had formally recognised having seen it) the Zurich institute suddenly came up with a new date, the very date I had mentioned in my conversations with them: some time in the 1960s. (Why and, mainly, how had they reached this new conclusion?)

Stranger still, I was informed that I should not be surprised at this twenty-year shift in dating as it depended on the preliminary "cleaning" of the samples being analysed and other "calibrations". (Yet another major unknown in the analysis.) It transpired that the percentage of carbon and hence the date of the work varies significantly depending on the preliminary treatment of the samples. Plunged in perplexity, I then

106.

106. *Painterly Realism of a Boy with a Knapsack*, 1915 (Cat. S-139), oil on canvas, 71.1 × 44.4 cm, MoMA, New York

[62] The difference is clearly explained in my introduction to the *Catalogue raisonné*. As a result of the incorrect date mentioned in the report, the media reports that gave 1915 as the date of *Red and Black Squares* were also false.

[63] The comments in this part of the analysis struck me as particularly well-founded for they agreed in every point with the remarks of Ann Hoenigswald, the first scholar to publish a solid stylistic analysis of Malewicz's pictorial technique (see Hoenigswald, *op. cit.*, 1997).

[64] As proof I would cite the report of the first examination of S-284 by the Zurich SIK, which contains information relative to the artist's pictorial style that corroborate both the work of Ann Hoenigswald and my own conclusions (see Nakov, *Malewicz*, 2007). I return to this subject below.

[65] Parallel to the conclusions produced in Zurich a similar carbon-14 study carried out in a laboratory at the University of Kiel arrived at altogether identical (!) findings.

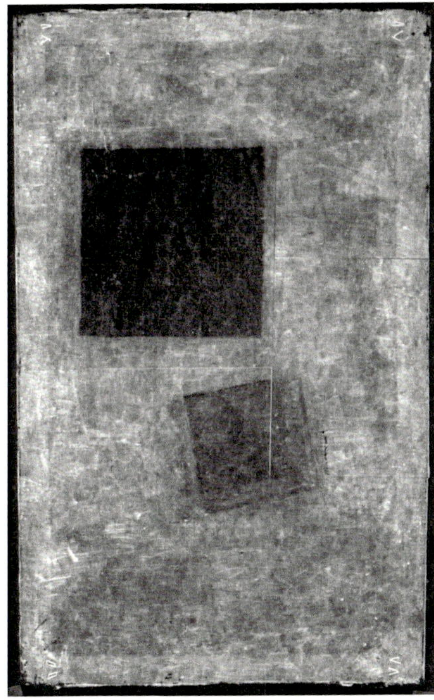

107.

107. *Painterly Realism of a Boy with a Knapsack* (Cat. S-139), X-ray

[66] In particular I contacted a Berlin laboratory renowned for its work in this area.

[67] The analysis was undertaken by Prof. Marek Krąpiec of the AGH (Akademia Górniczo-Hutnicza, Kraków, Poland). Some of the tests were carried out by the Absolute Dating Laboratory of the Center for Applied Isotope Studies at the University of Georgia, USA.

[68] See the report of 21 December 2020 (report on AMS C-14 dating in the Laboratory of Absolute Dating, Kraków [MKL]). This collaboration was necessary owing to the lack of proper instruments in Kraków (they are presently being installed).

consulted other carbon-14 specialists and learned that the dating of modern artworks could fluctuate by more than two decades and that, in view of this, carbon-14 testing was not really recommended for establishing a more or less precise date for the realisation of modern paintings.

In the face of the odd reticence of the Düsseldorf museum authorities concerning all earlier examinations of Hack's painting, I opted for a comparative approach. In my opinion S-141 belongs to a small homogenous group of three paintings (S-141, S-270 and S-284) in every way similar in texture as in their manner of execution. These works were treated as such not only by myself but also by Troels Andersen who, on the basis of these considerations, had rejected them all in the mid-1970s without having even set eyes on S-141. I therefore focused on one of these compositions, S-284.

The latter had previously been examined in early 2016 in a quite independent manner by the SIK laboratory in Zurich with a positive result and a rather ample commentary regarding the execution of the forms (with the difference that the carbon-14 method, unavailable at the time, had not been employed). In 2019 I finally succeeded in having the canvas tested again, this time using the carbon-14 method, by the same laboratory. Contrary to the findings of 2016 the results of this new test indicated a new date of composition in every way consistent with that of S-141 (mid-1970s). Intrigued by all these strange similarities I decided to have the same tests carried out in other German laboratories,[66] but my request met with refusals reflecting, in my opinion, an *esprit de corps* more than anything.

Finally, invited to teach at the Pontifical University in Kraków, Poland, I turned to the laboratory of the AGH (University of Science and Technology). The analysis in question was undertaken jointly with its sister institution at the University of Georgia in the USA (Absolute Dating Laboratory).[67] In December 2020 these institutions confirmed that S-284 dates from the first two decades of the 20th century and most likely from the years 1918–1921.[68] This was precisely the date I had suggested in 2002 in the *Catalogue raisonné* for the three compositions S-141, S-270 and S-284 on the sole basis of stylistic considerations, which are the art historian's only proper, if not exclusive, working material.

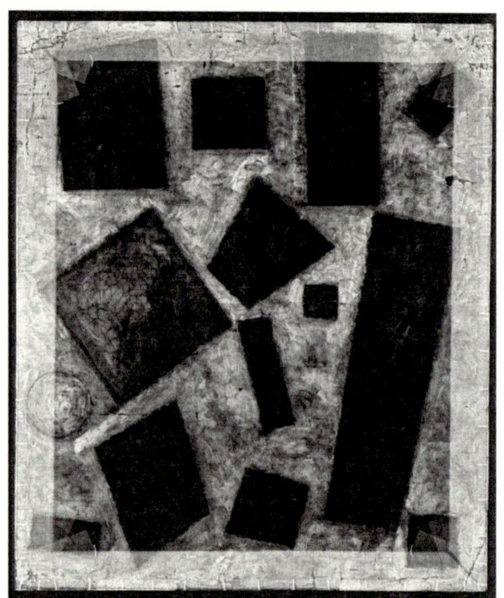

108.

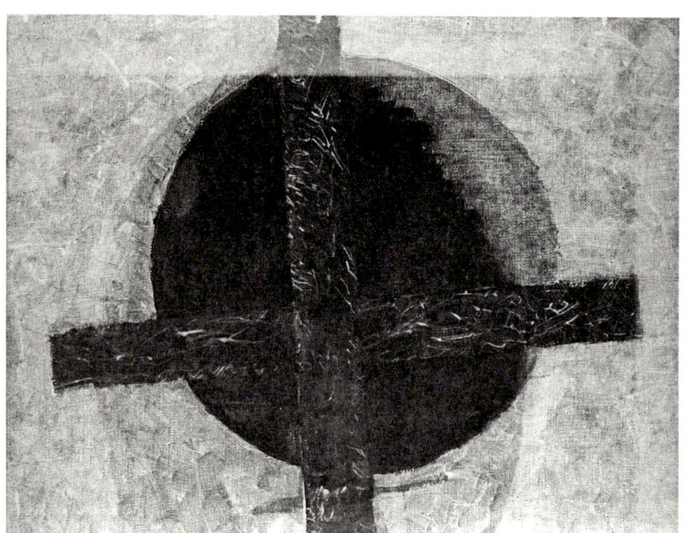

109.

Most of the participants of this extraordinary saga (Hack, Chashnik and Lamač) being no longer of this world, it was up to me to carry on with what I regarded as a duty to their memory and above all to Malewicz's work, which has always been the focus of my unrelenting dedication. As for the extravagant story of Malewicz's *Red and Black Squares*, it now strikes me that it merits more than just the text of an art historian; it calls for the pen of a contemporary Conan Doyle.

108. (Suprematist composition), 1915 (Cat. S-60), oil on canvas, 70 × 60 cm, Museum Ludwig, Cologne, X-ray

109. *Mystic Suprematism*, version of 1920–1922 (Cat. S-612), oil on canvas, 72.5 × 51 cm, Stedelijk Museum, Amsterdam. Motif explaining the artist's brush technique

DEFINITION OF THE TERM "SUPREMATISM"

In the critical texts accompanying the first appearance of Suprematism there is not a single indication about the origins of that word or its social resonance. Even the person who seems to me to have been in the best position to understand its philosophical implications – the painter and theorist Mikhail Matyushin – was somewhat taken aback by Malewicz's choice, and declared that he did not understand very well why the "new painterly realism" should be named "rather academically, Suprematism".[2]

Malewicz for his part never saw the point in explaining the source and meaning of the term Suprematism, the apodictic nature of which must immediately be underlined. One might think at first that it was dictated by circumstance and was intended to signal the position of the artist's new painting relative to the experiments that had preceded it, both his own and those of his colleagues. A close reading of *From Cubism and Futurism to Suprematism* (1916) nevertheless leads us to see a significant affirmation in the word "Suprematism". Accompanied by the adjective "non-objective", Suprematism signifies something other than just the assertion of a preponderant position in the "race for novelty" which, as Matyushin put it, "was the rage among Muscovites".[3]

The term Suprematism arrived at the conclusion of a vertiginous leapfrogging of stylistic "isms", which were more or less justified or justifiable and marked the formal bankruptcy of an evolution that is invariably and wrongly limited to "stylistic" considerations (Cubism, Orphism, Rayonism, various types of Futurism – Cubo-Futurism, Ego-futurism, *Kvero*-Futurism

[1] Translated by Michael Taylor from the edition of Malewicz's selected writings edited and introduced by Andréi Nakov, *Malévitch. Écrits*, Paris, 1975. Reprinted in 1986 and 1996.

[2] M. Matyushin, "Apropos the Exhibition of the Last Futurists", *Ocharovannyi Strannik*, Spring 1916, p. 17.

[3] *Ibidem*, p. 17: "One must be wary of everything here [in Moscow]. He who is the first to say something new is king. What is more, best friends will immediately steal any new idea [...] miscarriages of every sort of ism are rife in Moscow!"

and so forth – even *"toutisme"* [everythingism], the patently sarcastic resonance of which gives one a good indication of the artistic climate of the year 1915). In the face of this constant stylistic overhauling Malewicz opted for a term that was both formally and stylistically neutral, a term that escaped the superficial categories of formal appearances (or "distortions", in the by then obsolete language of Naturalist criticism). For Malewicz the new term designated the content of his system and led directly to the central issue of his creation – the ontological essence of his painting. "Suprematism" is a far cry from the flaccid intentions of Russia's so-called "Cubists" and "Fauvists" who blindly accepted labels that were less than flattering in the minds of critics.

In contrast, a determination to affirm a superior level of thought is manifest throughout Malewicz's evolution in 1915. The written explanations he posted among his paintings in the *0,10 – Last Futurist Exhibition* confirm the ideas contained in the manifesto of December 1915, which includes the phrase "supremacy of painting".[4] The artist was thereby proclaiming the supremacy of *pure* painting, that new language capable of attaining a new level of existence.

Possibly Malewicz considered other names before settling on the term "Suprematism". On the back of certain paintings executed after 1927 but reverting to the themes and form of his works of the 1910–1912 period, one finds the inscription *sverkhnaturalizm* (supernaturalism). Yet the fact that this return to the past was manifestly interpretative means that one should be extremely cautious about the actual existence of the term *sverkhnaturalizm* in the artist's vocabulary in 1910–1914.[5]

As a term referring to the concept of rejecting the "fictive appearances" of the material world, "super-naturalism" existed as of 1901 in the Russian edition of the German *Brockhaus Dictionary*.[6] On the other hand, the word "Suprematism" did not yet exist in the Russian language apart from Malewicz's sole use of it – as his fellow artists were quick to notice, as attested by a manuscript of Natalya Goncharova's datable to 1916.[7] However, on page 515 of volume VI of the *Słownik języka polskiego* (Dictionary of the Polish Language), edited by J. Karłowicz, A. Kryński and Wł. Niedźwiedzki, Warsaw, 1919, one finds the terms *supremacja* and *supremat*, as well as the adjective *supremacyjny* (suprematist). Their philosophic and

[4] My quotation marks.

[5] See Kovtun (ed.), *op. cit.*, 1976.

[6] F. A. Brockhaus, *Entsiklopedicheskiĭ Slovar* (Encyclopaedic Dictionary), St Petersburg, 1910, vol. 32, pp. 83–84. The *Bolshaya Sovietskaya Entsiklopedia* (Great Soviet Encyclopaedia) of 1956 (vol. 51, p. 301) includes the term "Suprematism" with the following definition: "[...] one of the extremist movements of reactionary formalist art [...] devoid of visual meaning [...] based on a combination of variously coloured surface-planes having outlines of the greatest simplicity".

[7] The reference of N. Goncharova concerning the term "Suprematism" qualified by Goncharova as a "forcefully foreign language" figures in a sketch-book of 1916, kept in the Victoria & Albert Museum, London, *cf.* L. Salmina-Haskell, *Catalogue of Russian Drawings*, London: Victoria & Albert Museum, 1972, p. 49.

religious connotation and their use in the canon law of the Polish Catholic Church are very closely related to the logic of Malewicz's "hierarchical" use of the term. Consequently one can put forward without any great risk of going wrong that in the artist's mouth the word "Suprematism" in Russian was a loan from Polish. It is significant that in order to express certain key concepts he resorted to Polish words in Russian dress, so to speak. For example, a Suprematist drawing in the collection of the Musée national d'art moderne in Paris, includes an inscription containing the Polish word *tarcza* (disk) in Cyrillic characters. (The word does not appear in any Russian dictionary.) The idea of the supremacy of a new type of thought over the totality of the quantitative discourse of traditional logic and the need for going beyond it qualitatively in a radically different discourse is central to Piotr Uspenski's philosophical opus *Tertium Organum* (1911). The superior level of thought in Uspenski's book corresponds to the noumenal logic that will triumph in the future, according to Malewicz. The sources of this idea are to be found in the work of Charles Hinton who, as early as 1866, alluded explicitly to the coming supremacy of a novel kind of thinking.[8]

Understood in the philosophical context of Uspenski's system, Suprematism appears logically in Malewicz's work as the most appropriate term for designating the new stage of noumenal deductive thought. The imaginative corollaries that accompanied this discovery correspond perfectly to the psychological stereotypes Gaston Bachelard established. Thus in both Malewicz's compositions and Uspenski's writing we encounter symbols of vertical ascension (spirituality) contrasting with quantitative advances of a material nature (horizontal accumulation).

The purely linguistic considerations developed thus far acquire an extra weight and lead to a further dimension when one looks at the artist's background. The rapport of his family, especially on his father's side, with the Church in Poland was not limited to customary practices that could be described roughly as a sort of superficial Polish patriotism. Lucjan Malewicz, the older brother of the painter's father, was a Catholic priest in Kiev. Regarded as one of the ringleaders of the Polish uprising of 1863, he was hung as an example and buried at the Baikove cemetery ("the cross on his grave could

8 Ch. H. Hinton, *Scientific Romances*, London, 1886, in particular vol. 2 (1912), p. 3.

be seen from very far away", according to Victoria Zaitseva, the artist's younger sister). Seweryn Malewicz, the father, insisted on his children undertaking regular pilgrimages to this grave. What is more he was adamant that his older son, Kazimir, become a Catholic priest in turn. This paternal fixation gave rise to quarrels in the family, for Kazimir, backed by his mother, wanted to take up painting – which he did eventually. Strangely enough, this resistance to the father turned out to be more formal in the end than real (in the philosophical sense of both terms) when one considers that Malewicz devoted his life to a kind of evangelisation of the painting of his century. From his father the artist acquired a number of "superior" values, which he transformed into a philosophical and moral discourse serving a new "Church", as he puts it in his text "On Poetry" (1919). The word "Suprematism", borrowed from the canonic terminology of Polish Catholicism, sums up his ideas perfectly.

As for the term "non-objective" (*bespredmetnyi*), which appears to be the indispensable accompaniment of "Suprematism" in Malewicz's writings, it explains his thought by orientating it towards the noumenal field defined by Uspenski. Malewicz's pronouncement that he had freed painting from the tyranny of objects should be placed alongside the negation of objective reality (knowing things through the senses rather than through the deductive intellect) advocated by the author of *Tertium Organum*. However, one also encounters the term "abstract" (*abstraktnyi*) in Malewicz's writings, though very rarely before 1919. It is more frequent under the pen of certain students of the Vitebsk UNOVIS group (Nina Kogan). Malewicz having differentiated between *bespredmetnyi* (non-objective) and *abstraktnyi* (abstract) in his own texts, there can be no confusing the two terms.

Andréi Nakov
Malewicz: Beyond Censorship
© Andréi Nakov, Paris, 2021

Translated from the French
by Michael Taylor

Editor:
Agnieszka Smołucha-Sładkowska

Editorial assistance:
Katarzyna Chrzanowska
Joanna Wolańska

Layout:
Andréi Nakov
Agnieszka Czuba

Printing:
Lettra-Graphic
www.lettra-graphic.com.pl

Publisher:

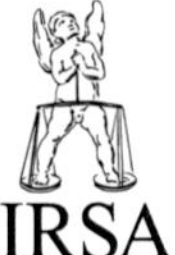

IRSA Publishing House
Plac Matejki 7/8
31-157 Kraków
tel. (+48 12) 421 90 30
e-mail: irsa@irsa.com.pl

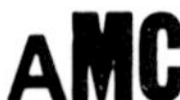

Published with the support
of the Archive of Modern Conflict AMC

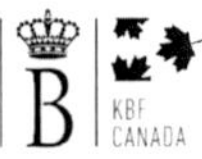

Funding partly provided by KBF CANADA

ISBN 978-83-89831-43-9